FEAR ITSELF
THUNDERBOLTS

WRITER
JEFF PARKER

ARTISTS
KEV WALKER
(ISSUE #158)

DECLAN SHALVEY
(ISSUES #160-161)

VALENTINE DE LANDRO
WITH MATTHEW SOUTHWORTH (ISSUE #162)

COLOR ART
FRANK MARTIN
WITH FABIO D'AURIA (ISSUES #161-162)

THUNDERBOLTS #159

"UNDERBOLTS"
WRITER
JEFF PARKER
ARTIST
DECLAN SHALVEY
COLOR ART
FRANK MARTIN

"THE GHOST & MR. WALKER"
WRITER
JEN VAN METER
ARTIST
ERIC CANETE
COLOR ART
FABIO D'AURIA

"GROUP THERAPY"
WRITER
JOE CARAMAGNA
ARTIST
VALENTINE DE LANDRO
COLOR ART
CHRIS SOTOMAYOR

"DOUBLE CROSS"
WRITER
FRANK TIERI
ARTIST
MATTHEW SOUTHWORTH

LETTERERS
ALBERT DESCHESNE & DAVE SHARPE

COVER ARTISTS
KEV WALKER & FRANK MARTIN (ISSUES #158-159)
J.S. ROSSBACH (ISSUES #160-161)

M

ASSISTA...
RACHEL PINNELAS   **TOM BRENNAN**

COLLECTION EDITOR: CORY LEVINE
ASSISTANT EDITORS: ALEX STARBUCK & NELSON RIBEIRO
EDITORS, SPECIAL PROJECTS: JENNIFER GRÜNWALD & MARK D. BEAZLEY
SENIOR EDITOR, SPECIAL PROJECTS: JEFF YOUNGQUIST
SENIOR VICE PRESIDENT OF SALES: DAVID GABRIEL
SVP OF BRAND PLANNING & COMMUNICATIONS: MICHAEL PASCIULLO
BOOK DESIGN: JEFF POWELL

EDITOR IN CHIEF: AXEL ALONSO
CHIEF CREATIVE OFFICER: JOE QUESADA
PUBLISHER: DAN BUCKLEY
EXECUTIVE PRODUCER: ALAN FINE

PREVIOUSLY

THEIR BASE IS A SUPERMAX FACILITY KNOWN AS THE RAFT. THEIR TRANSPORT IS A SWAMP MONSTER. THEIR MISSION LEADER IS THE BULLETPROOF AVENGER KNOWN AS LUKE CAGE. A HANDPICKED TEAM OF INMATES HAVE THE CHANCE TO GO OUTSIDE PRISON WALLS AS LONG AS THEY USE THEIR POWERS TO DEAL WITH THE WORST THE WORLD HAS TO OFFER — THEY ARE THE THUNDERBOLTS!

AFTER A BRUTAL MISSION AGAINST OCCULT DEMONS OVERSEAS, LUKE CAGE SUSPENDS AN ERRATIC JUGGERNAUT FROM THE THUNDERBOLTS A-TEAM.

THE THUNDERBOLTS B-TEAM, A NEWLY RECRUITED BACKUP REGIMENT LED BY MACH-V AND FIXER, LEAVE FOR THEIR FIRST MISSION: THRONGS OF THE UNDEAD HAVE RISEN AT THE WORLD'S LARGEST GRAVEYARD IN NAJAF, IRAQ. THE 'BOLTS HAVE TO PUT THEM DOWN BEFORE THE CRADLE OF CIVILIZATION IS ROBBED OF LIVES!

WITH THE B-TEAM OVERWHELMED BY ZOMBIES, LUKE CAGE SENDS THE A-TEAM OUT TO PROVIDE BACKUP. BUT SOMETHING BIGGER IS ABOUT TO LAND ON THE RAFT...

FEAR ITSELF: THUNDERBOLTS. Contains material originally published in magazine form as THUNDERBOLTS #158-162. First printing 2011. Hardcover ISBN# 978-0-7851-5798-4. Softcover ISBN# 978-0-7851-5223-1. Published by MARVEL WORLDWIDE, INC., a subsidiary of MARVEL ENTERTAINMENT, LLC. OFFICE OF PUBLICATION: 135 West 50th Street, New York, NY 10020. Copyright © 2011 and 2012 Marvel Characters, Inc. All rights reserved. $19.99 per copy in the U.S. and $21.99 in Canada (GST R127032852). Softcover: $15.99 per copy in the U.S. and $17.99 in Canada (GST #R127032852). Canadian Agreement #40668537. All characters featured in this issue and the distinctive names and likenesses thereof, and all related indicia are trademarks of Marvel Characters, Inc. No similarity between any of the names, characters, persons, and/or institutions in this magazine with those of any living or dead person or institution is intended, and any such similarity which may exist is purely coincidental. **Printed in the U.S.A.** ALAN FINE, EVP - Office of the President, Marvel Worldwide, Inc. and EVP & CMO Marvel Characters B.V.; DAN BUCKLEY, Publisher & President - Print, Animation & Digital Divisions; JOE QUESADA, Chief Creative Officer; DAVID BOGART, SVP of Business Affairs & Talent Management; TOM BREVOORT, SVP of Publishing; C.B. CEBULSKI, SVP of Creator & Content Development; DAVID GABRIEL, SVP of Publishing Sales & Circulation; MICHAEL PASCIULLO, SVP of Brand Planning & Communications; JIM O'KEEFE, VP of Operations & Logistics; DAN CARR, Executive Director of Publishing Technology; SUSAN CRESPI, Editorial Operations Manager; ALEX MORALES, Publishing Operations Manager; STAN LEE, Chairman Emeritus. For information regarding advertising in Marvel Comics or on Marvel.com, please contact John Dokes, SVP Integrated Sales and Marketing, at jdokes@marvel.com. For Marvel subscription inquiries, please call 800-217-9158. **Manufactured between 11/28/2011 and 1/2/2012 (hardcover), and 11/28/2011 and 8/13/2012 (softcover), by R.R. DONNELLEY, INC., SALEM, VA, USA.**

10 9 8 7 6 5 4 3 2 1

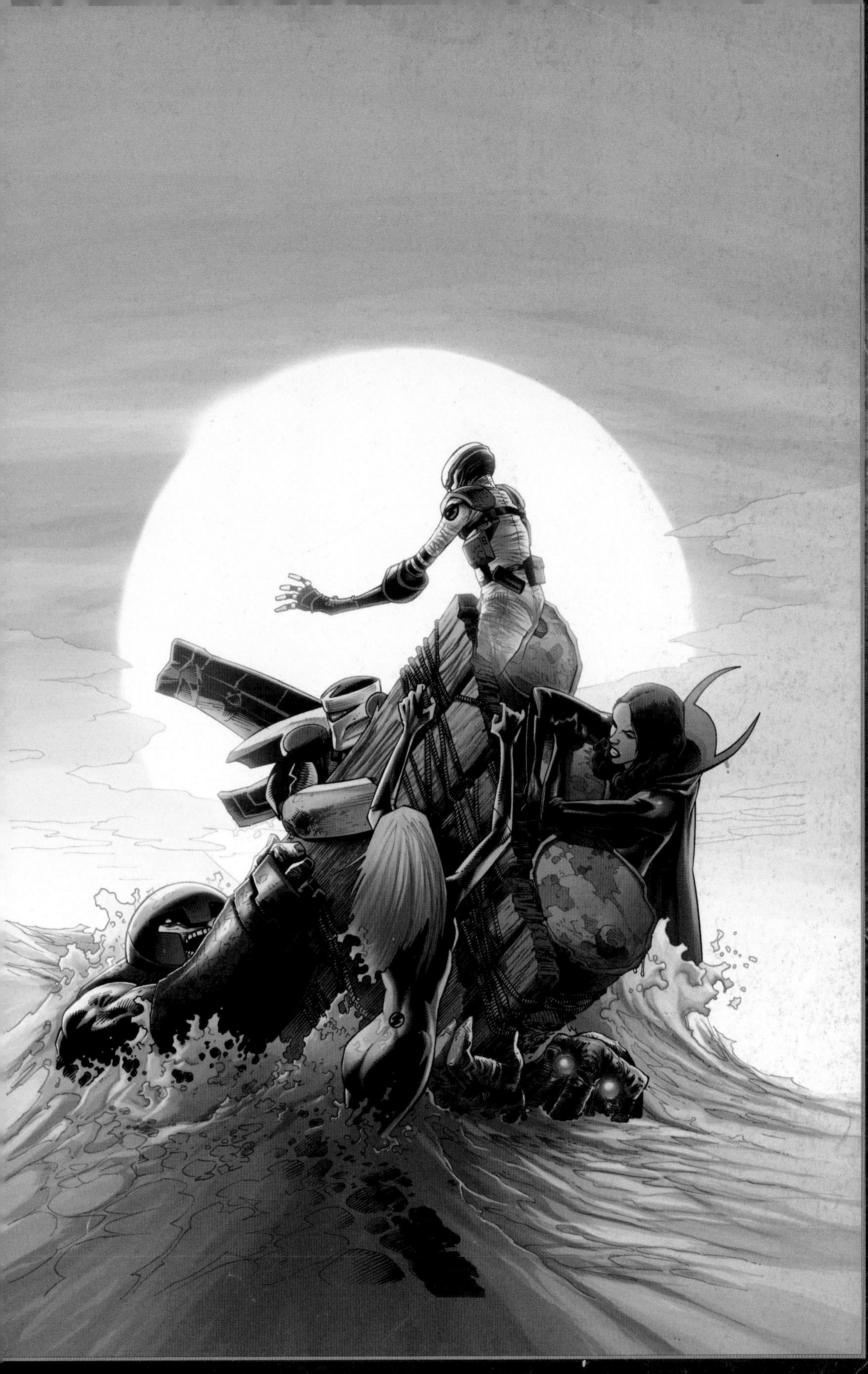

THUNDERBOLTS #158

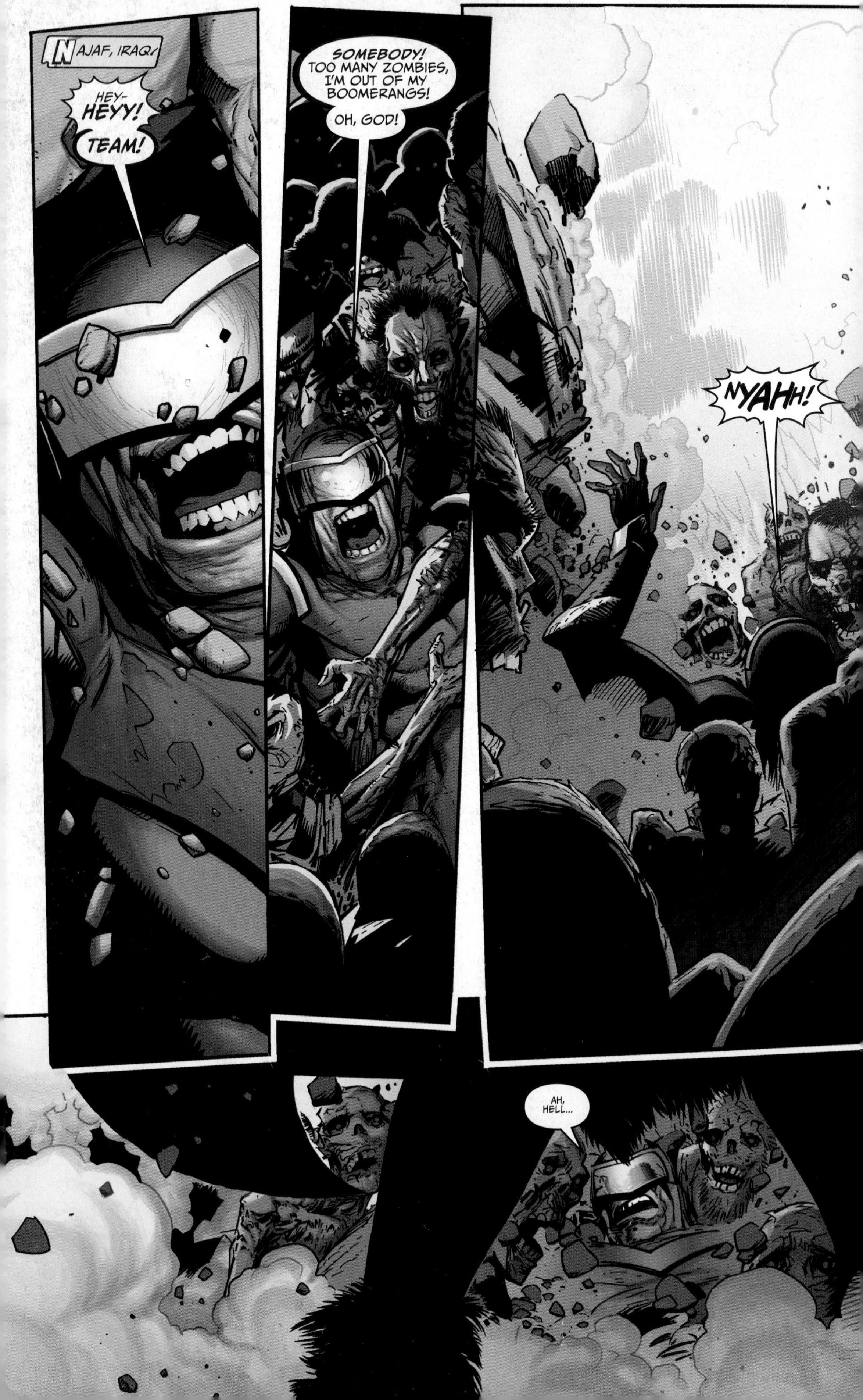
NAJAF, IRAQ.
HEY-HEYY!
TEAM!
SOMEBODY! TOO MANY ZOMBIES, I'M OUT OF MY BOOMERANGS!
OH, GOD!
NYAHH!
AH, HELL...

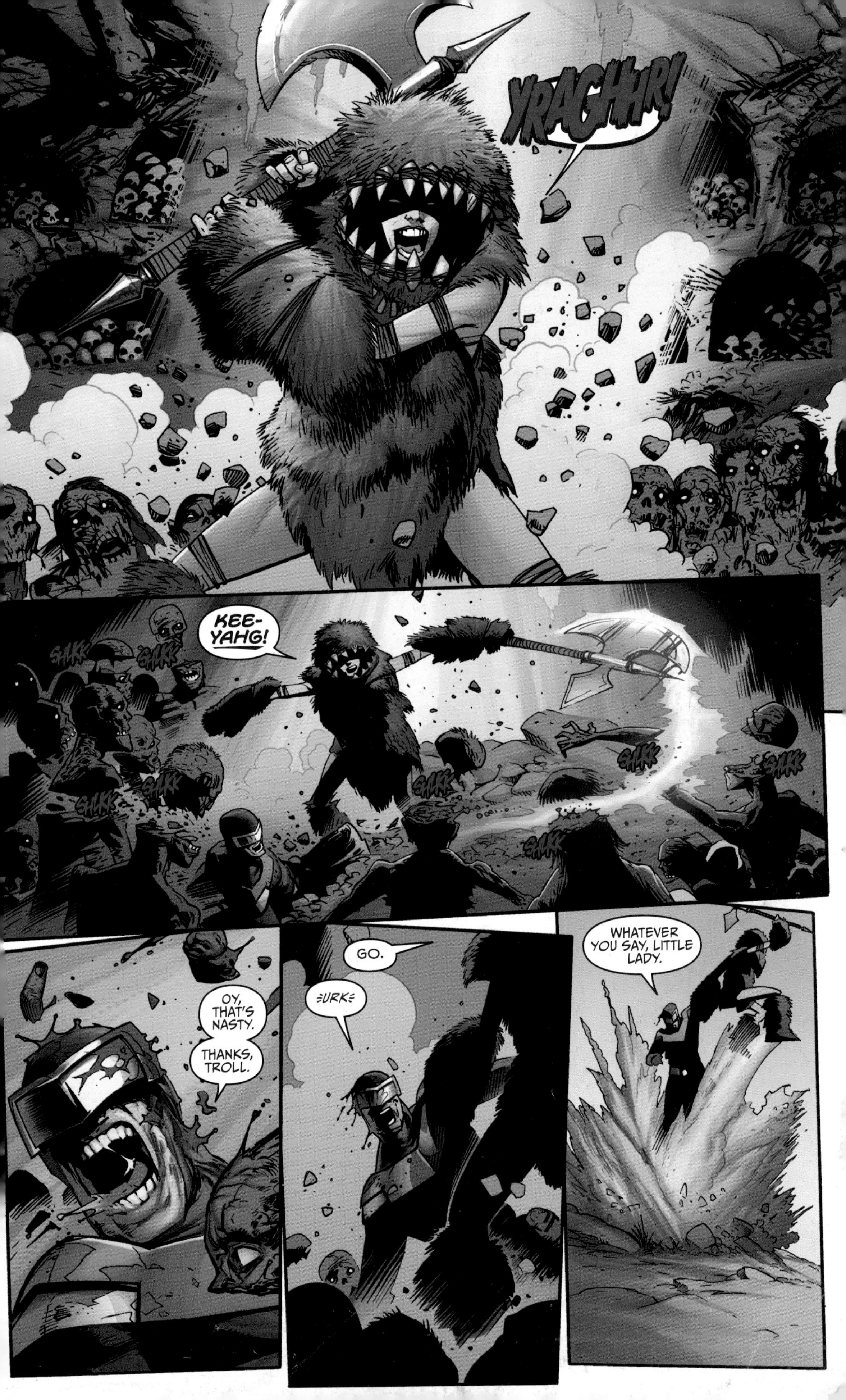
YRAGHHR!
KEE-YAHG!
SHAKK
SHAKK
SHAKK
SHAKK
SHAKK
SHAKK
SHAKK
SHAKK
OY, THAT'S NASTY.
THANKS, TROLL.
GO.
URK
WHATEVER YOU SAY, LITTLE LADY.

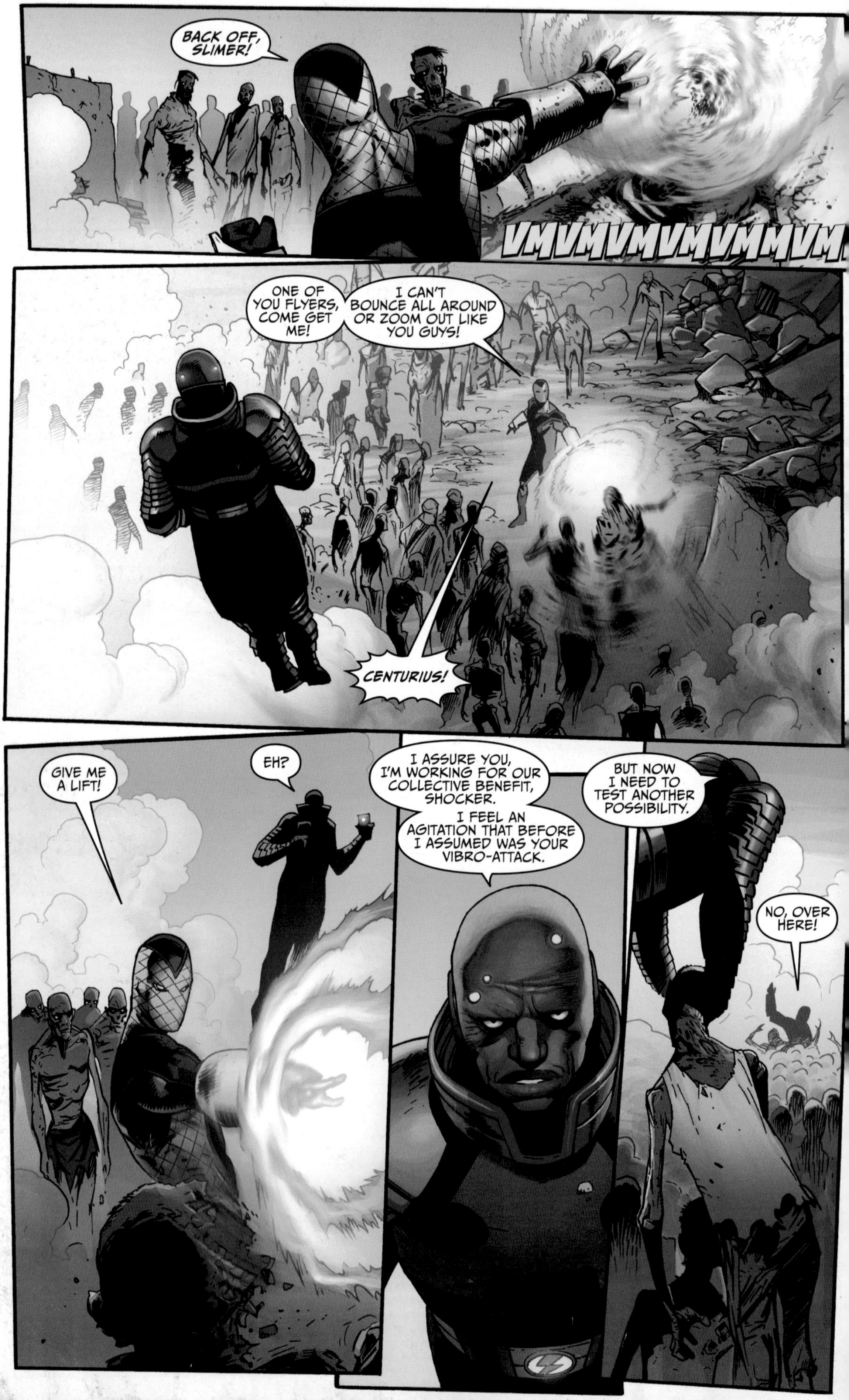
BACK OFF, SLIMER!
VMVMVMVMVMVMMVM
ONE OF YOU FLYERS, COME GET ME!
I CAN'T BOUNCE ALL AROUND OR ZOOM OUT LIKE YOU GUYS!
CENTURIUS!
GIVE ME A LIFT!
EH?
I ASSURE YOU, I'M WORKING FOR OUR COLLECTIVE BENEFIT, SHOCKER.
I FEEL AN AGITATION THAT BEFORE I ASSUMED WAS YOUR VIBRO-ATTACK.
BUT NOW I NEED TO TEST ANOTHER POSSIBILITY.
NO, OVER HERE!

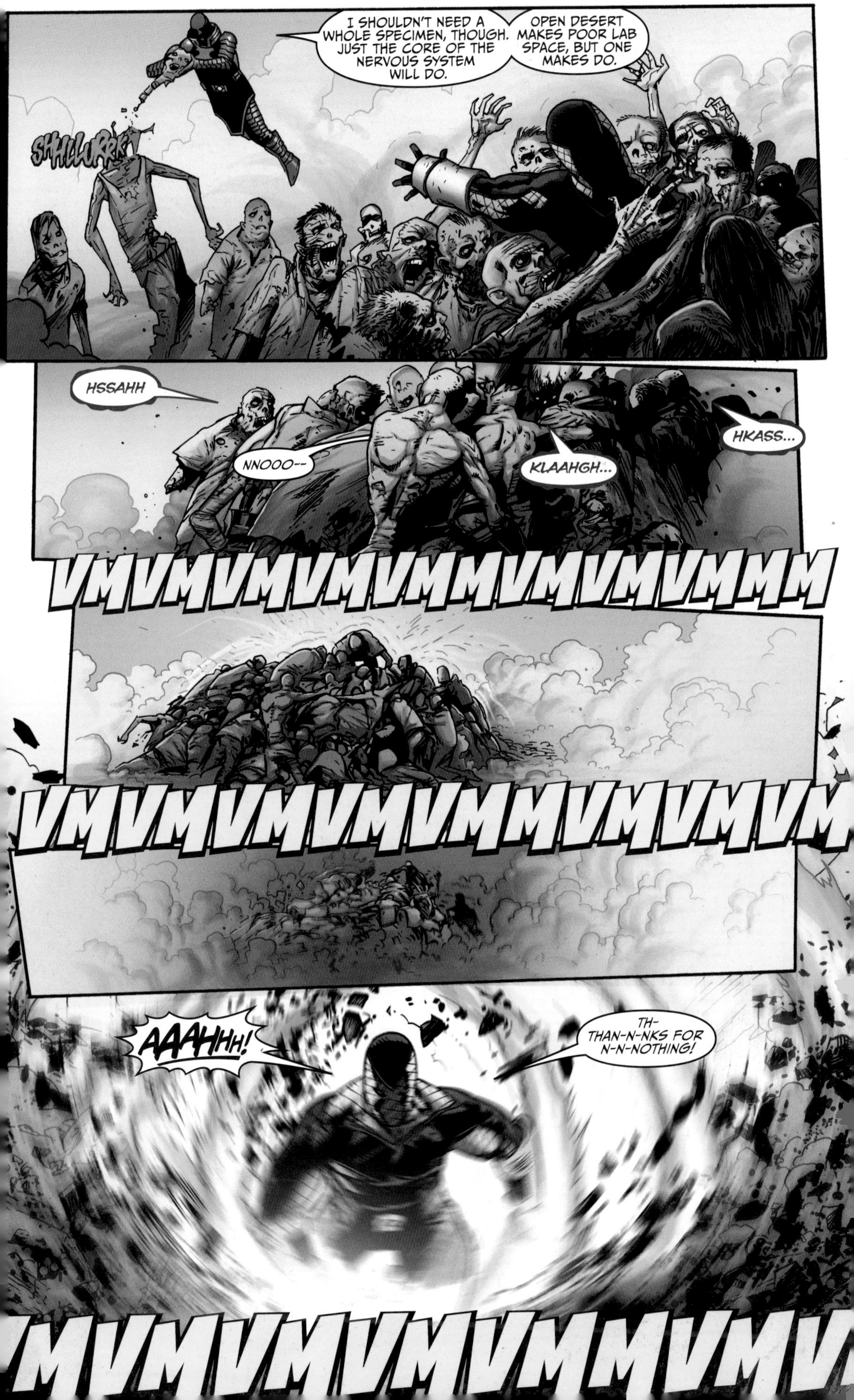

I SHOULDN'T NEED A WHOLE SPECIMEN, THOUGH. JUST THE CORE OF THE NERVOUS SYSTEM WILL DO.
OPEN DESERT MAKES POOR LAB SPACE, BUT ONE MAKES DO.
SHHLURRK
HSSAHH
NNOOO--
KLAAHGH...
HKASS...
VMVMVMVMVMMVMVMVMMM
VMVMVMVMVMMVMVMVM
AAAHHH!
TH- THAN-N-NKS FOR N-N-NOTHING!
MVMVMVMVMMVMV

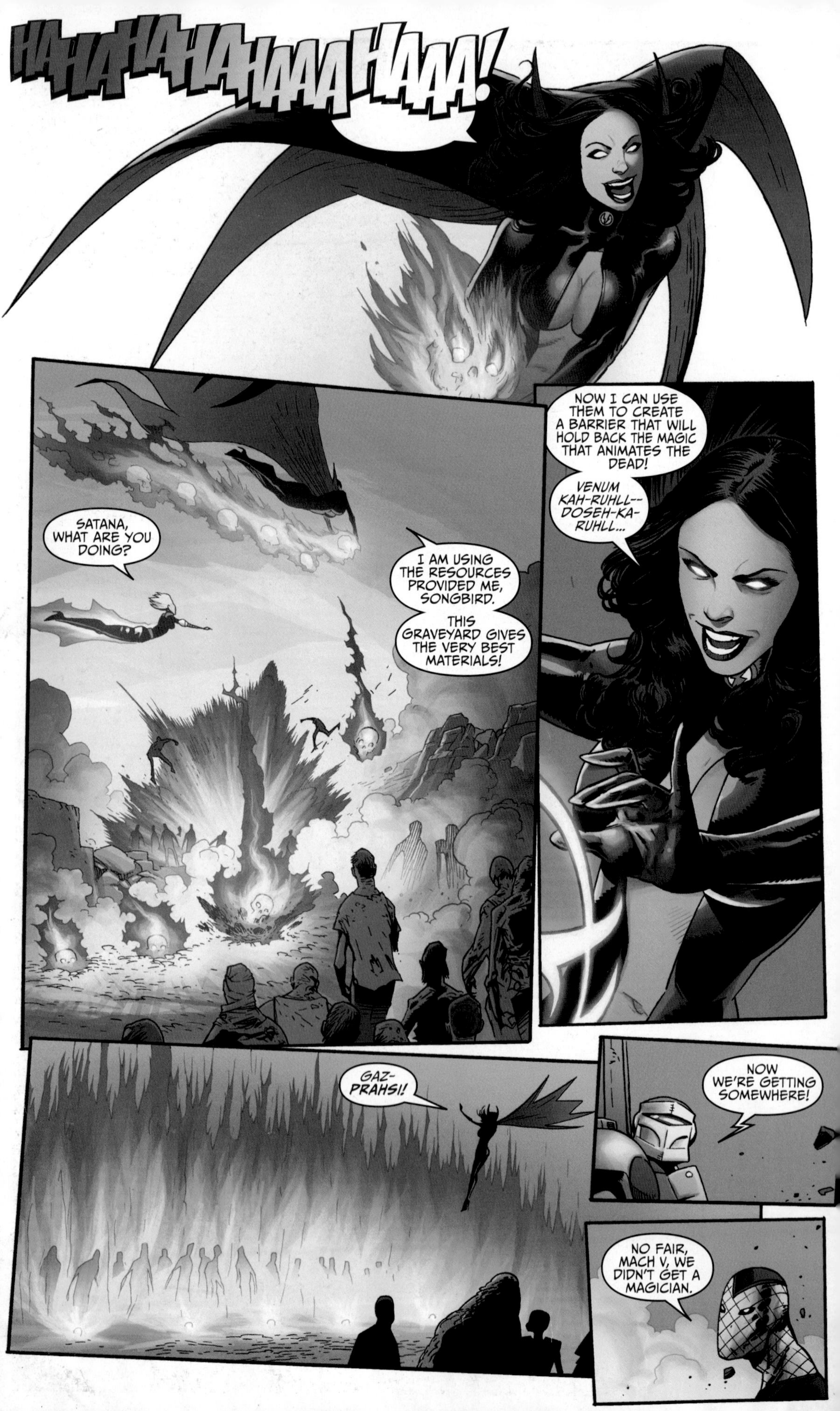
HAHAHAHAHAAAHAAA!
SATANA, WHAT ARE YOU DOING?
I AM USING THE RESOURCES PROVIDED ME, SONGBIRD.
THIS GRAVEYARD GIVES THE VERY BEST MATERIALS!
NOW I CAN USE THEM TO CREATE A BARRIER THAT WILL HOLD BACK THE MAGIC THAT ANIMATES THE DEAD!
VENUM KAH-RUHLL-- DOSEH-KA-RUHLL...
GAZ-PRAHSI!
NOW WE'RE GETTING SOMEWHERE!
NO FAIR, MACH V, WE DIDN'T GET A MAGICIAN.

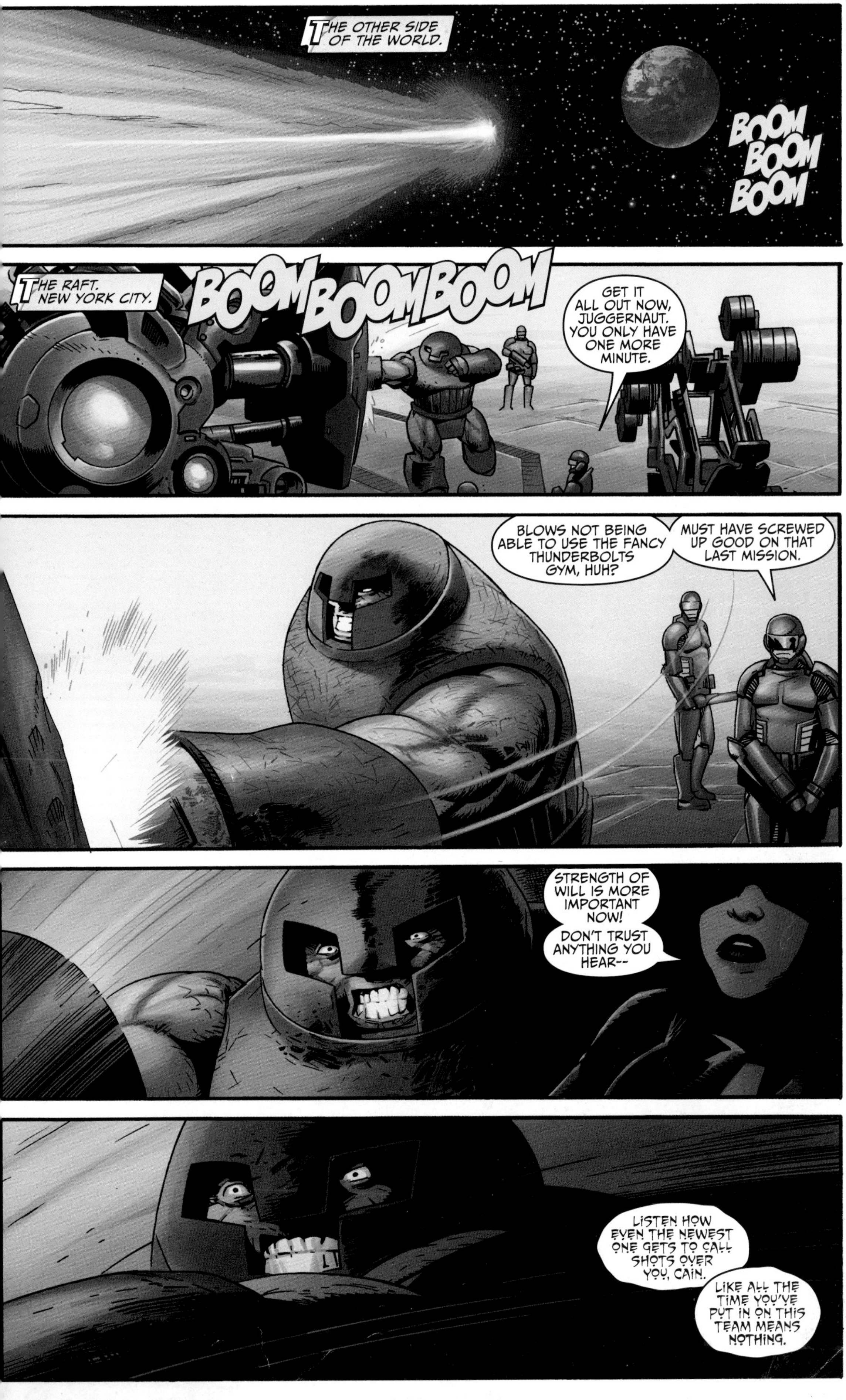
THE OTHER SIDE OF THE WORLD.
BOOM BOOM BOOM
THE RAFT. NEW YORK CITY.
BOOM BOOM BOOM
GET IT ALL OUT NOW, JUGGERNAUT. YOU ONLY HAVE ONE MORE MINUTE.
BLOWS NOT BEING ABLE TO USE THE FANCY THUNDERBOLTS GYM, HUH?
MUST HAVE SCREWED UP GOOD ON THAT LAST MISSION.
STRENGTH OF WILL IS MORE IMPORTANT NOW!
DON'T TRUST ANYTHING YOU HEAR--
LISTEN HOW EVEN THE NEWEST ONE GETS TO CALL SHOTS OVER YOU, CAIN.
LIKE ALL THE TIME YOU'VE PUT IN ON THIS TEAM MEANS NOTHING.

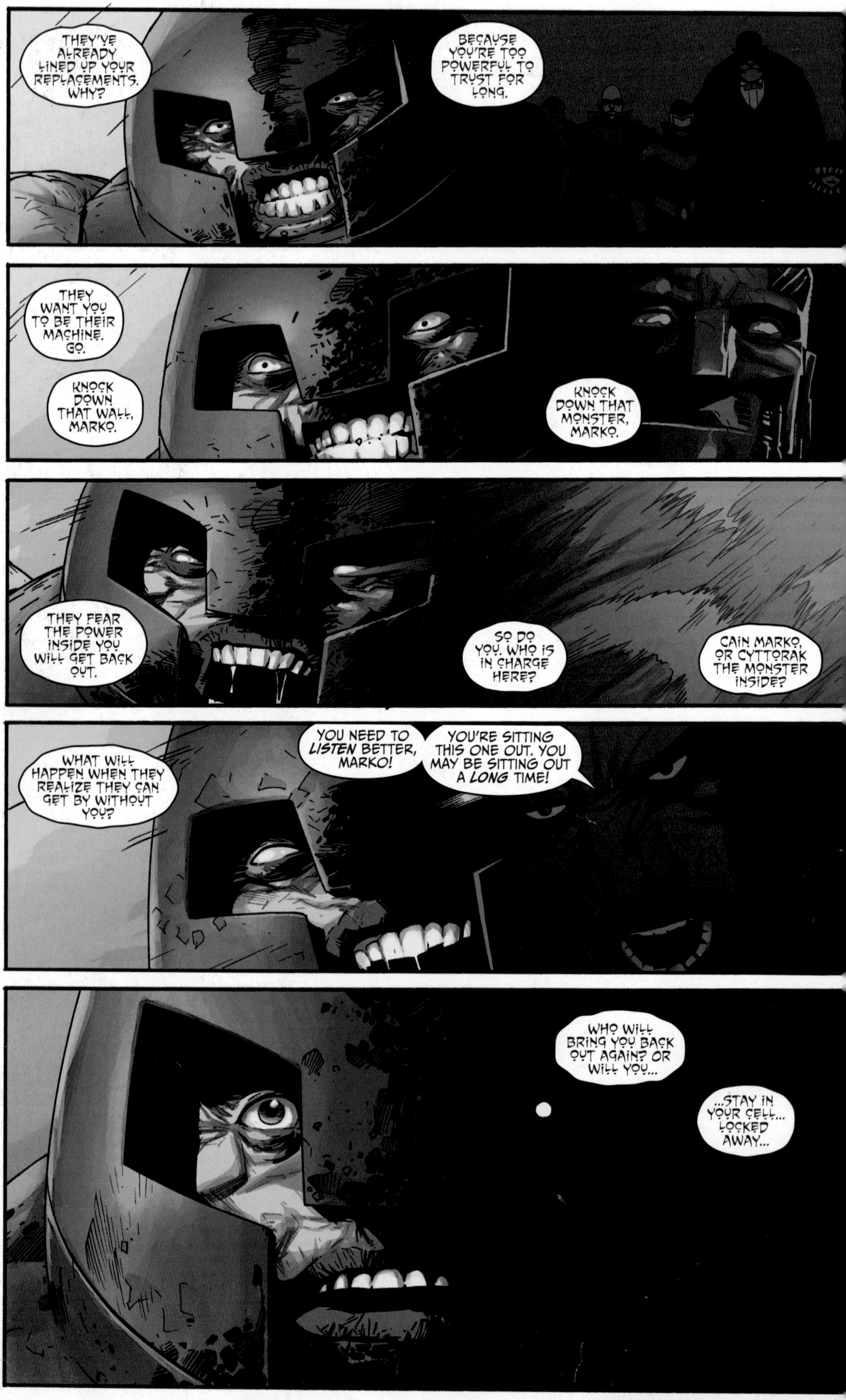
THEY'VE ALREADY LINED UP YOUR REPLACEMENTS. WHY?
BECAUSE YOU'RE TOO POWERFUL TO TRUST FOR LONG.
THEY WANT YOU TO BE THEIR MACHINE. GO.
KNOCK DOWN THAT WALL, MARKO.
KNOCK DOWN THAT MONSTER, MARKO.
THEY FEAR THE POWER INSIDE YOU WILL GET BACK OUT.
SO DO YOU. WHO IS IN CHARGE HERE?
CAIN MARKO, OR CYTTORAK THE MONSTER INSIDE?
WHAT WILL HAPPEN WHEN THEY REALIZE THEY CAN GET BY WITHOUT YOU?
YOU NEED TO LISTEN BETTER, MARKO!
YOU'RE SITTING THIS ONE OUT. YOU MAY BE SITTING OUT A LONG TIME!
WHO WILL BRING YOU BACK OUT AGAIN? OR WILL YOU...
...STAY IN YOUR CELL... LOCKED AWAY...

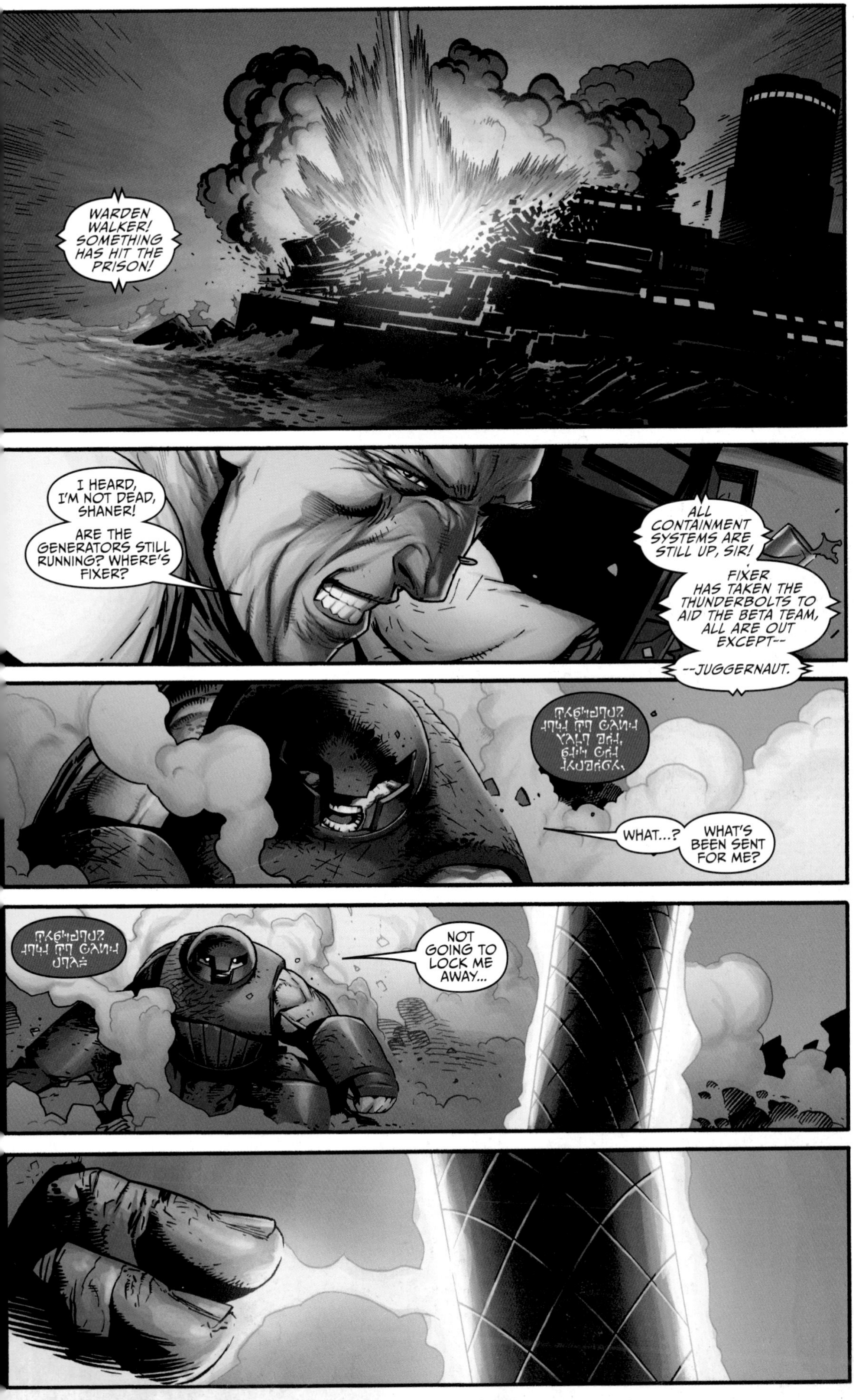
WARDEN WALKER! SOMETHING HAS HIT THE PRISON!
I HEARD, I'M NOT DEAD, SHANER!
ARE THE GENERATORS STILL RUNNING? WHERE'S FIXER?
ALL CONTAINMENT SYSTEMS ARE STILL UP, SIR!
FIXER HAS TAKEN THE THUNDERBOLTS TO AID THE BETA TEAM, ALL ARE OUT EXCEPT--
--JUGGERNAUT.
WHAT...?
WHAT'S BEEN SENT FOR ME?
NOT GOING TO LOCK ME AWAY...

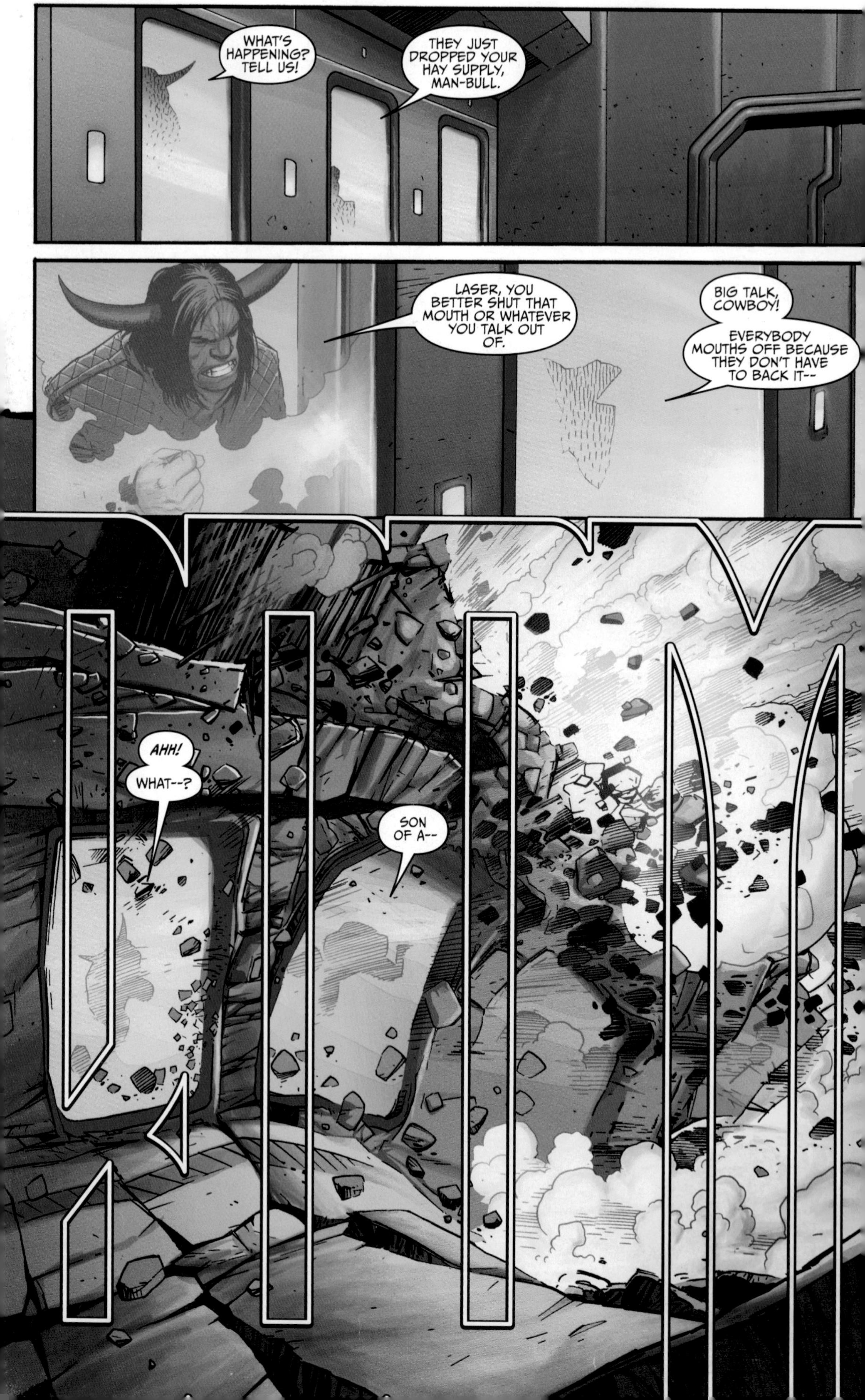
WHAT'S HAPPENING? TELL US!
THEY JUST DROPPED YOUR HAY SUPPLY, MAN-BULL.
LASER, YOU BETTER SHUT THAT MOUTH OR WHATEVER YOU TALK OUT OF.
BIG TALK, COWBOY!
EVERYBODY MOUTHS OFF BECAUSE THEY DON'T HAVE TO BACK IT--
AHH!
WHAT--?
SON OF A--

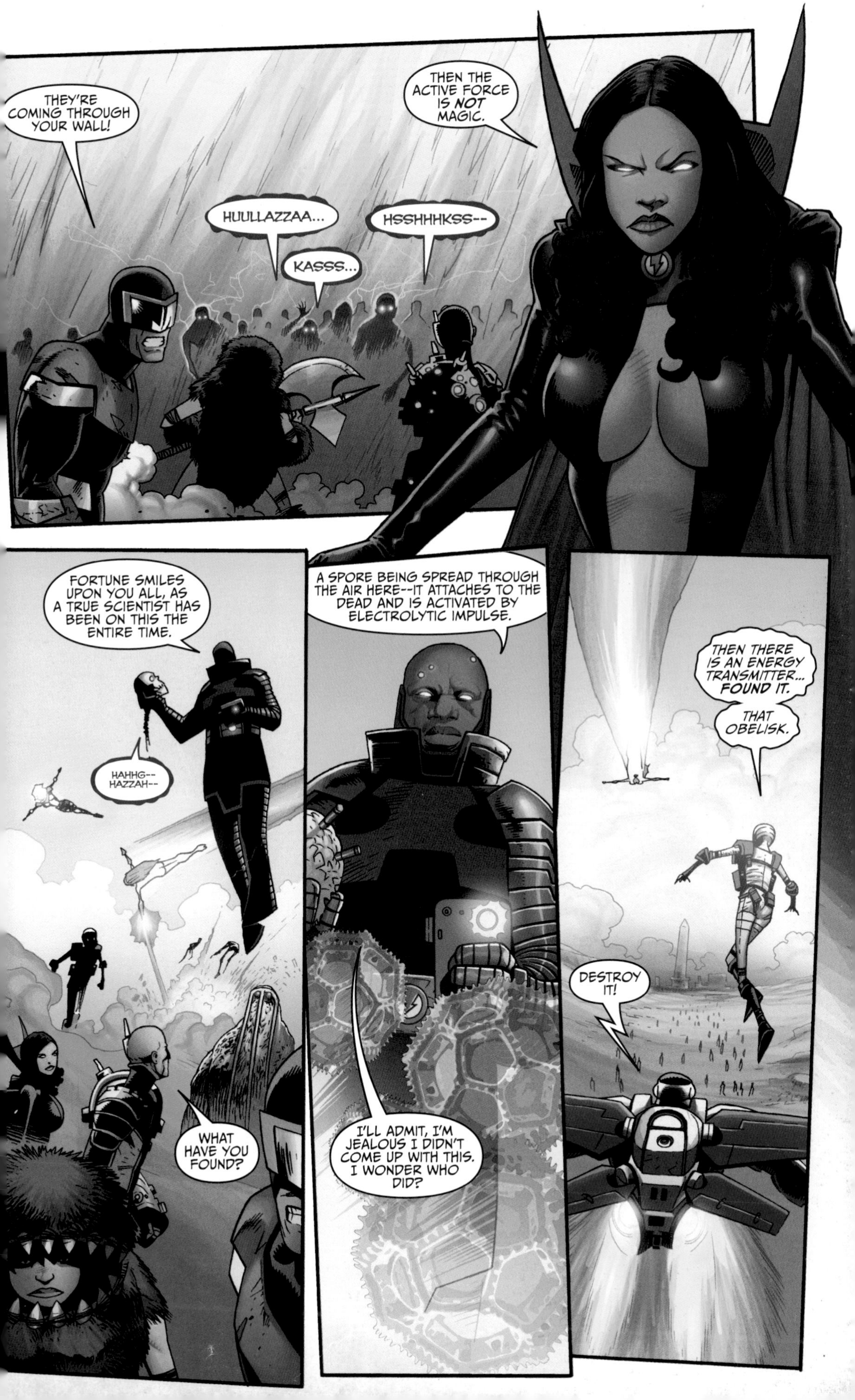

THEY'RE COMING THROUGH YOUR WALL!
THEN THE ACTIVE FORCE IS NOT MAGIC.
HUULLAZZAA...
KASSS...
HSSHHHKSS--
FORTUNE SMILES UPON YOU ALL, AS A TRUE SCIENTIST HAS BEEN ON THIS THE ENTIRE TIME.
HAHHG-- HAZZAH--
WHAT HAVE YOU FOUND?
A SPORE BEING SPREAD THROUGH THE AIR HERE--IT ATTACHES TO THE DEAD AND IS ACTIVATED BY ELECTROLYTIC IMPULSE.
I'LL ADMIT, I'M JEALOUS I DIDN'T COME UP WITH THIS. I WONDER WHO DID?
THEN THERE IS AN ENERGY TRANSMITTER... FOUND IT.
THAT OBELISK.
DESTROY IT!

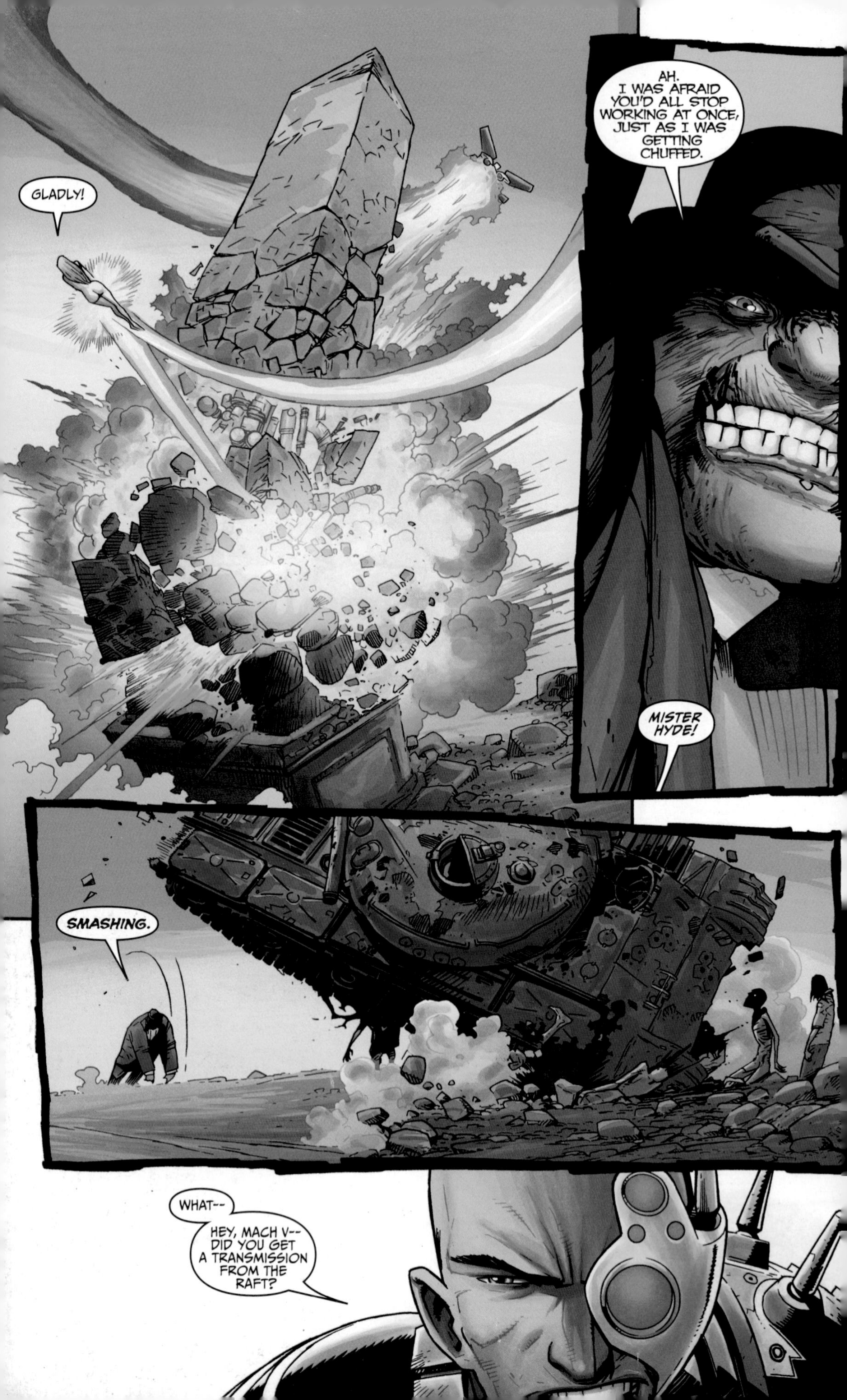
GLADLY!
AH. I WAS AFRAID YOU'D ALL STOP WORKING AT ONCE, JUST AS I WAS GETTING CHUFFED.
MISTER HYDE!
SMASHING.
WHAT--
HEY, MACH V-- DID YOU GET A TRANSMISSION FROM THE RAFT?

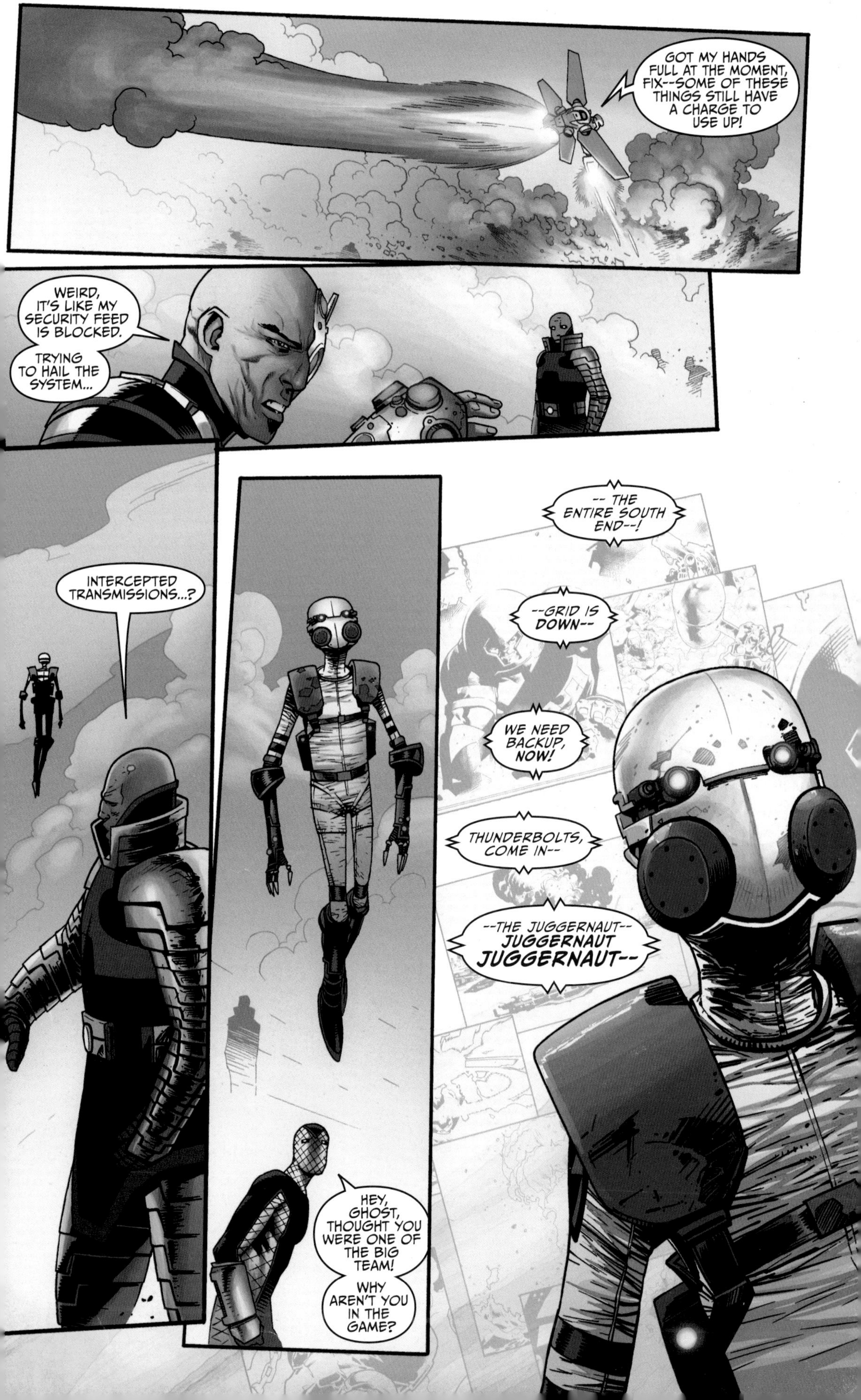

GOT MY HANDS FULL AT THE MOMENT, FIX--SOME OF THESE THINGS STILL HAVE A CHARGE TO USE UP!
WEIRD, IT'S LIKE MY SECURITY FEED IS BLOCKED.
TRYING TO HAIL THE SYSTEM...
INTERCEPTED TRANSMISSIONS...?
-- THE ENTIRE SOUTH END--!
--GRID IS DOWN--
WE NEED BACKUP, NOW!
THUNDERBOLTS, COME IN--
--THE JUGGERNAUT-- JUGGERNAUT JUGGERNAUT--
HEY, GHOST, THOUGHT YOU WERE ONE OF THE BIG TEAM!
WHY AREN'T YOU IN THE GAME?

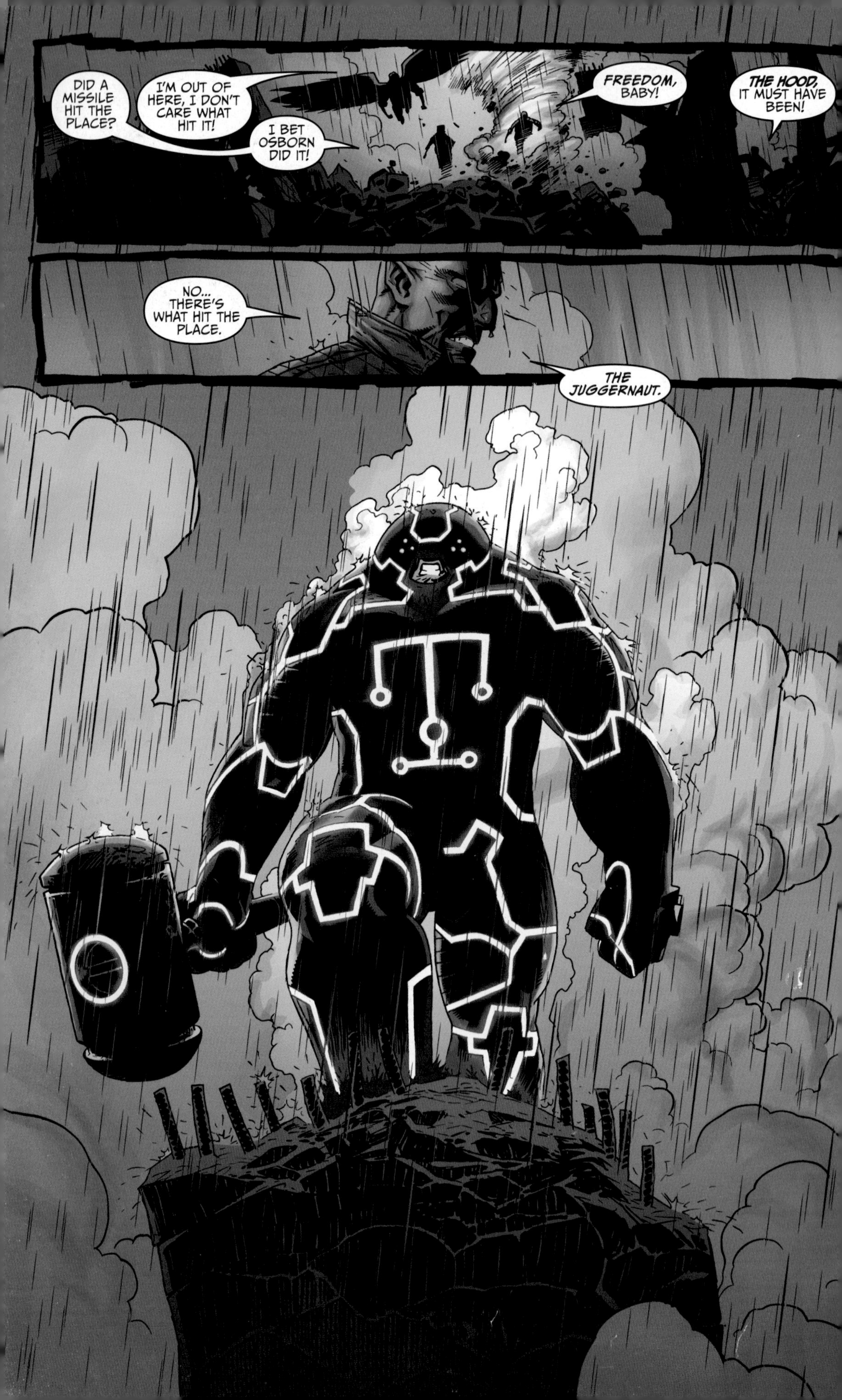

DID A MISSILE HIT THE PLACE?
I'M OUT OF HERE, I DON'T CARE WHAT HIT IT!
I BET OSBORN DID IT!
FREEDOM, BABY!
THE HOOD, IT MUST HAVE BEEN!
NO... THERE'S WHAT HIT THE PLACE.
THE JUGGERNAUT.

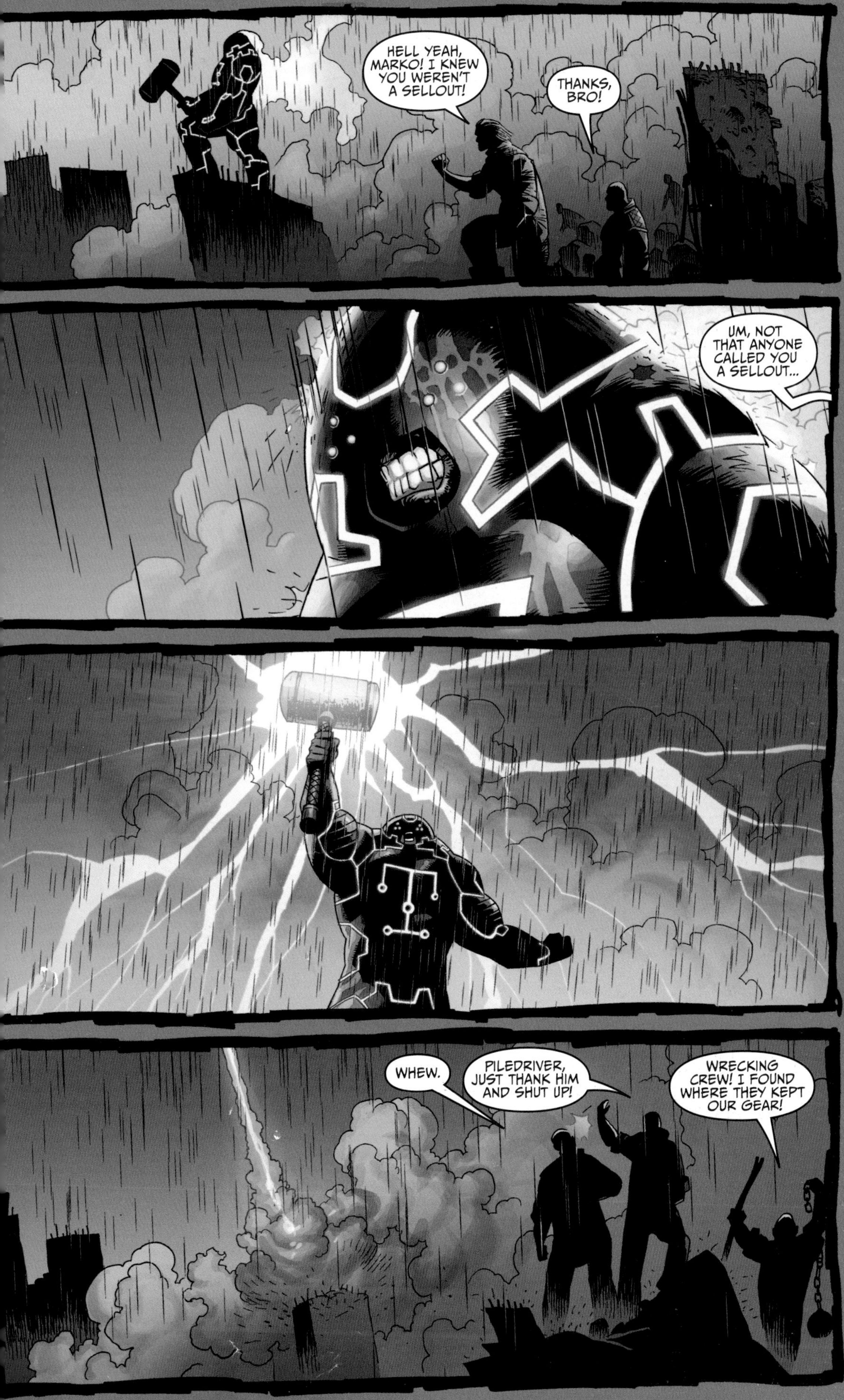
HELL YEAH, MARKO! I KNEW YOU WEREN'T A SELLOUT!
THANKS, BRO!
UM, NOT THAT ANYONE CALLED YOU A SELLOUT...
WHEW.
PILEDRIVER, JUST THANK HIM AND SHUT UP!
WRECKING CREW! I FOUND WHERE THEY KEPT OUR GEAR!

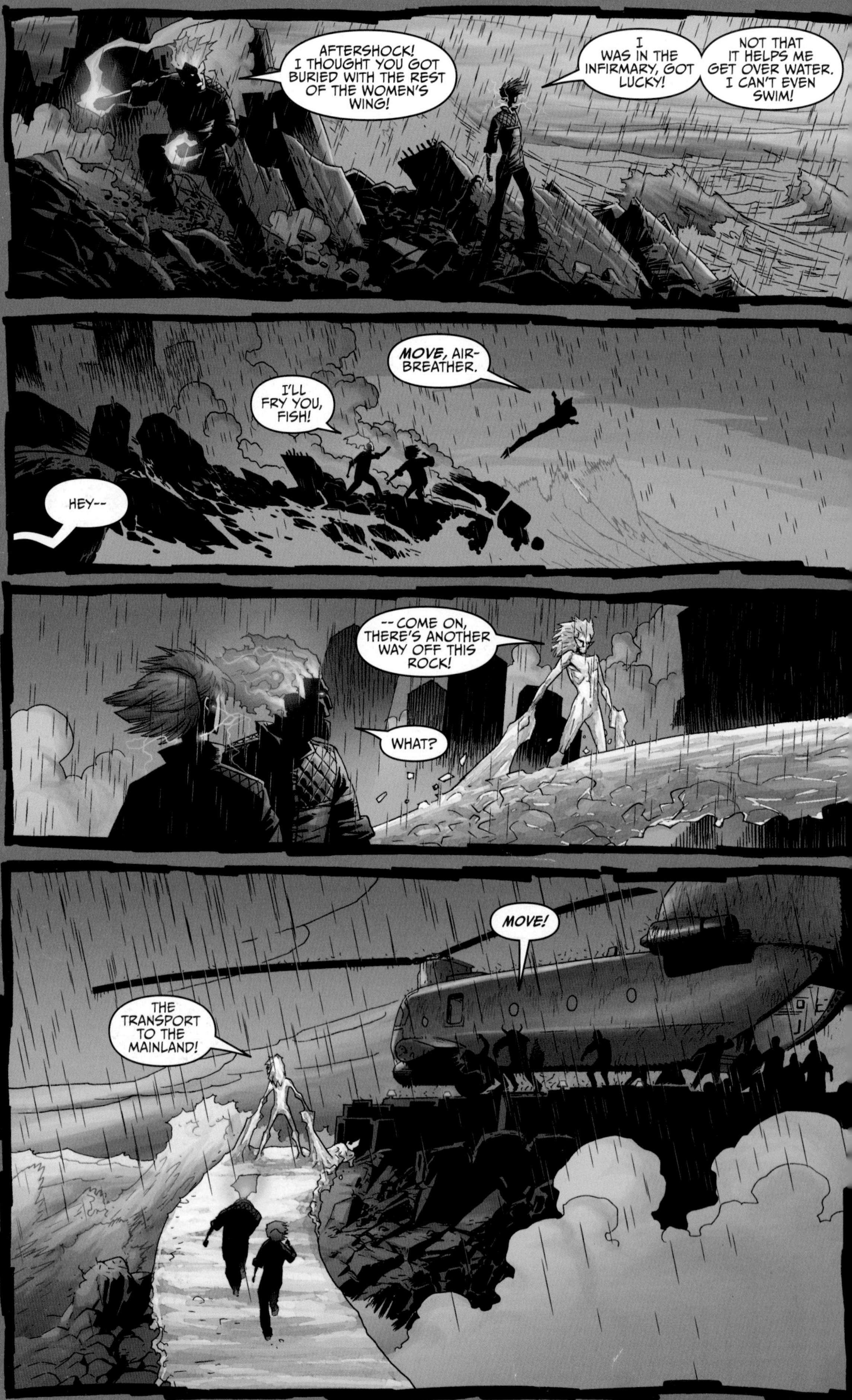
AFTERSHOCK! I THOUGHT YOU GOT BURIED WITH THE REST OF THE WOMEN'S WING!
I WAS IN THE INFIRMARY, GOT LUCKY!
NOT THAT IT HELPS ME GET OVER WATER. I CAN'T EVEN SWIM!
MOVE, AIR-BREATHER.
I'LL FRY YOU, FISH!
HEY--
--COME ON, THERE'S ANOTHER WAY OFF THIS ROCK!
WHAT?
THE TRANSPORT TO THE MAINLAND!
MOVE!

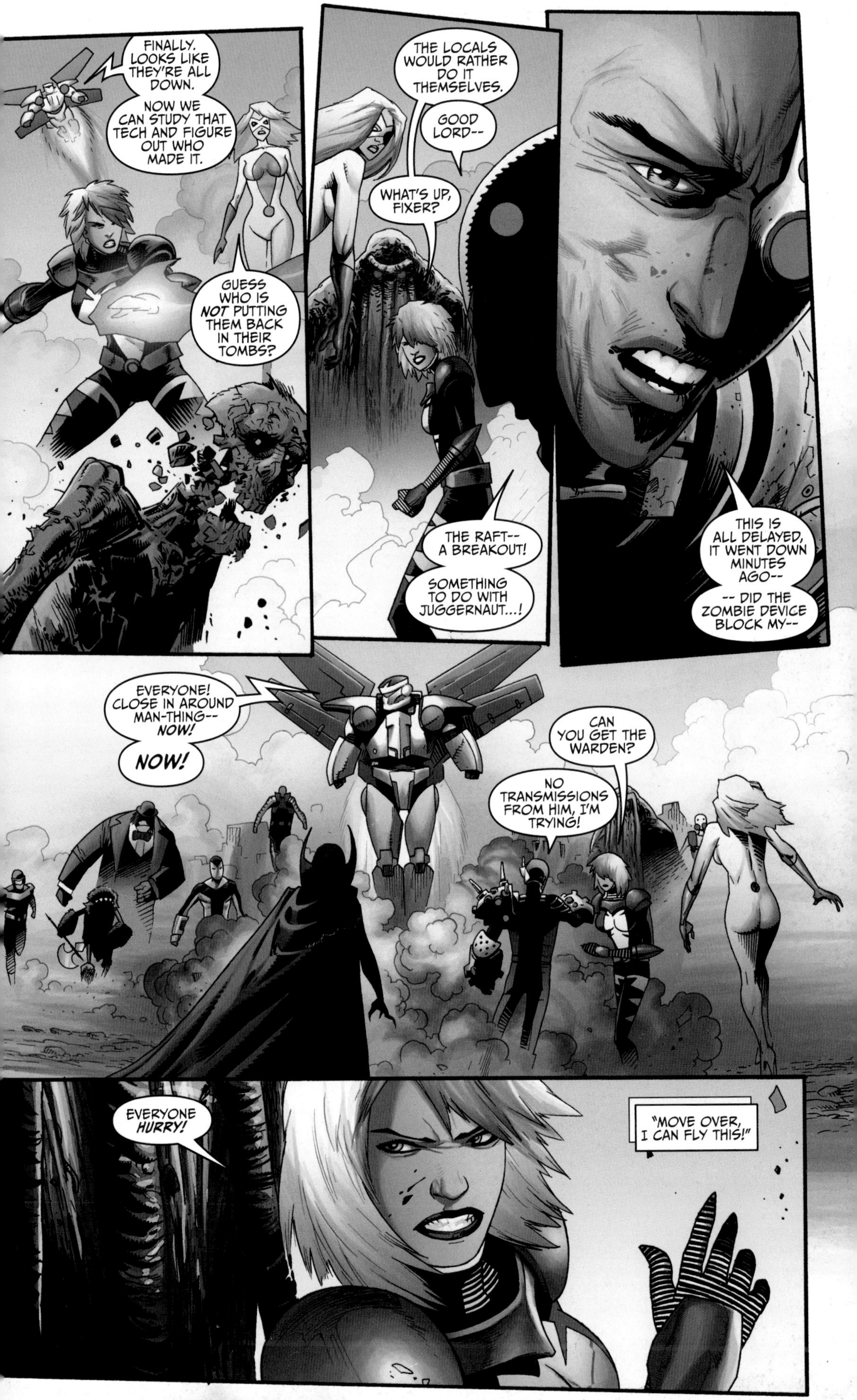

FINALLY. LOOKS LIKE THEY'RE ALL DOWN.
NOW WE CAN STUDY THAT TECH AND FIGURE OUT WHO MADE IT.
GUESS WHO IS *NOT* PUTTING THEM BACK IN THEIR TOMBS?
THE LOCALS WOULD RATHER DO IT THEMSELVES.
GOOD LORD--
WHAT'S UP, FIXER?
THE RAFT-- A BREAKOUT!
SOMETHING TO DO WITH JUGGERNAUT...!
THIS IS ALL DELAYED, IT WENT DOWN MINUTES AGO--
-- DID THE ZOMBIE DEVICE BLOCK MY--
EVERYONE! CLOSE IN AROUND MAN-THING-- *NOW!*
NOW!
CAN YOU GET THE WARDEN?
NO TRANSMISSIONS FROM HIM, I'M TRYING!
EVERYONE *HURRY!*
"MOVE OVER, I CAN FLY THIS!"

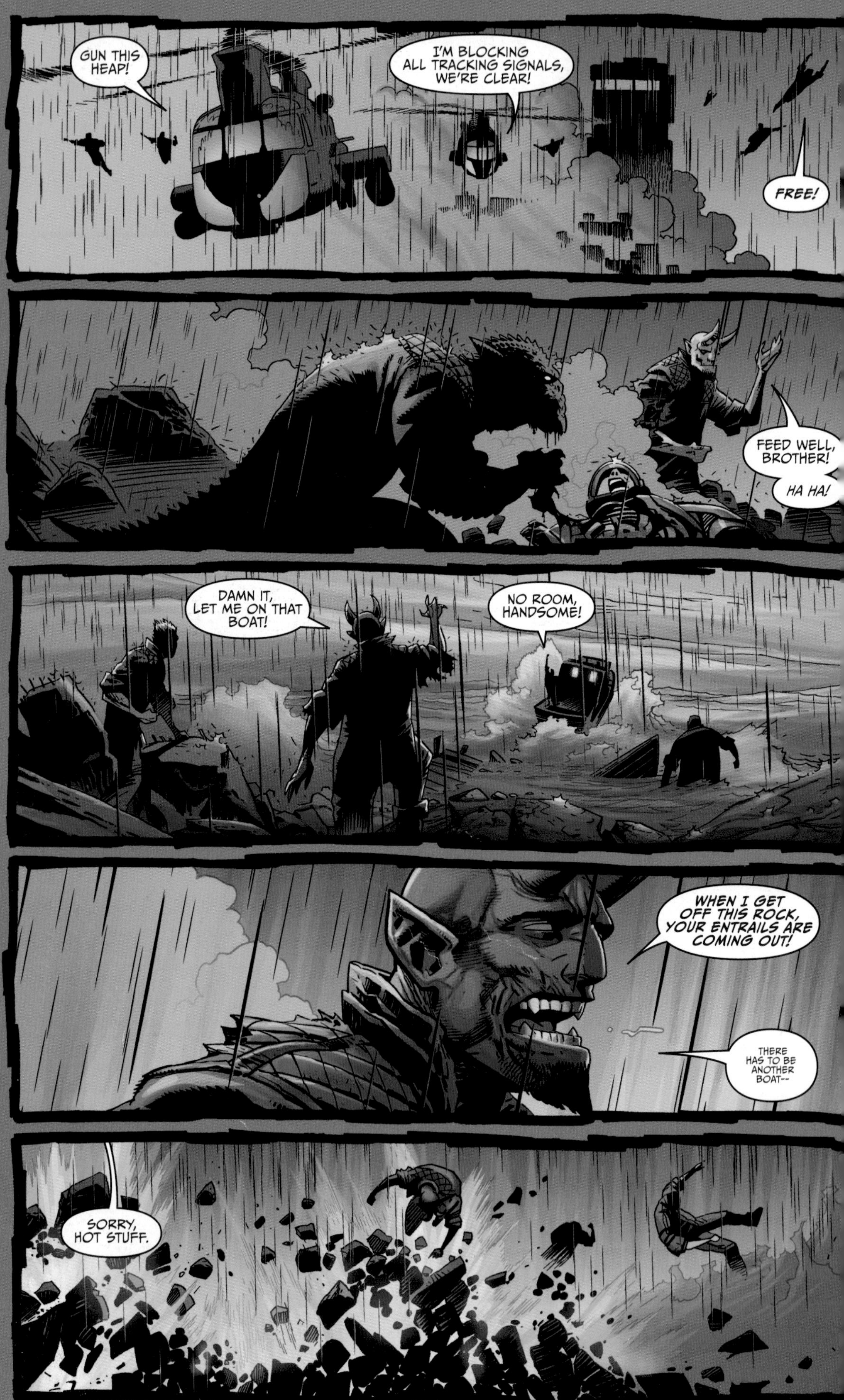
GUN THIS HEAP!
I'M BLOCKING ALL TRACKING SIGNALS, WE'RE CLEAR!
FREE!
FEED WELL, BROTHER!
HA HA!
DAMN IT, LET ME ON THAT BOAT!
NO ROOM, HANDSOME!
WHEN I GET OFF THIS ROCK, YOUR ENTRAILS ARE COMING OUT!
THERE HAS TO BE ANOTHER BOAT--
SORRY, HOT STUFF.

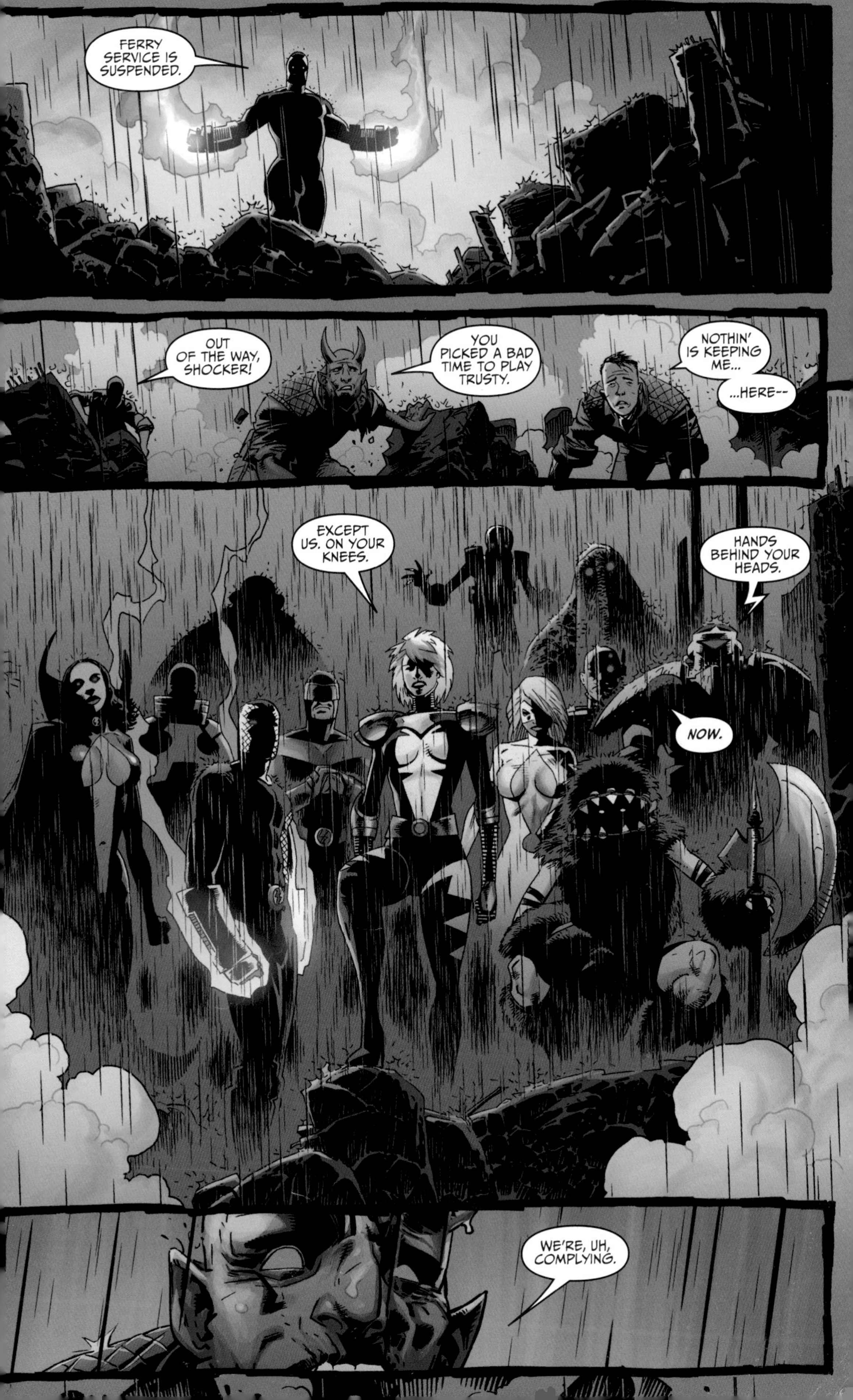
FERRY SERVICE IS SUSPENDED.
OUT OF THE WAY, SHOCKER!
YOU PICKED A BAD TIME TO PLAY TRUSTY.
NOTHIN' IS KEEPING ME...
...HERE--
EXCEPT US. ON YOUR KNEES.
HANDS BEHIND YOUR HEADS.
NOW.
WE'RE, UH, COMPLYING.

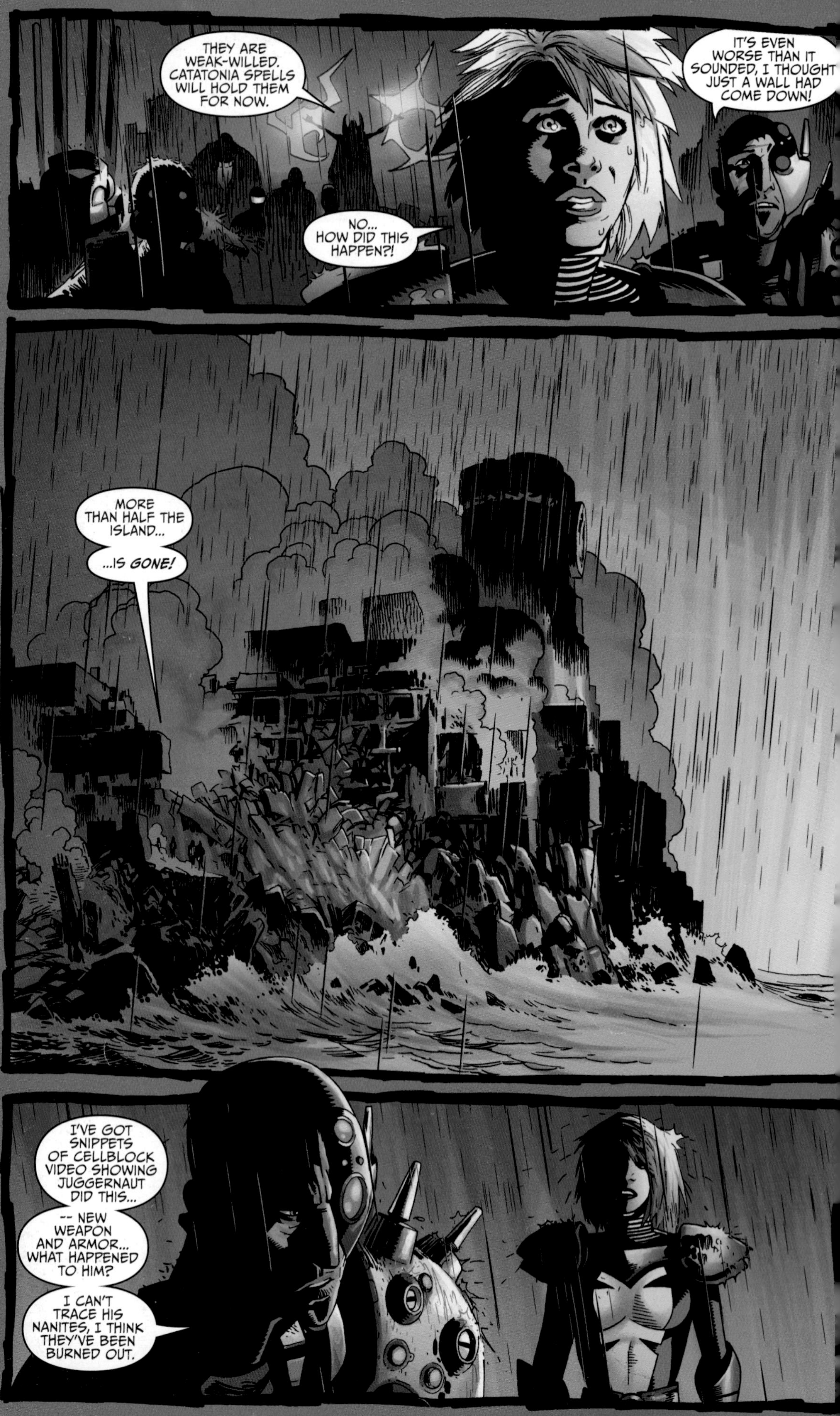
THEY ARE WEAK-WILLED. CATATONIA SPELLS WILL HOLD THEM FOR NOW.
IT'S EVEN WORSE THAN IT SOUNDED, I THOUGHT JUST A WALL HAD COME DOWN!
NO... HOW DID THIS HAPPEN?!
MORE THAN HALF THE ISLAND...
...IS GONE!
I'VE GOT SNIPPETS OF CELLBLOCK VIDEO SHOWING JUGGERNAUT DID THIS...
-- NEW WEAPON AND ARMOR... WHAT HAPPENED TO HIM?
I CAN'T TRACE HIS NANITES, I THINK THEY'VE BEEN BURNED OUT.

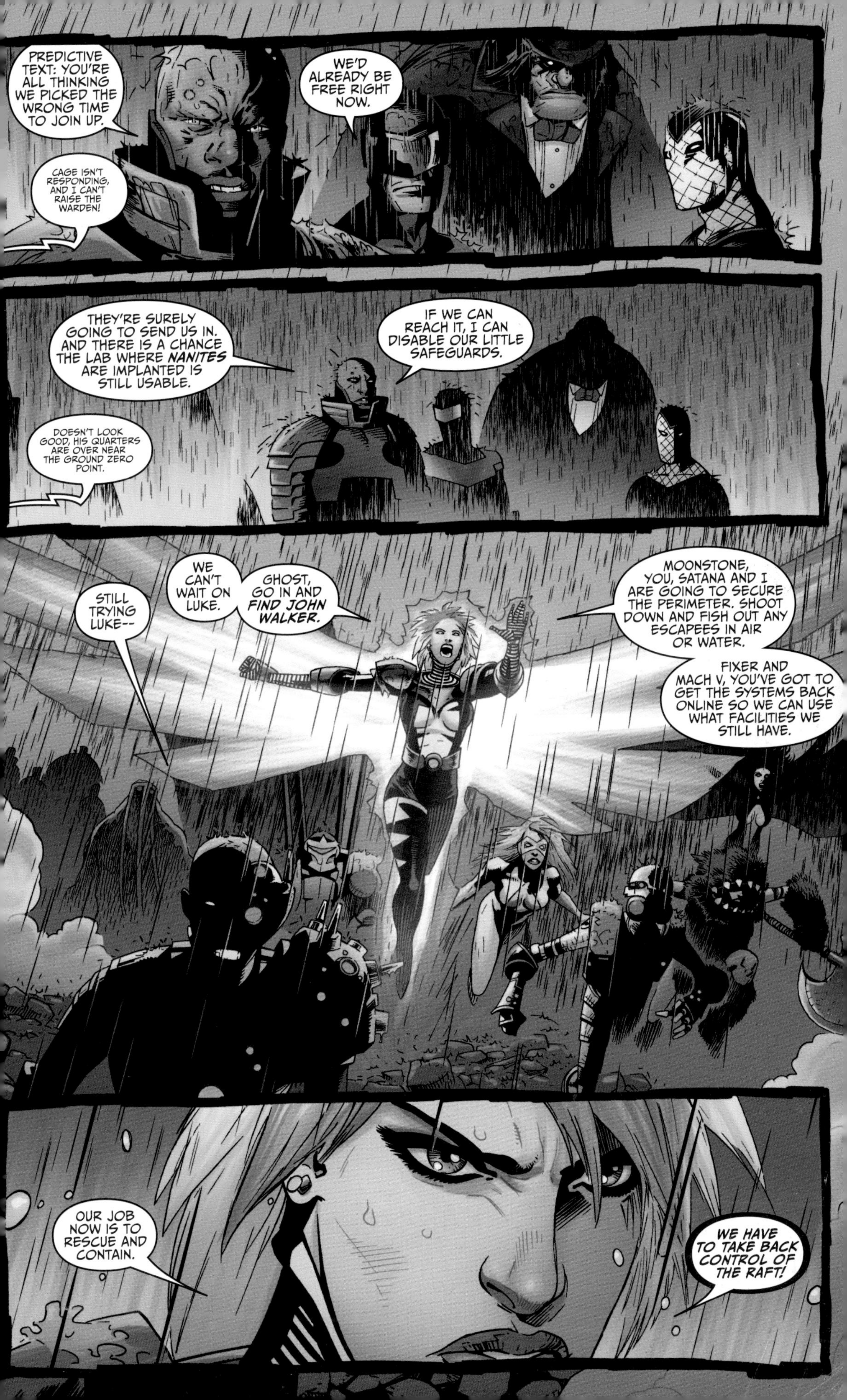
PREDICTIVE TEXT: YOU'RE ALL THINKING WE PICKED THE WRONG TIME TO JOIN UP.
WE'D ALREADY BE FREE RIGHT NOW.
CAGE ISN'T RESPONDING, AND I CAN'T RAISE THE WARDEN!
THEY'RE SURELY GOING TO SEND US IN. AND THERE IS A CHANCE THE LAB WHERE NANITES ARE IMPLANTED IS STILL USABLE.
IF WE CAN REACH IT, I CAN DISABLE OUR LITTLE SAFEGUARDS.
DOESN'T LOOK GOOD, HIS QUARTERS ARE OVER NEAR THE GROUND ZERO POINT.
STILL TRYING LUKE--
WE CAN'T WAIT ON LUKE.
GHOST, GO IN AND FIND JOHN WALKER.
MOONSTONE, YOU, SATANA AND I ARE GOING TO SECURE THE PERIMETER. SHOOT DOWN AND FISH OUT ANY ESCAPEES IN AIR OR WATER.
FIXER AND MACH V, YOU'VE GOT TO GET THE SYSTEMS BACK ONLINE SO WE CAN USE WHAT FACILITIES WE STILL HAVE.
OUR JOB NOW IS TO RESCUE AND CONTAIN.
WE HAVE TO TAKE BACK CONTROL OF THE RAFT!

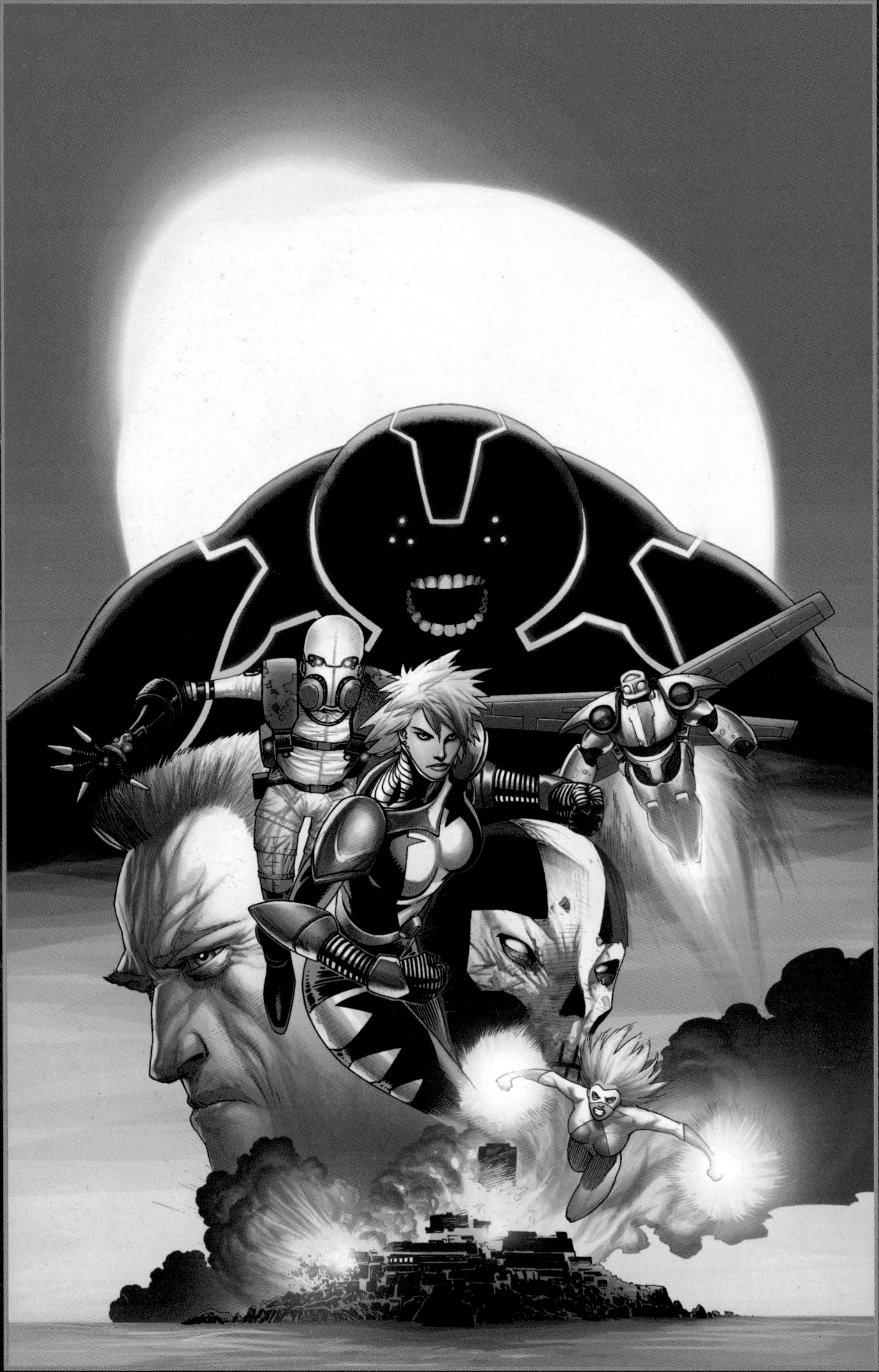

THUNDERBOLTS #159

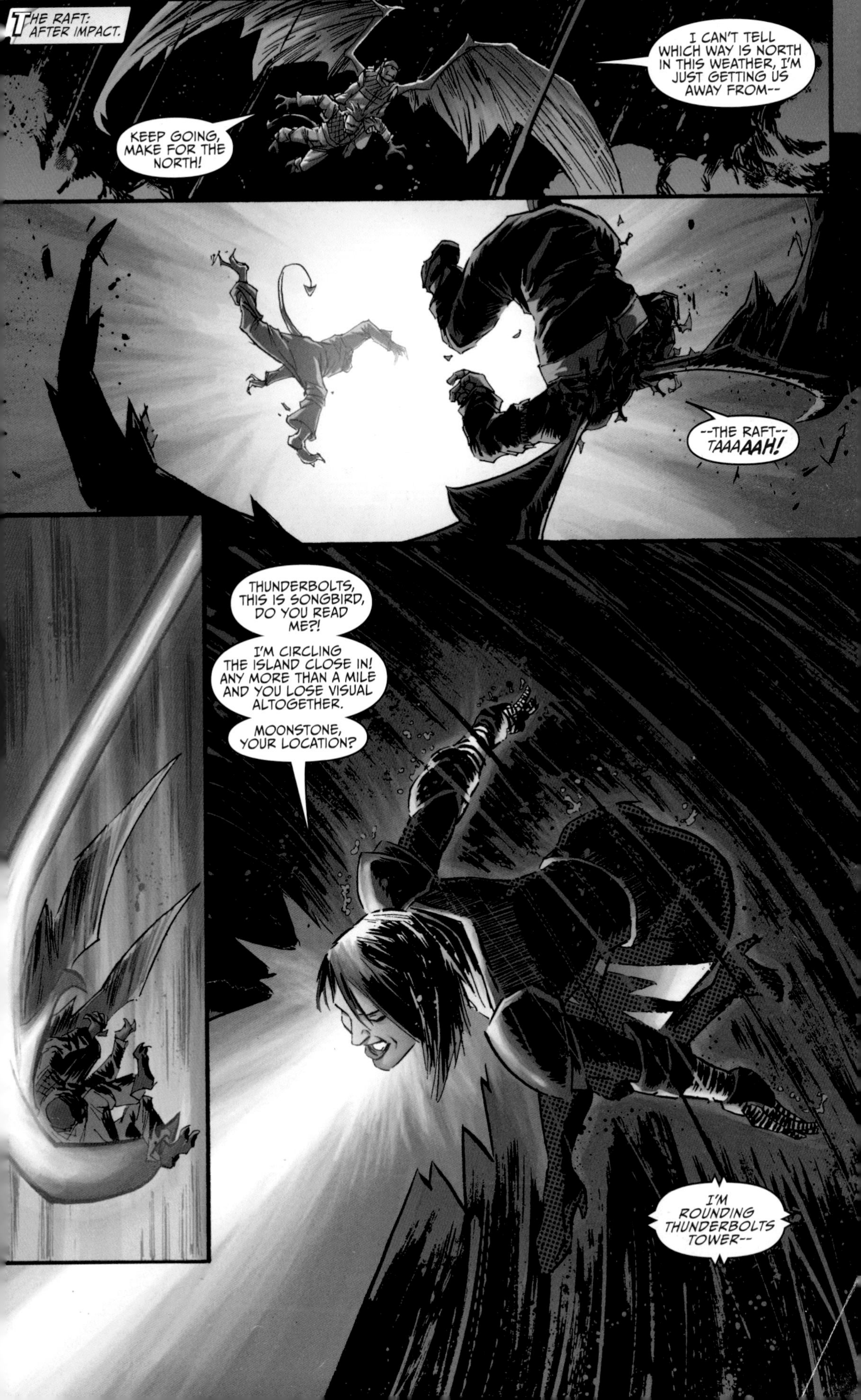
THE RAFT: AFTER IMPACT.
KEEP GOING, MAKE FOR THE NORTH!
I CAN'T TELL WHICH WAY IS NORTH IN THIS WEATHER, I'M JUST GETTING US AWAY FROM--
--THE RAFT-- TAAAAAH!
THUNDERBOLTS, THIS IS SONGBIRD, DO YOU READ ME?!
I'M CIRCLING THE ISLAND CLOSE IN! ANY MORE THAN A MILE AND YOU LOSE VISUAL ALTOGETHER.
MOONSTONE, YOUR LOCATION?
I'M ROUNDING THUNDERBOLTS TOWER--

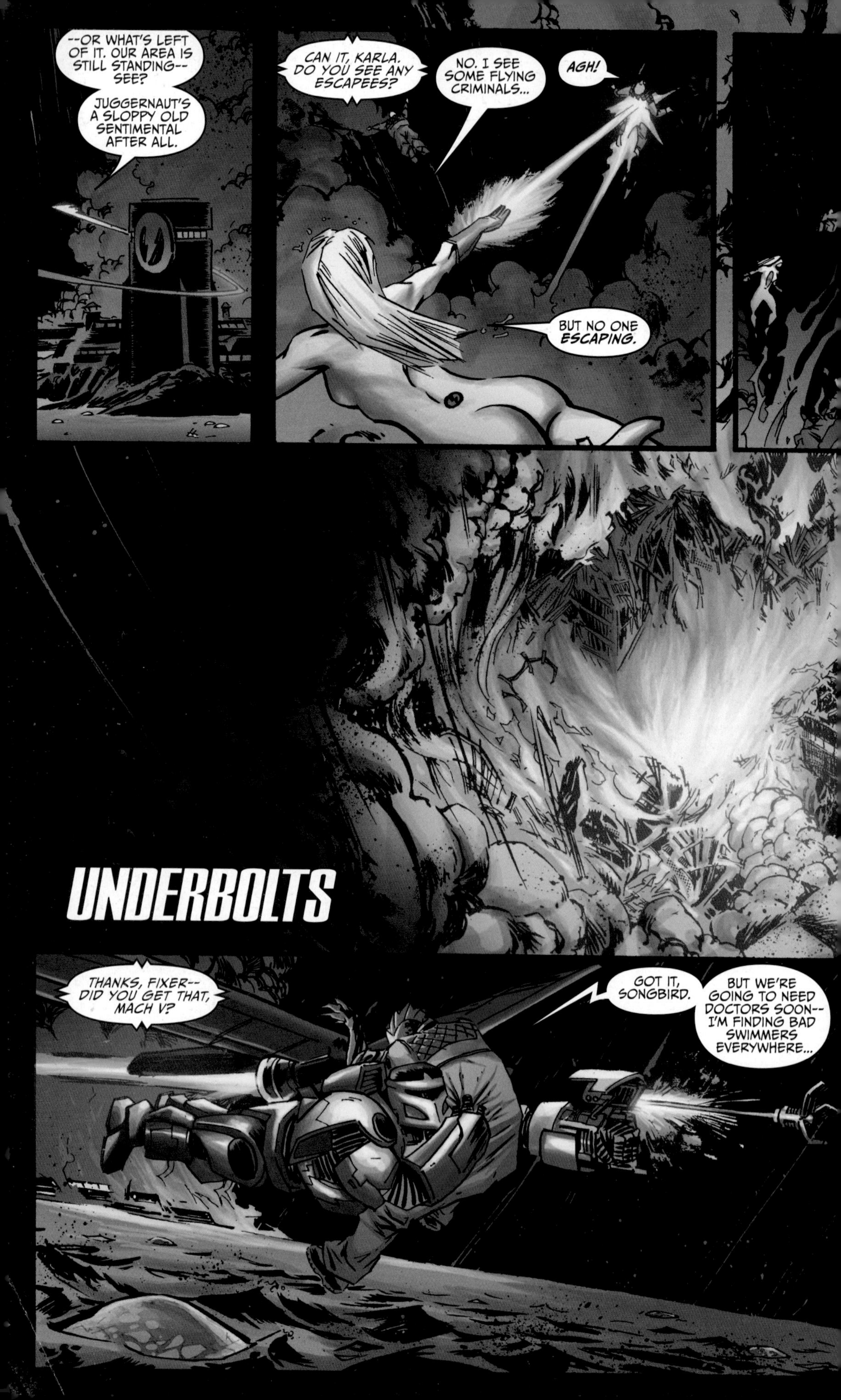

--OR WHAT'S LEFT OF IT. OUR AREA IS STILL STANDING--SEE?
JUGGERNAUT'S A SLOPPY OLD SENTIMENTAL AFTER ALL.
CAN IT, KARLA. DO YOU SEE ANY ESCAPEES?
NO. I SEE SOME FLYING CRIMINALS...
AGH!
BUT NO ONE ESCAPING.
UNDERBOLTS
THANKS, FIXER--DID YOU GET THAT, MACH V?
GOT IT, SONGBIRD.
BUT WE'RE GOING TO NEED DOCTORS SOON--I'M FINDING BAD SWIMMERS EVERYWHERE...

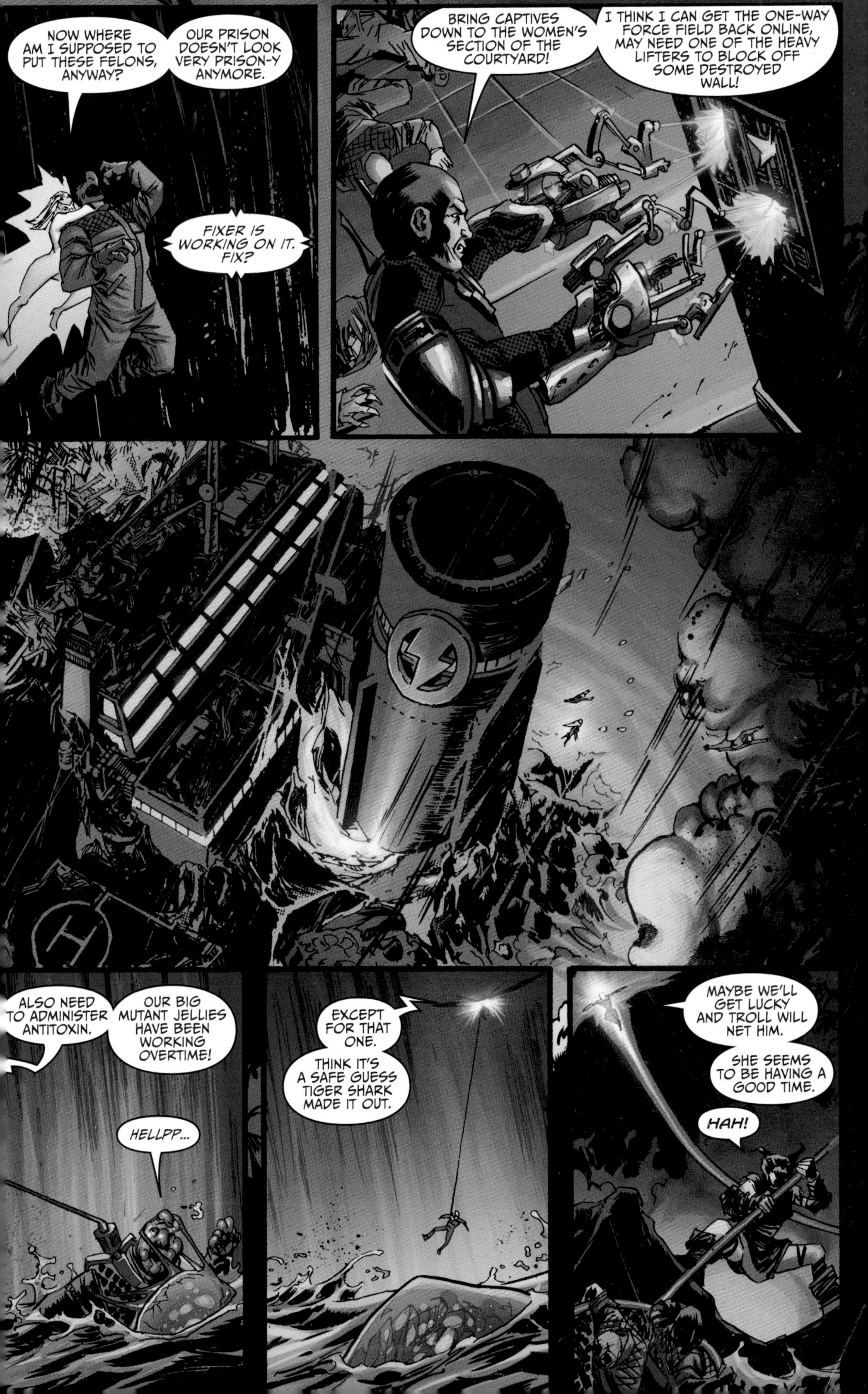
NOW WHERE AM I SUPPOSED TO PUT THESE FELONS, ANYWAY?
OUR PRISON DOESN'T LOOK VERY PRISON-Y ANYMORE.
FIXER IS WORKING ON IT. FIX?
BRING CAPTIVES DOWN TO THE WOMEN'S SECTION OF THE COURTYARD!
I THINK I CAN GET THE ONE-WAY FORCE FIELD BACK ONLINE, MAY NEED ONE OF THE HEAVY LIFTERS TO BLOCK OFF SOME DESTROYED WALL!
ALSO NEED TO ADMINISTER ANTITOXIN.
OUR BIG MUTANT JELLIES HAVE BEEN WORKING OVERTIME!
HELLPP...
EXCEPT FOR THAT ONE.
THINK IT'S A SAFE GUESS TIGER SHARK MADE IT OUT.
MAYBE WE'LL GET LUCKY AND TROLL WILL NET HIM.
SHE SEEMS TO BE HAVING A GOOD TIME.
HAH!

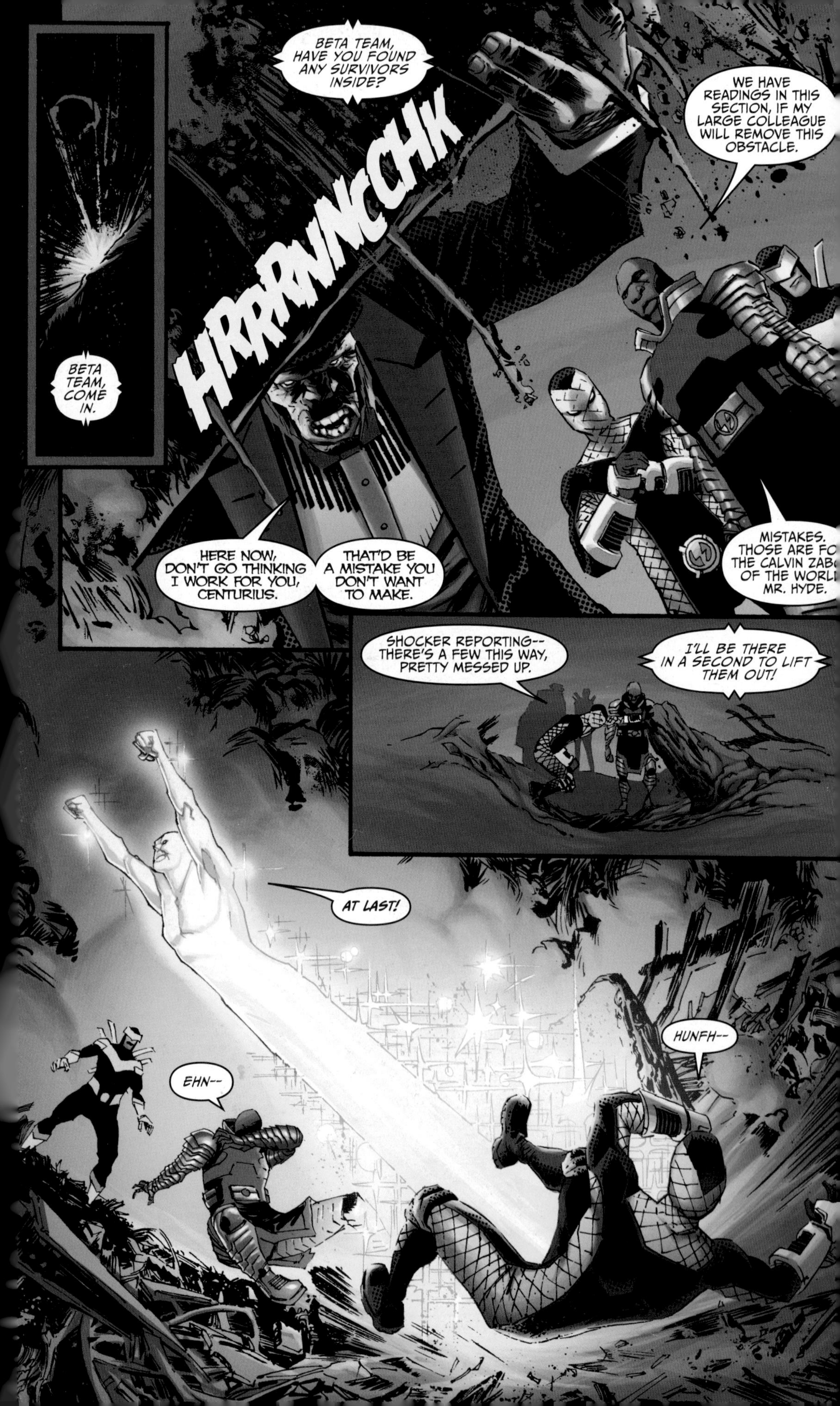
BETA TEAM, COME IN.
BETA TEAM, HAVE YOU FOUND ANY SURVIVORS INSIDE?
HRRRNNCCHK
WE HAVE READINGS IN THIS SECTION, IF MY LARGE COLLEAGUE WILL REMOVE THIS OBSTACLE.
HERE NOW, DON'T GO THINKING I WORK FOR YOU, CENTURIUS.
THAT'D BE A MISTAKE YOU DON'T WANT TO MAKE.
MISTAKES. THOSE ARE FO THE CALVIN ZAB OF THE WORL MR. HYDE.
SHOCKER REPORTING-- THERE'S A FEW THIS WAY, PRETTY MESSED UP.
I'LL BE THERE IN A SECOND TO LIFT THEM OUT!
AT LAST!
HUNFH--
EHN--

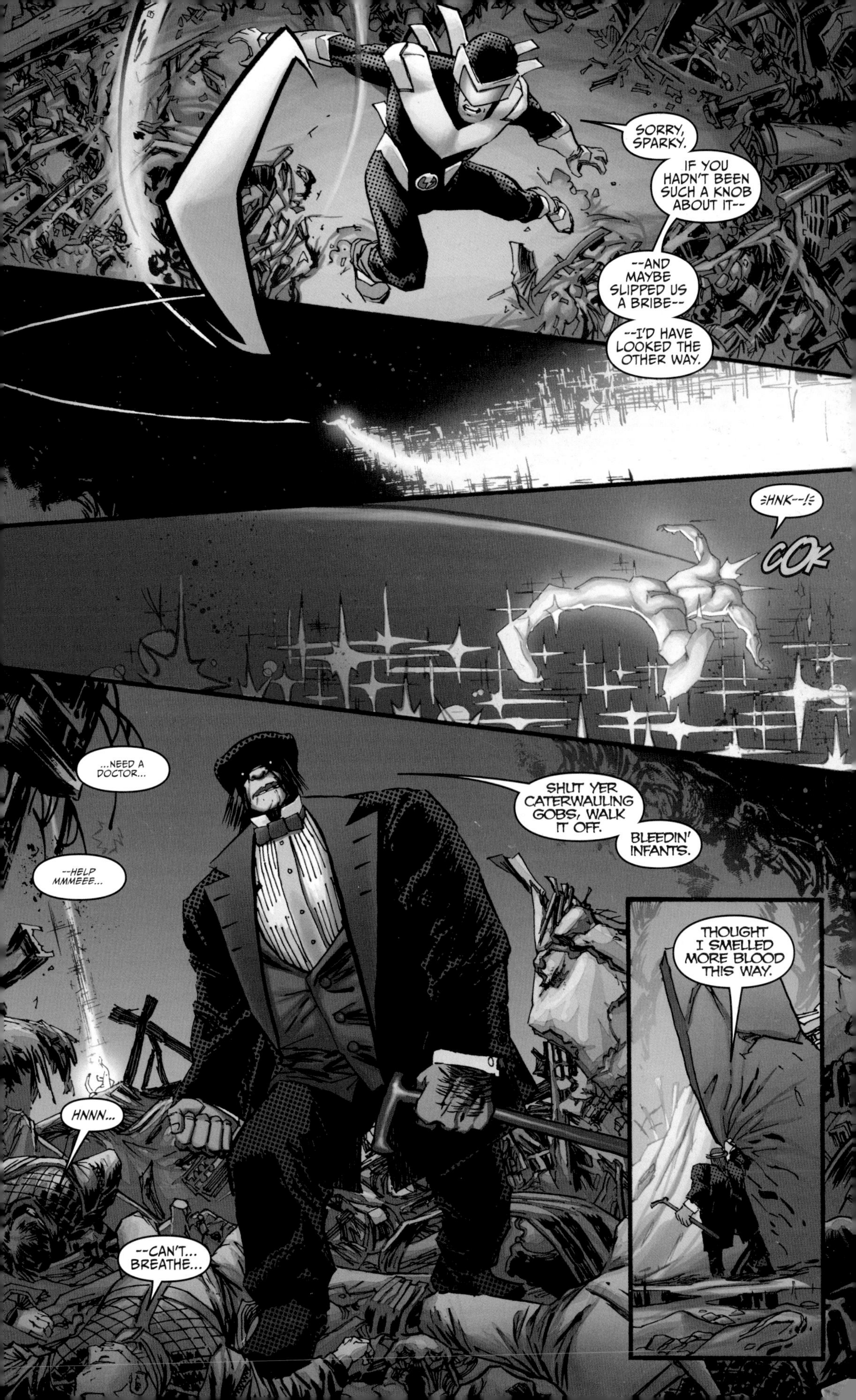
SORRY, SPARKY.
IF YOU HADN'T BEEN SUCH A KNOB ABOUT IT--
--AND MAYBE SLIPPED US A BRIBE--
--I'D HAVE LOOKED THE OTHER WAY.
HNK--!
COK
...NEED A DOCTOR...
SHUT YER CATERWAULING GOBS, WALK IT OFF.
BLEEDIN' INFANTS.
--HELP MMMEEE...
THOUGHT I SMELLED MORE BLOOD THIS WAY.
HNNN...
--CAN'T... BREATHE...

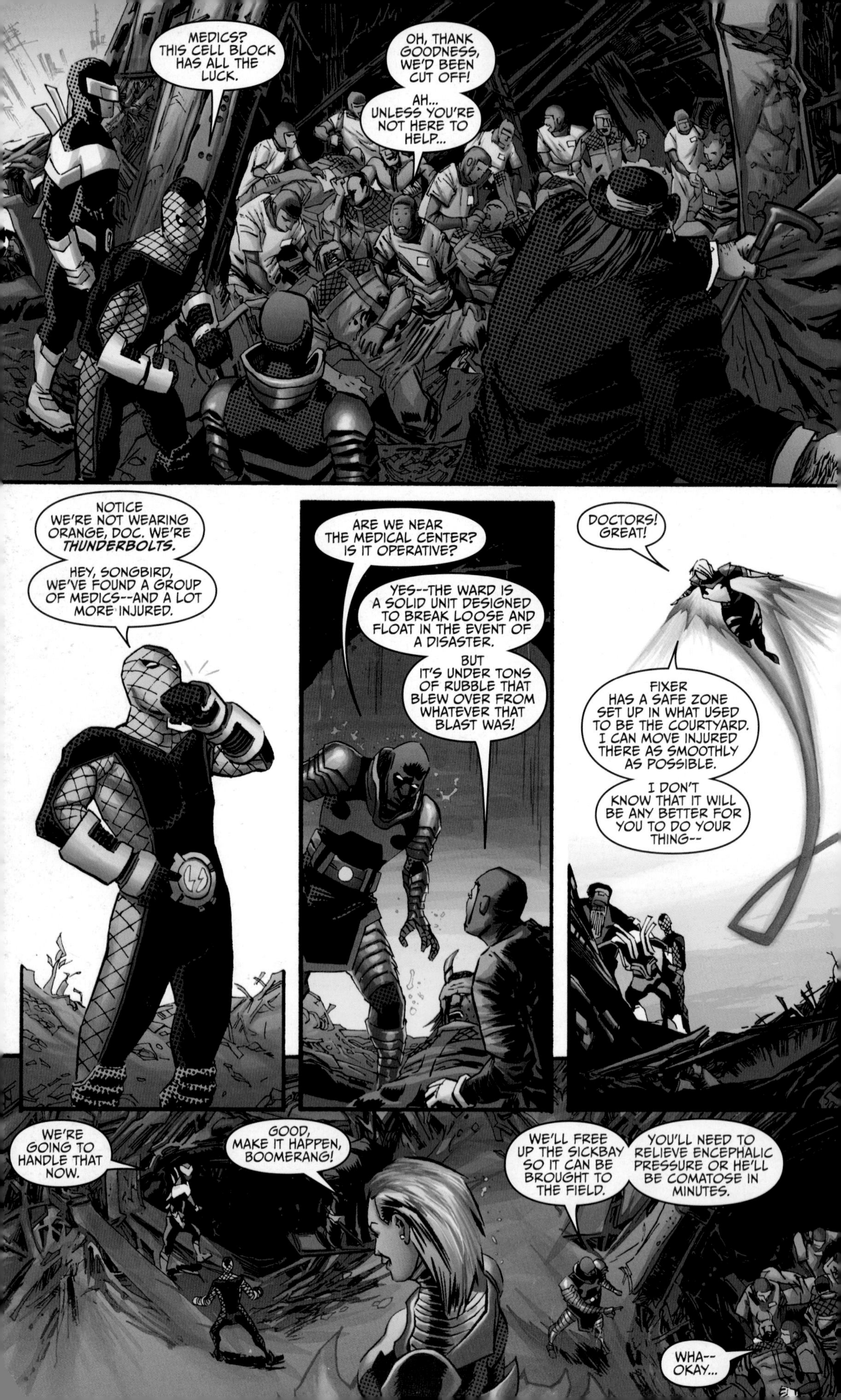
MEDICS? THIS CELL BLOCK HAS ALL THE LUCK.
OH, THANK GOODNESS, WE'D BEEN CUT OFF!
AH... UNLESS YOU'RE NOT HERE TO HELP...
NOTICE WE'RE NOT WEARING ORANGE, DOC. WE'RE THUNDERBOLTS.
HEY, SONGBIRD, WE'VE FOUND A GROUP OF MEDICS--AND A LOT MORE INJURED.
ARE WE NEAR THE MEDICAL CENTER? IS IT OPERATIVE?
YES--THE WARD IS A SOLID UNIT DESIGNED TO BREAK LOOSE AND FLOAT IN THE EVENT OF A DISASTER.
BUT IT'S UNDER TONS OF RUBBLE THAT BLEW OVER FROM WHATEVER THAT BLAST WAS!
DOCTORS! GREAT!
FIXER HAS A SAFE ZONE SET UP IN WHAT USED TO BE THE COURTYARD. I CAN MOVE INJURED THERE AS SMOOTHLY AS POSSIBLE.
I DON'T KNOW THAT IT WILL BE ANY BETTER FOR YOU TO DO YOUR THING--
WE'RE GOING TO HANDLE THAT NOW.
GOOD, MAKE IT HAPPEN, BOOMERANG!
WE'LL FREE UP THE SICKBAY SO IT CAN BE BROUGHT TO THE FIELD.
YOU'LL NEED TO RELIEVE ENCEPHALIC PRESSURE OR HE'LL BE COMATOSE IN MINUTES.
WHA-- OKAY...

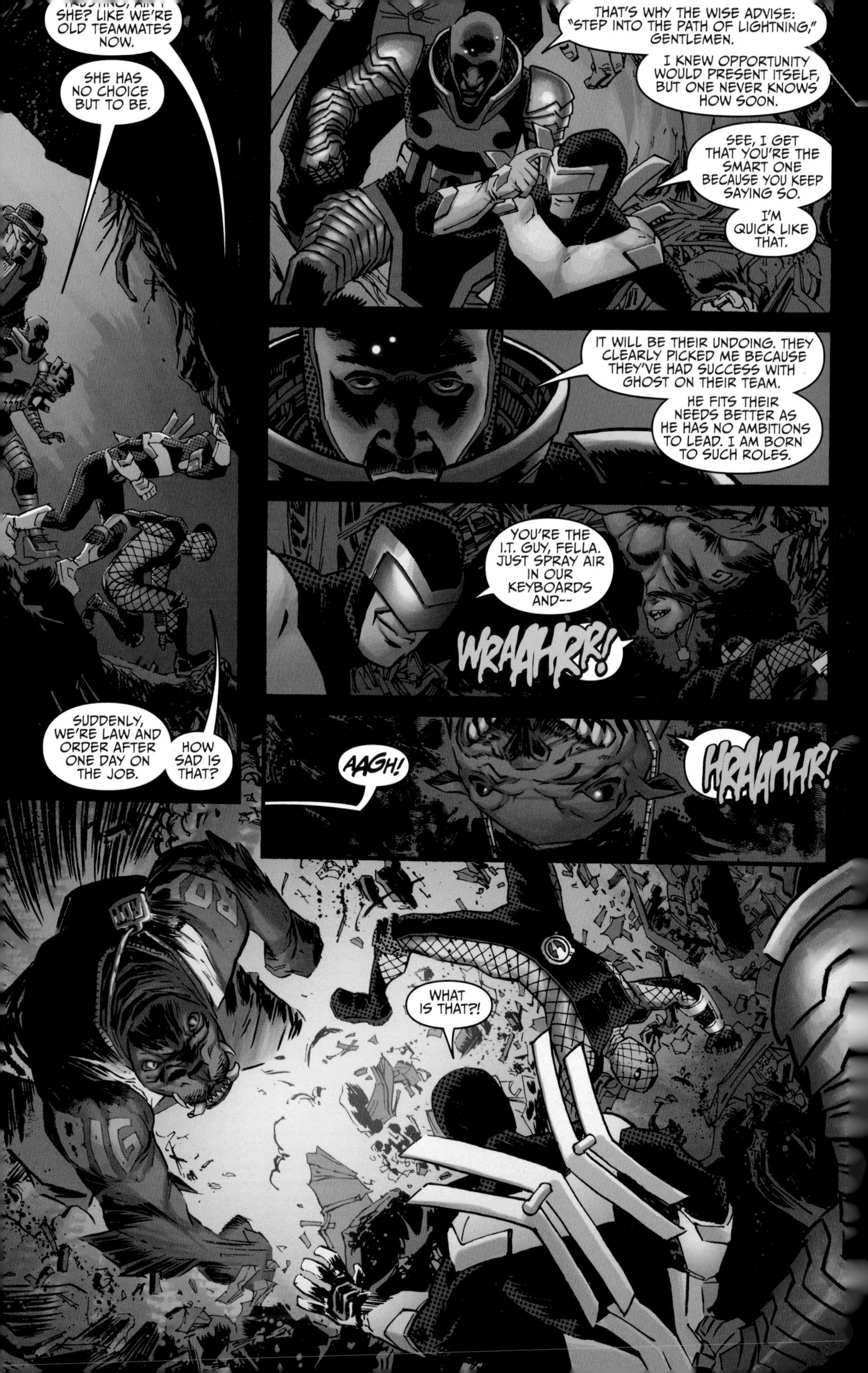
SHE? LIKE WE'RE OLD TEAMMATES NOW.
SHE HAS NO CHOICE BUT TO BE.
THAT'S WHY THE WISE ADVISE: "STEP INTO THE PATH OF LIGHTNING," GENTLEMEN.
I KNEW OPPORTUNITY WOULD PRESENT ITSELF, BUT ONE NEVER KNOWS HOW SOON.
SEE, I GET THAT YOU'RE THE SMART ONE BECAUSE YOU KEEP SAYING SO.
I'M QUICK LIKE THAT.
IT WILL BE THEIR UNDOING. THEY CLEARLY PICKED ME BECAUSE THEY'VE HAD SUCCESS WITH GHOST ON THEIR TEAM.
HE FITS THEIR NEEDS BETTER AS HE HAS NO AMBITIONS TO LEAD. I AM BORN TO SUCH ROLES.
YOU'RE THE I.T. GUY, FELLA. JUST SPRAY AIR IN OUR KEYBOARDS AND--
WRAAHRR!
SUDDENLY, WE'RE LAW AND ORDER AFTER ONE DAY ON THE JOB.
HOW SAD IS THAT?
AAGH!
HRAAHHR!
WHAT IS THAT?!

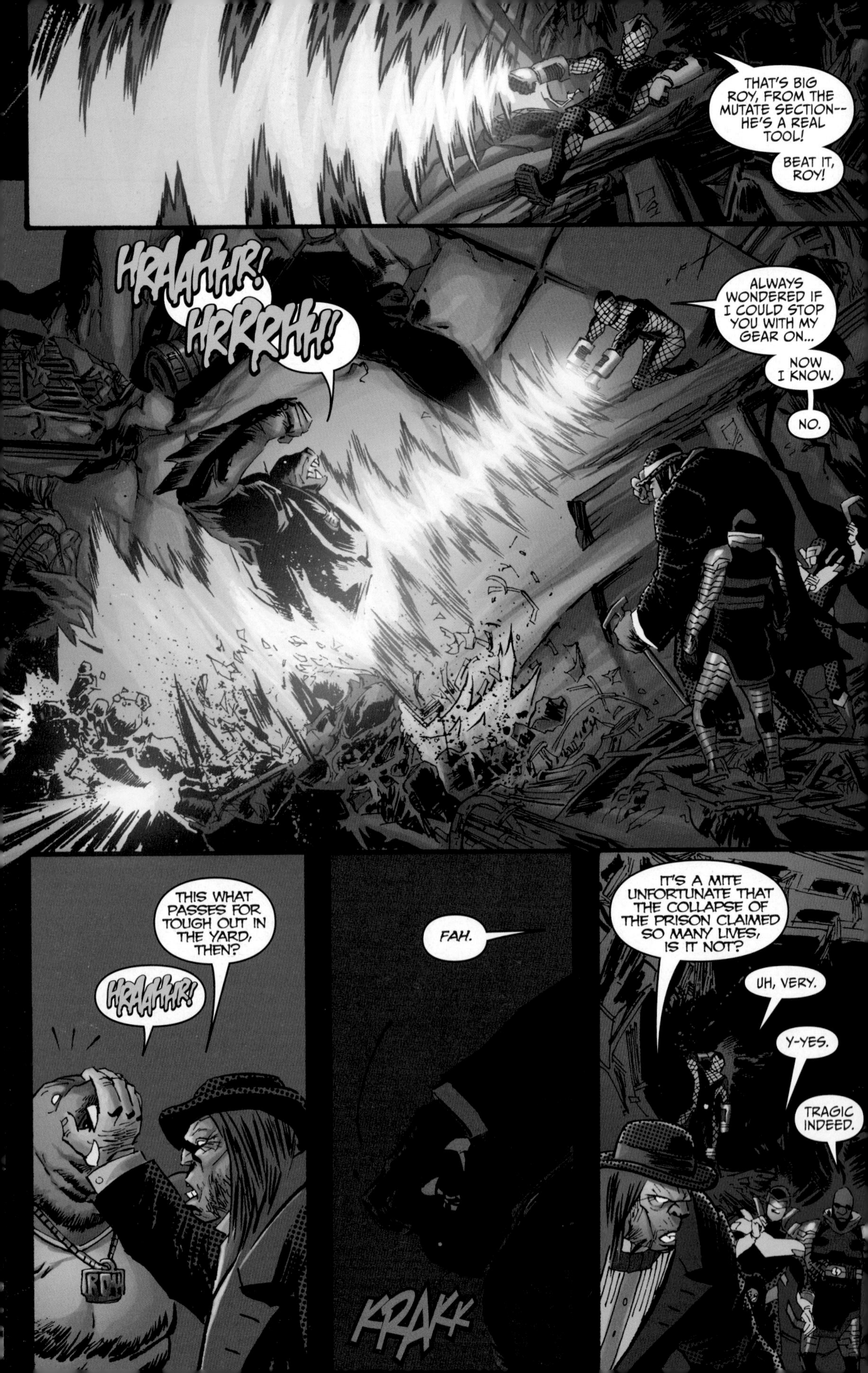
THAT'S BIG ROY, FROM THE MUTATE SECTION-- HE'S A REAL TOOL!
BEAT IT, ROY!
HRAAHHR! HRRRHH!
ALWAYS WONDERED IF I COULD STOP YOU WITH MY GEAR ON...
NOW I KNOW.
NO.
THIS WHAT PASSES FOR TOUGH OUT IN THE YARD, THEN?
HRAAHHR!
FAH.
KRAKK
IT'S A MITE UNFORTUNATE THAT THE COLLAPSE OF THE PRISON CLAIMED SO MANY LIVES, IS IT NOT?
UH, VERY.
Y-YES.
TRAGIC INDEED.

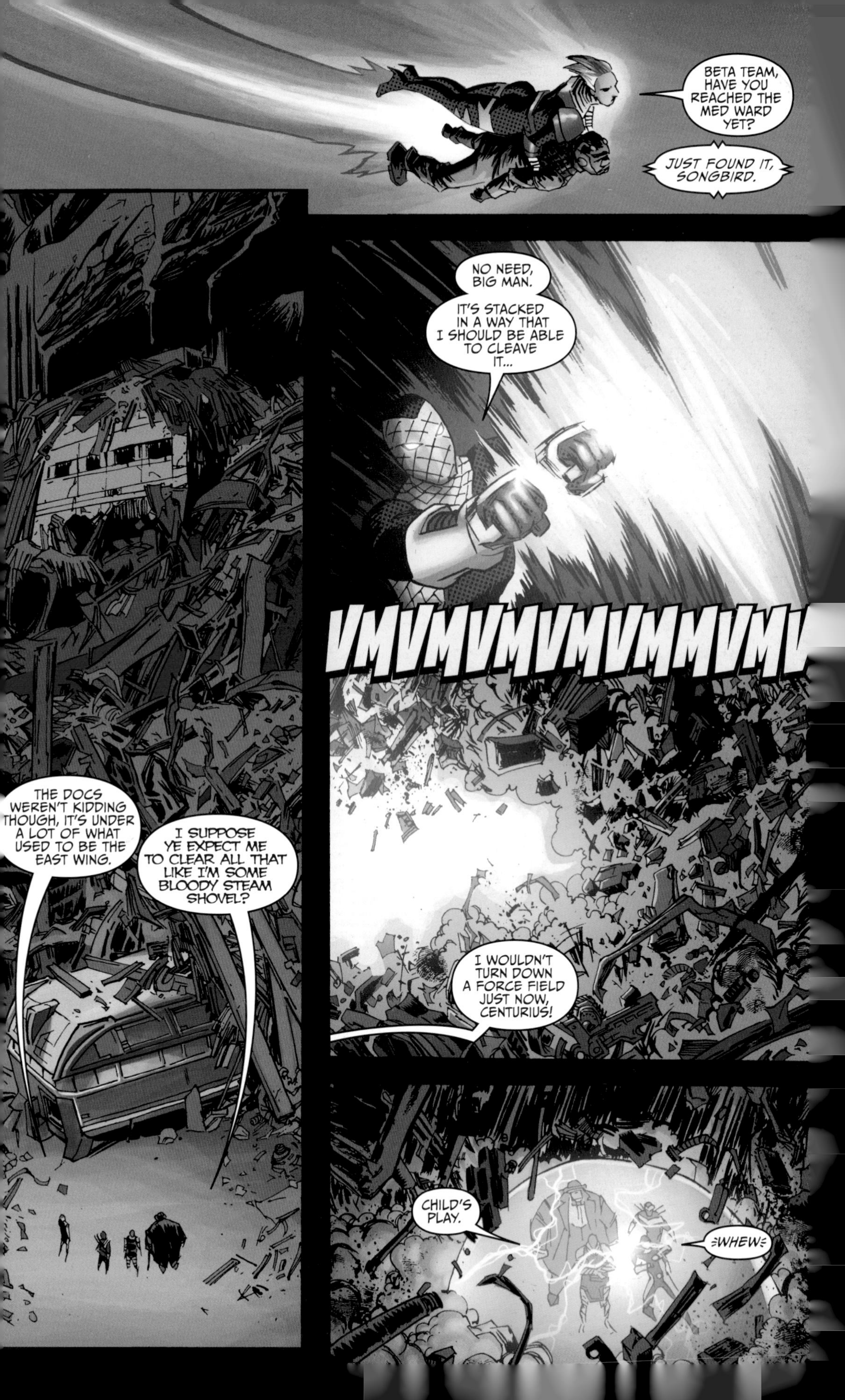
BETA TEAM, HAVE YOU REACHED THE MED WARD YET?
JUST FOUND IT, SONGBIRD.
THE DOCS WEREN'T KIDDING THOUGH, IT'S UNDER A LOT OF WHAT USED TO BE THE EAST WING.
I SUPPOSE YE EXPECT ME TO CLEAR ALL THAT LIKE I'M SOME BLOODY STEAM SHOVEL?
NO NEED, BIG MAN.
IT'S STACKED IN A WAY THAT I SHOULD BE ABLE TO CLEAVE IT...
VMVMVMVMVMMVMV
I WOULDN'T TURN DOWN A FORCE FIELD JUST NOW, CENTURIUS!
CHILD'S PLAY.
WHEW

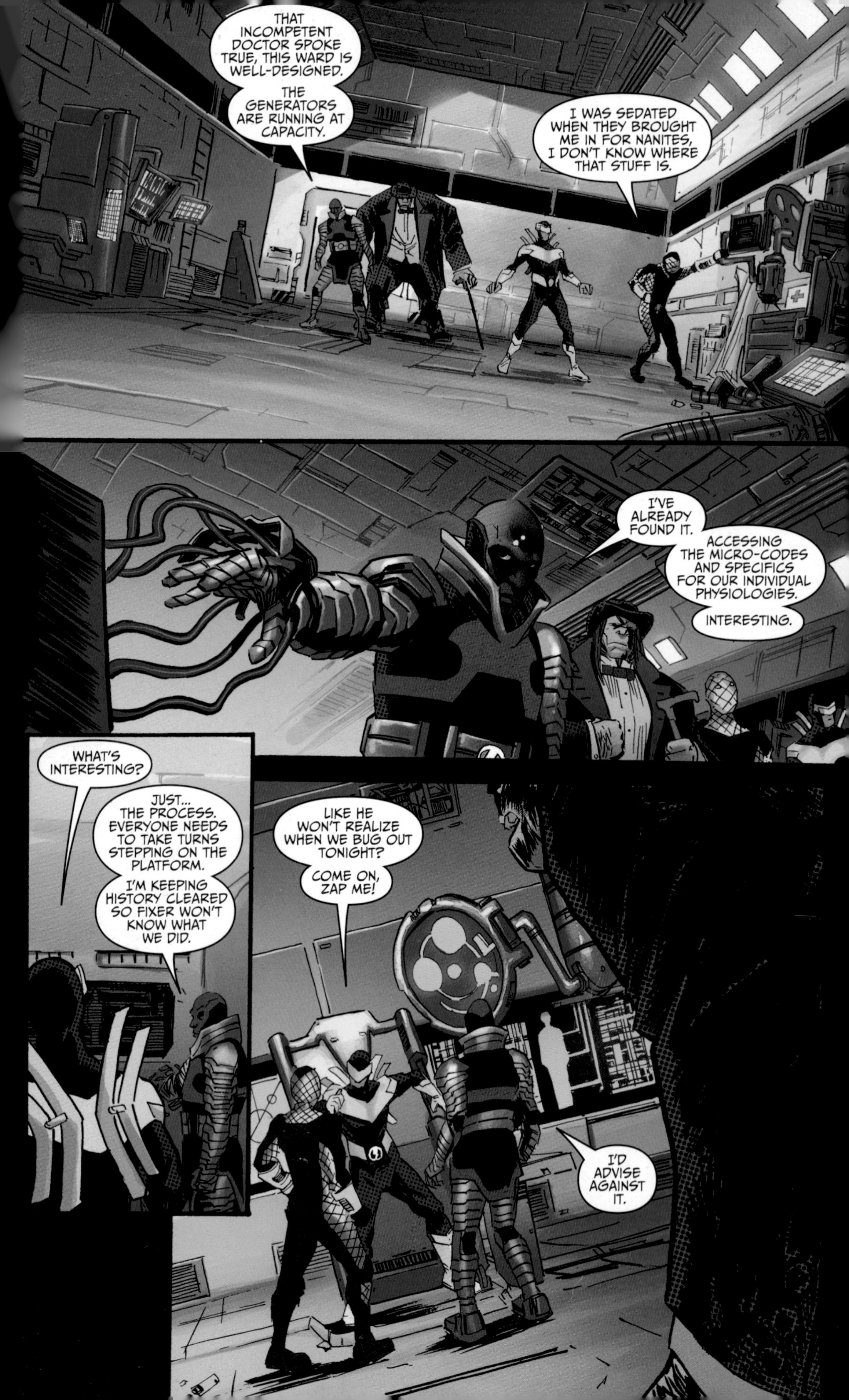
THAT INCOMPETENT DOCTOR SPOKE TRUE, THIS WARD IS WELL-DESIGNED.
THE GENERATORS ARE RUNNING AT CAPACITY.
I WAS SEDATED WHEN THEY BROUGHT ME IN FOR NANITES, I DON'T KNOW WHERE THAT STUFF IS.
I'VE ALREADY FOUND IT.
ACCESSING THE MICRO-CODES AND SPECIFICS FOR OUR INDIVIDUAL PHYSIOLOGIES.
INTERESTING.
WHAT'S INTERESTING?
JUST... THE PROCESS. EVERYONE NEEDS TO TAKE TURNS STEPPING ON THE PLATFORM.
I'M KEEPING HISTORY CLEARED SO FIXER WON'T KNOW WHAT WE DID.
LIKE HE WON'T REALIZE WHEN WE BUG OUT TONIGHT?
COME ON, ZAP ME!
I'D ADVISE AGAINST IT.

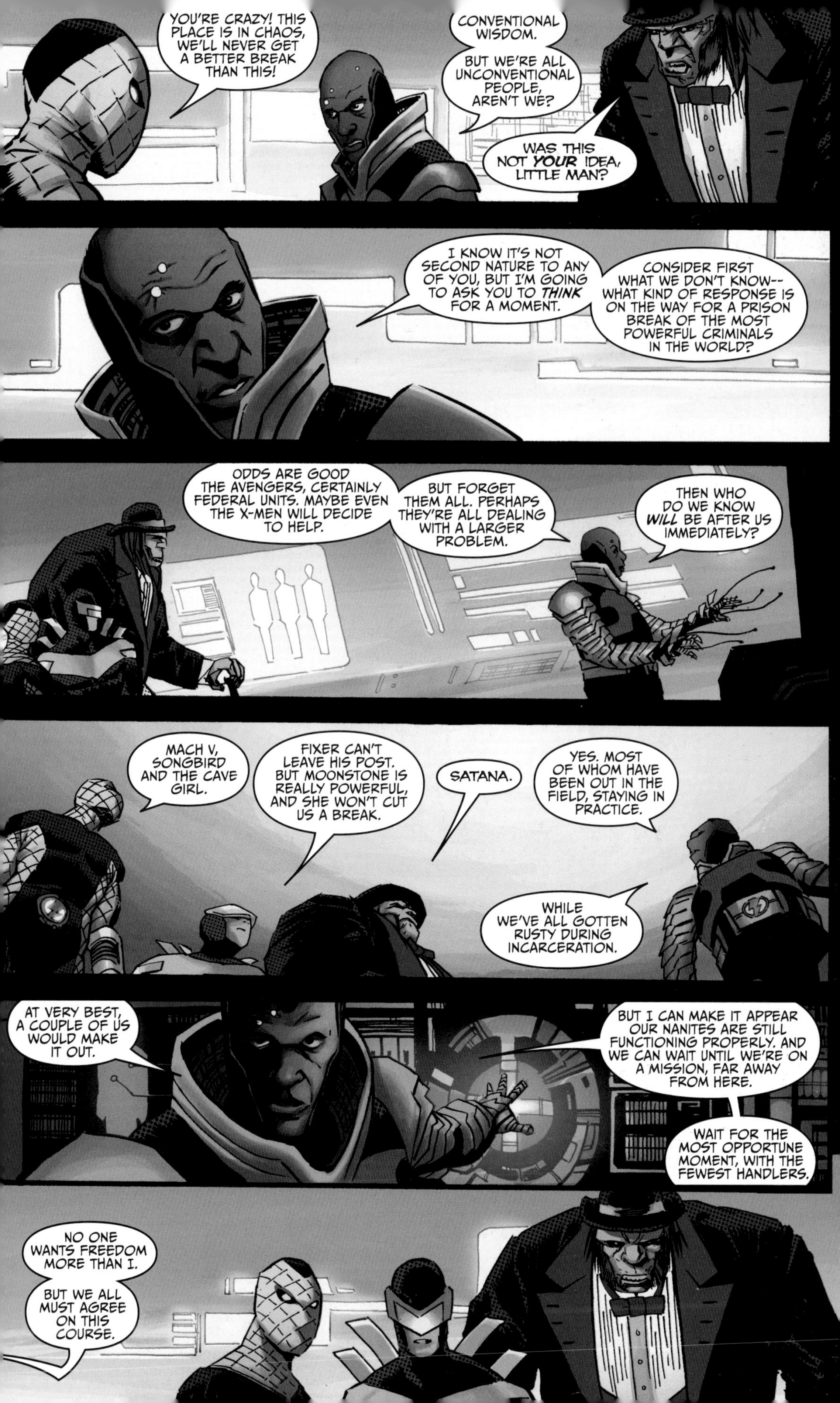

YOU'RE CRAZY! THIS PLACE IS IN CHAOS, WE'LL NEVER GET A BETTER BREAK THAN THIS!
CONVENTIONAL WISDOM.
BUT WE'RE ALL UNCONVENTIONAL PEOPLE, AREN'T WE?
WAS THIS NOT **YOUR** IDEA, LITTLE MAN?
I KNOW IT'S NOT SECOND NATURE TO ANY OF YOU, BUT I'M GOING TO ASK YOU TO ***THINK*** FOR A MOMENT.
CONSIDER FIRST WHAT WE DON'T KNOW-- WHAT KIND OF RESPONSE IS ON THE WAY FOR A PRISON BREAK OF THE MOST POWERFUL CRIMINALS IN THE WORLD?
ODDS ARE GOOD THE AVENGERS, CERTAINLY FEDERAL UNITS. MAYBE EVEN THE X-MEN WILL DECIDE TO HELP.
BUT FORGET THEM ALL. PERHAPS THEY'RE ALL DEALING WITH A LARGER PROBLEM.
THEN WHO DO WE KNOW ***WILL*** BE AFTER US IMMEDIATELY?
MACH V, SONGBIRD AND THE CAVE GIRL.
FIXER CAN'T LEAVE HIS POST. BUT MOONSTONE IS REALLY POWERFUL, AND SHE WON'T CUT US A BREAK.
SATANA.
YES. MOST OF WHOM HAVE BEEN OUT IN THE FIELD, STAYING IN PRACTICE.
WHILE WE'VE ALL GOTTEN RUSTY DURING INCARCERATION.
AT VERY BEST, A COUPLE OF US WOULD MAKE IT OUT.
BUT I CAN MAKE IT APPEAR OUR NANITES ARE STILL FUNCTIONING PROPERLY. AND WE CAN WAIT UNTIL WE'RE ON A MISSION, FAR AWAY FROM HERE.
WAIT FOR THE MOST OPPORTUNE MOMENT, WITH THE FEWEST HANDLERS.
NO ONE WANTS FREEDOM MORE THAN I.
BUT WE ALL MUST AGREE ON THIS COURSE.

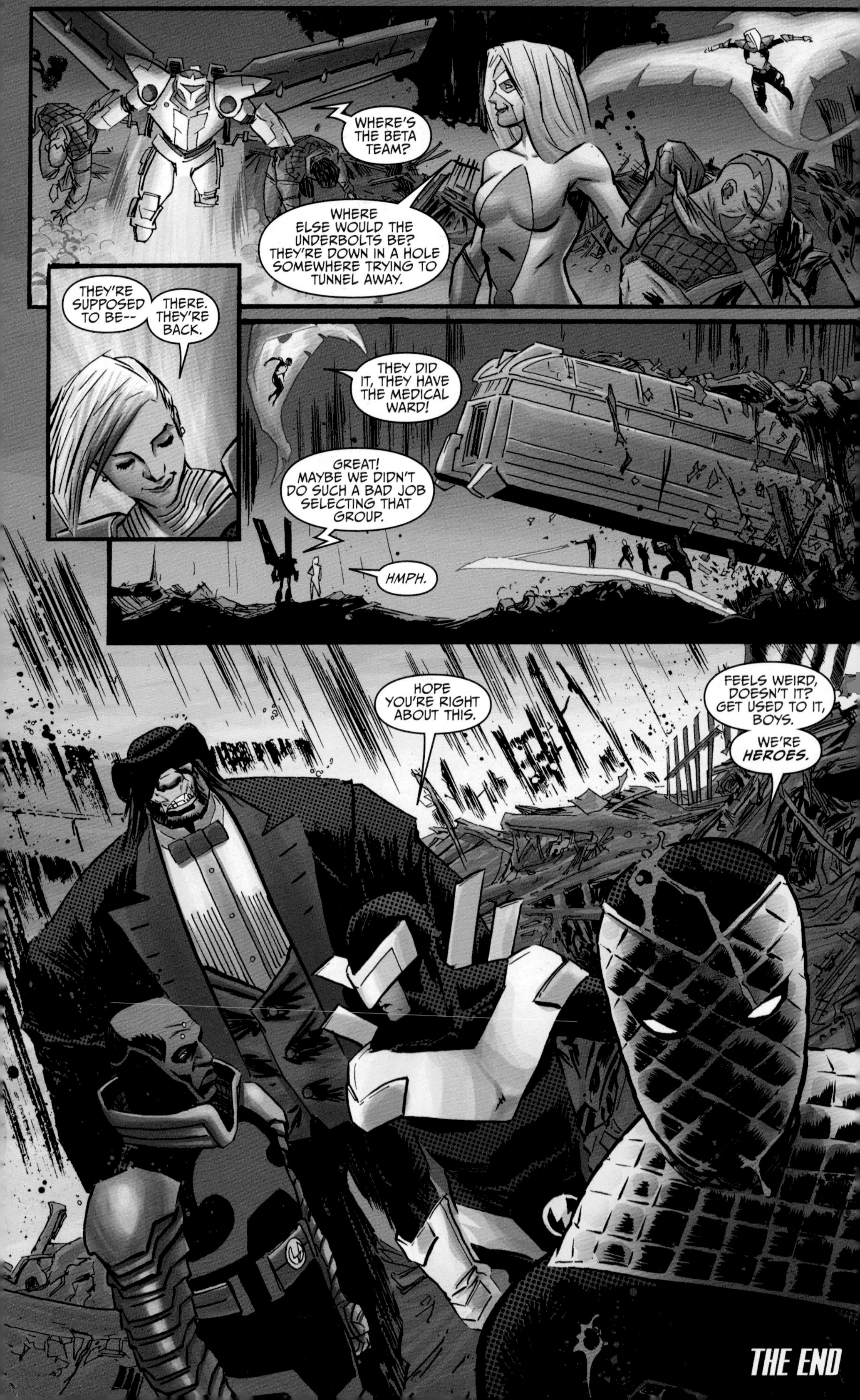
WHERE'S THE BETA TEAM?
WHERE ELSE WOULD THE UNDERBOLTS BE? THEY'RE DOWN IN A HOLE SOMEWHERE TRYING TO TUNNEL AWAY.
THEY'RE SUPPOSED TO BE--
THERE. THEY'RE BACK.
THEY DID IT, THEY HAVE THE MEDICAL WARD!
GREAT! MAYBE WE DIDN'T DO SUCH A BAD JOB SELECTING THAT GROUP.
HMPH.
HOPE YOU'RE RIGHT ABOUT THIS.
FEELS WEIRD, DOESN'T IT? GET USED TO IT, BOYS.
WE'RE HEROES.
THE END

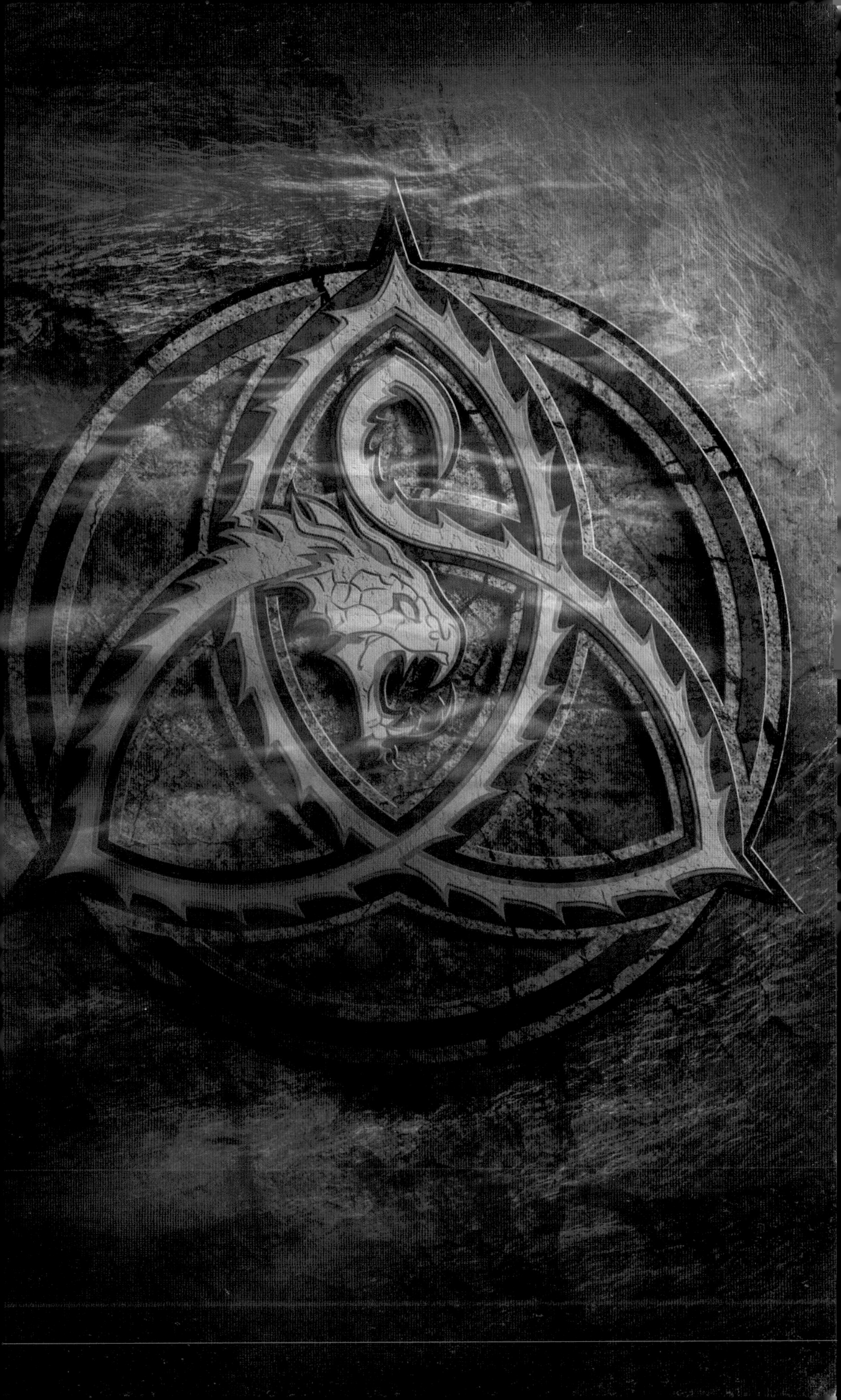

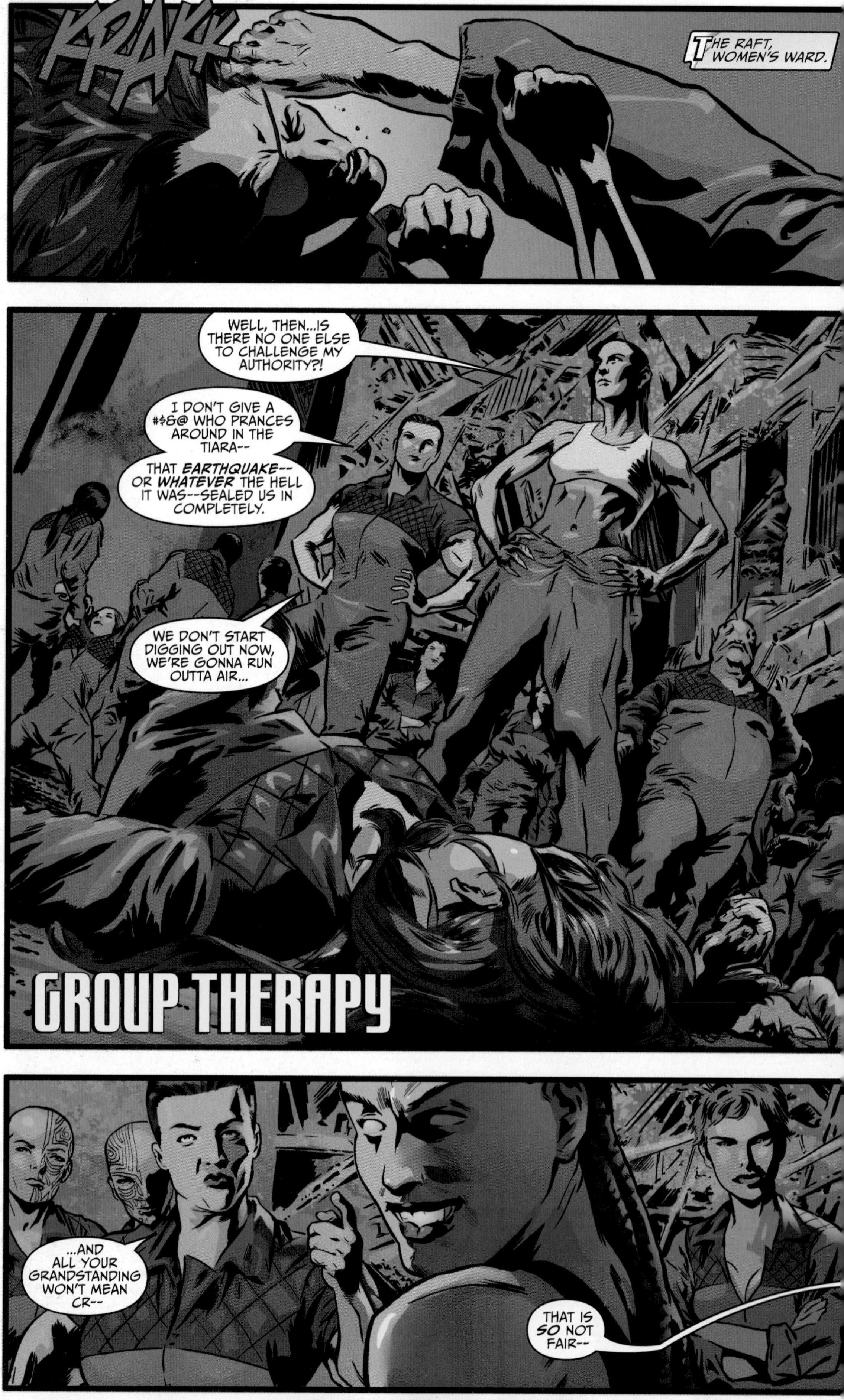
KRAKK
THE RAFT, WOMEN'S WARD.
WELL, THEN...IS THERE NO ONE ELSE TO CHALLENGE MY AUTHORITY?!
I DON'T GIVE A #$&@ WHO PRANCES AROUND IN THE TIARA--
THAT EARTHQUAKE-- OR WHATEVER THE HELL IT WAS--SEALED US IN COMPLETELY.
WE DON'T START DIGGING OUT NOW, WE'RE GONNA RUN OUTTA AIR...
GROUP THERAPY
...AND ALL YOUR GRANDSTANDING WON'T MEAN CR--
THAT IS SO NOT FAIR--

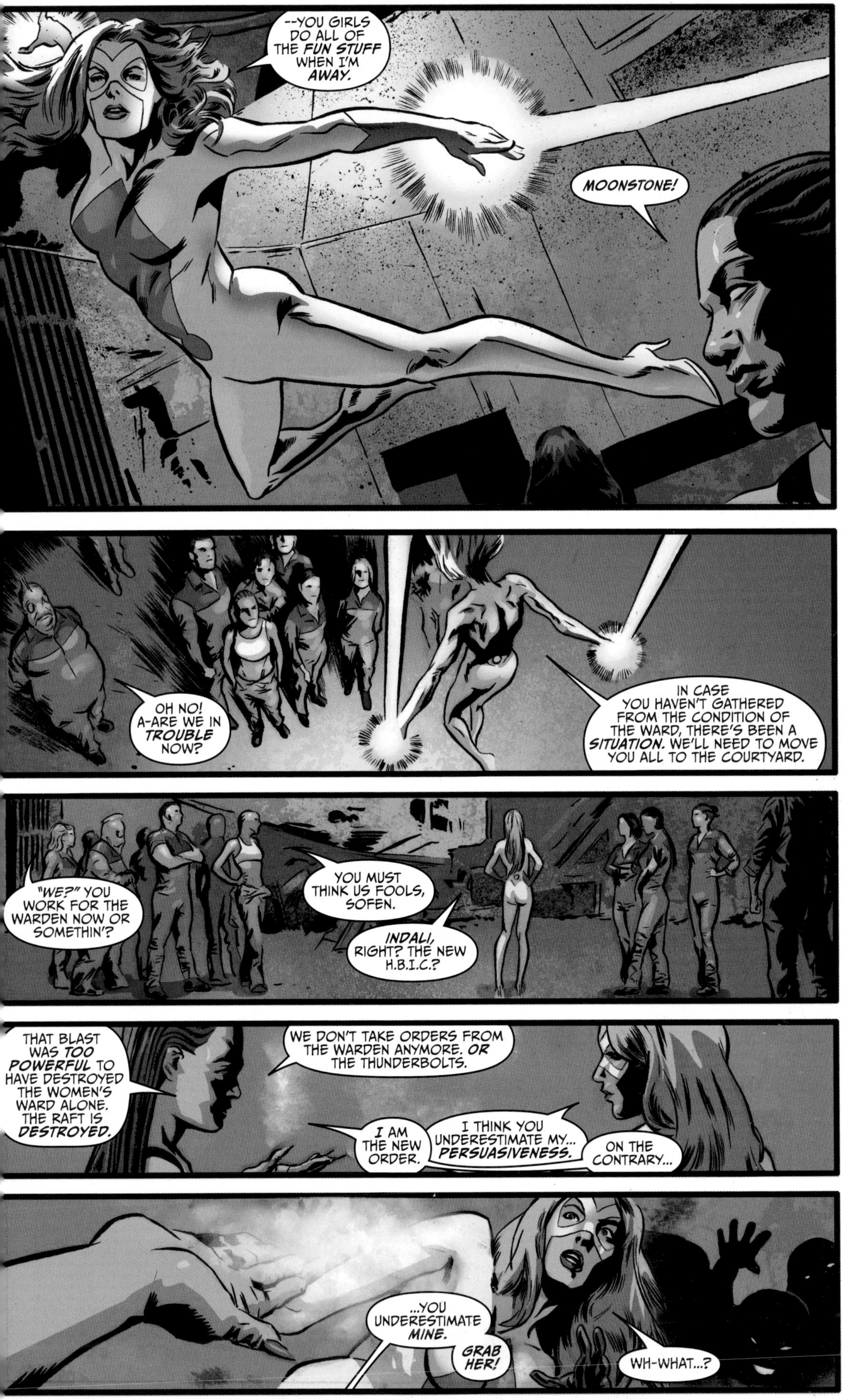
--YOU GIRLS DO ALL OF THE FUN STUFF WHEN I'M AWAY.
MOONSTONE!
OH NO! A-ARE WE IN TROUBLE NOW?
IN CASE YOU HAVEN'T GATHERED FROM THE CONDITION OF THE WARD, THERE'S BEEN A SITUATION. WE'LL NEED TO MOVE YOU ALL TO THE COURTYARD.
"WE?" YOU WORK FOR THE WARDEN NOW OR SOMETHIN'?
YOU MUST THINK US FOOLS, SOFEN.
INDALI, RIGHT? THE NEW H.B.I.C.?
THAT BLAST WAS TOO POWERFUL TO HAVE DESTROYED THE WOMEN'S WARD ALONE. THE RAFT IS DESTROYED.
WE DON'T TAKE ORDERS FROM THE WARDEN ANYMORE. OR THE THUNDERBOLTS.
I AM THE NEW ORDER.
I THINK YOU UNDERESTIMATE MY... PERSUASIVENESS.
ON THE CONTRARY...
...YOU UNDERESTIMATE MINE.
GRAB HER!
WH-WHAT...?

M-MY POWERS--

--THEY AREN'T WORKING!

YESSSSS...

WHILE THE REST OF *YOU COWS* HAVE HAD YOUR POWERS DAMPENED BY THE RAFT'S SECURITY...

...MINE WERE NEVER CONSIDERED A THREAT TO THEM FROM THE CONFINES OF MY CELL. BUT THEN, THEY NEVER COUNTED ON ME GETTING OUT.

I CAN CLOUD THE SUPERHUMAN ABILITIES OF *ANYONE* IN MY PROXIMITY-- THE CLOSER YOU ARE, THE STRONGER MY HOLD--

--EVEN ON THOSE GRANTED YOU BY YOUR *MOONSTONE.*

NO!

AAHHH! MY GILLS!

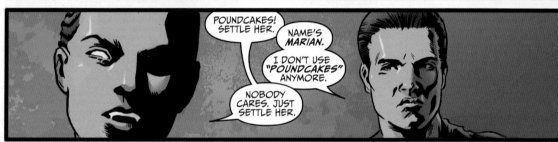

POUNDCAKES! SETTLE HER.

NAME'S MARIAN.

I DON'T USE *"POUNDCAKES"* ANYMORE.

NOBODY CARES. JUST SETTLE HER.

WOOM

I THIRST FOR THE TASTE OF FREEDOM. AND YOU WILL LEAD ME TO THE DRINK...

...OR *PERISH* AT MY *HAND!*

OUR AIRCRAFT--OUR BOATS--ALL GONE ALREADY.

I HAVE NO INTEREST IN YOUR LIFEBOATS...

...I WANT TO TAKE THE CADILLAC.

LEAD ME TO THE *MAN-THING!*

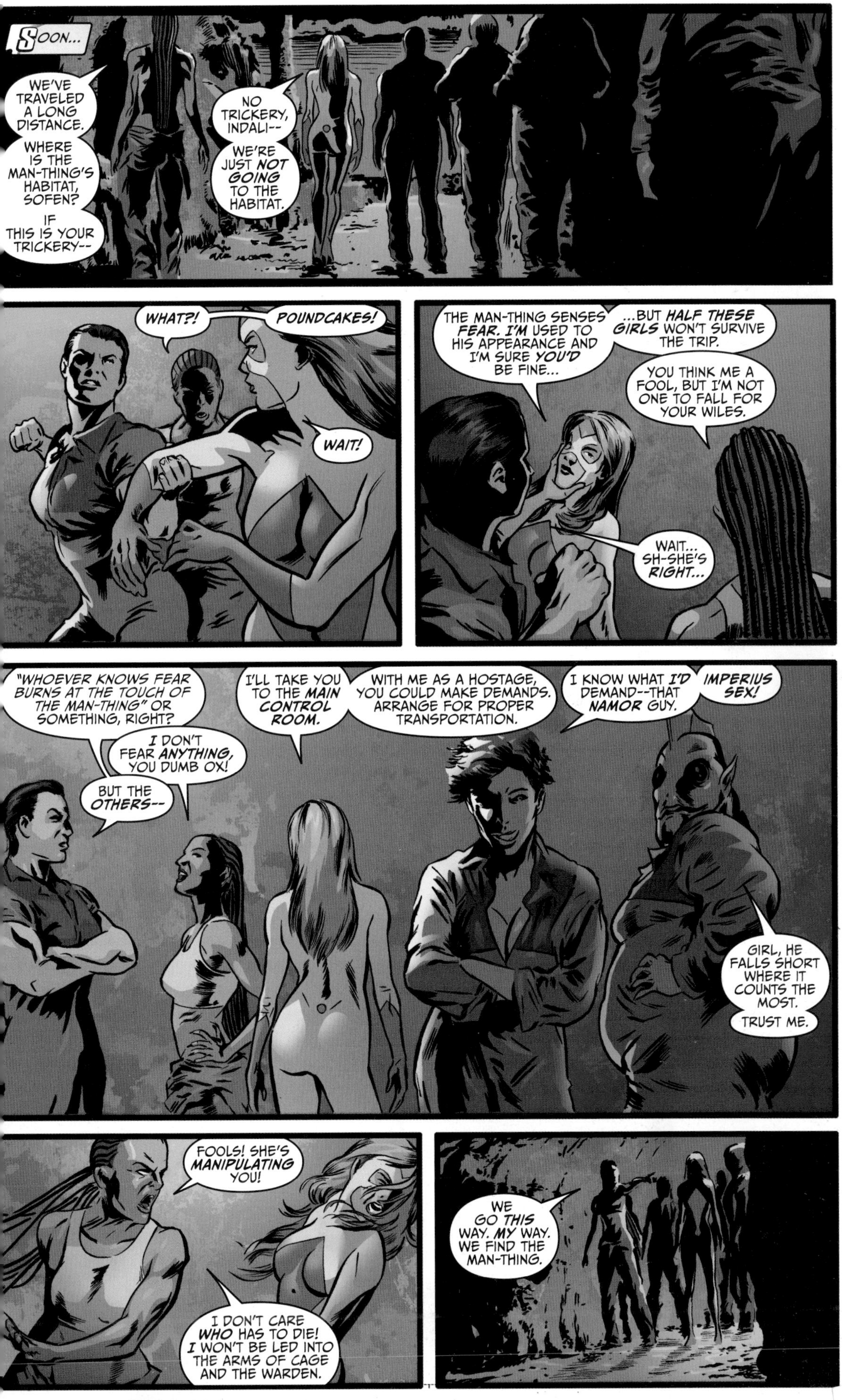
SOON...
WE'VE TRAVELED A LONG DISTANCE.
WHERE IS THE MAN-THING'S HABITAT, SOFEN?
IF THIS IS YOUR TRICKERY--
NO TRICKERY, INDALI--
WE'RE JUST NOT GOING TO THE HABITAT.
WHAT?!
POUNDCAKES!
WAIT!
THE MAN-THING SENSES FEAR. I'M USED TO HIS APPEARANCE AND I'M SURE YOU'D BE FINE...
...BUT HALF THESE GIRLS WON'T SURVIVE THE TRIP.
YOU THINK ME A FOOL, BUT I'M NOT ONE TO FALL FOR YOUR WILES.
WAIT... SH-SHE'S RIGHT...
"WHOEVER KNOWS FEAR BURNS AT THE TOUCH OF THE MAN-THING" OR SOMETHING, RIGHT?
I DON'T FEAR ANYTHING, YOU DUMB OX!
BUT THE OTHERS--
I'LL TAKE YOU TO THE MAIN CONTROL ROOM.
WITH ME AS A HOSTAGE, YOU COULD MAKE DEMANDS. ARRANGE FOR PROPER TRANSPORTATION.
I KNOW WHAT I'D DEMAND--THAT NAMOR GUY.
IMPERIUS SEX!
GIRL, HE FALLS SHORT WHERE IT COUNTS THE MOST.
TRUST ME.
FOOLS! SHE'S MANIPULATING YOU!
I DON'T CARE WHO HAS TO DIE! I WON'T BE LED INTO THE ARMS OF CAGE AND THE WARDEN.
WE GO THIS WAY. MY WAY. WE FIND THE MAN-THING.

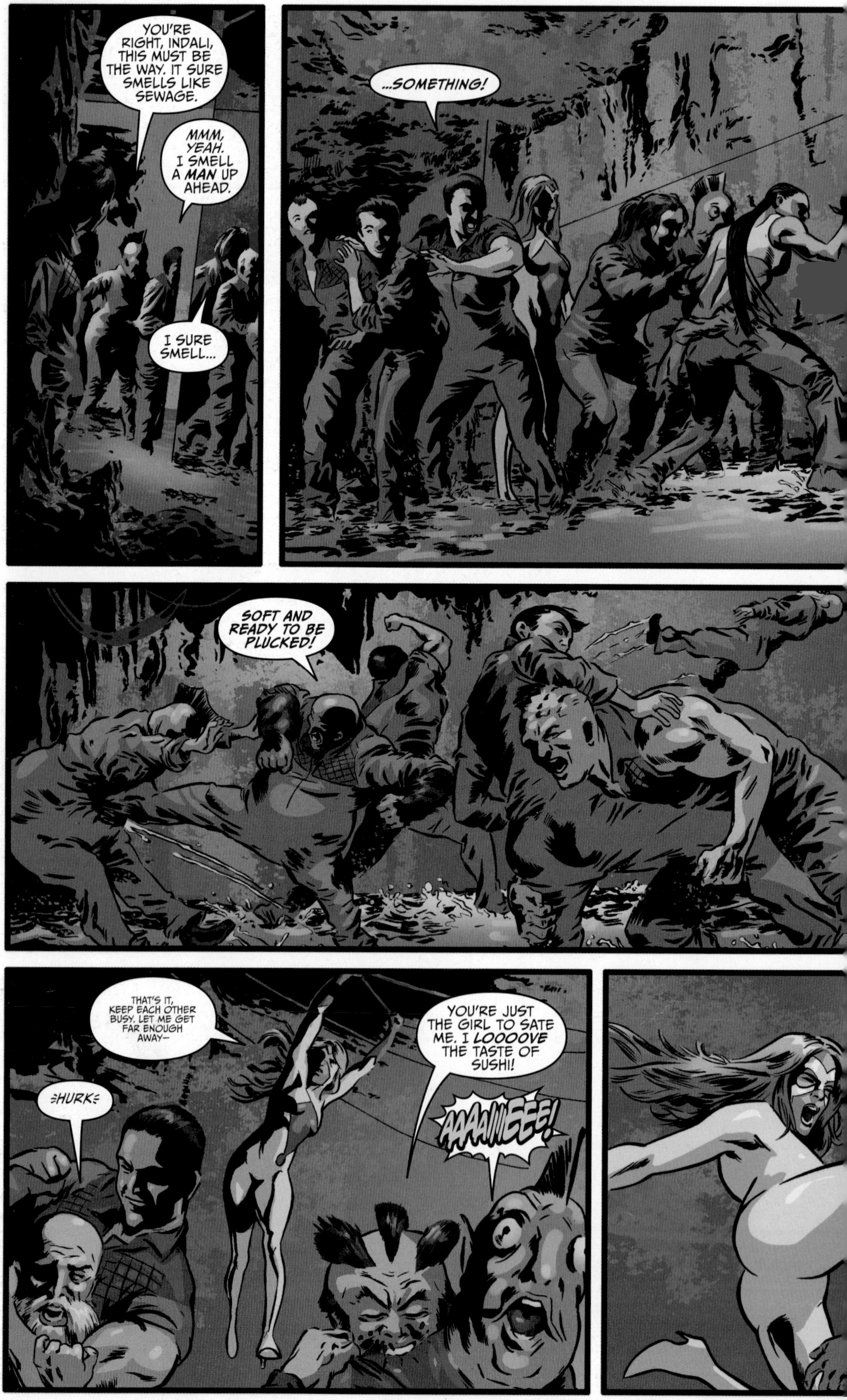

YOU'RE RIGHT, INDALI, THIS MUST BE THE WAY. IT SURE SMELLS LIKE SEWAGE.
MMM, YEAH. I SMELL A MAN UP AHEAD.
I SURE SMELL...
...SOMETHING!
SOFT AND READY TO BE PLUCKED!
THAT'S IT, KEEP EACH OTHER BUSY. LET ME GET FAR ENOUGH AWAY—
HURK
YOU'RE JUST THE GIRL TO SATE ME. I LOOOOVE THE TASTE OF SUSHI!
AAAAIIIEEE!

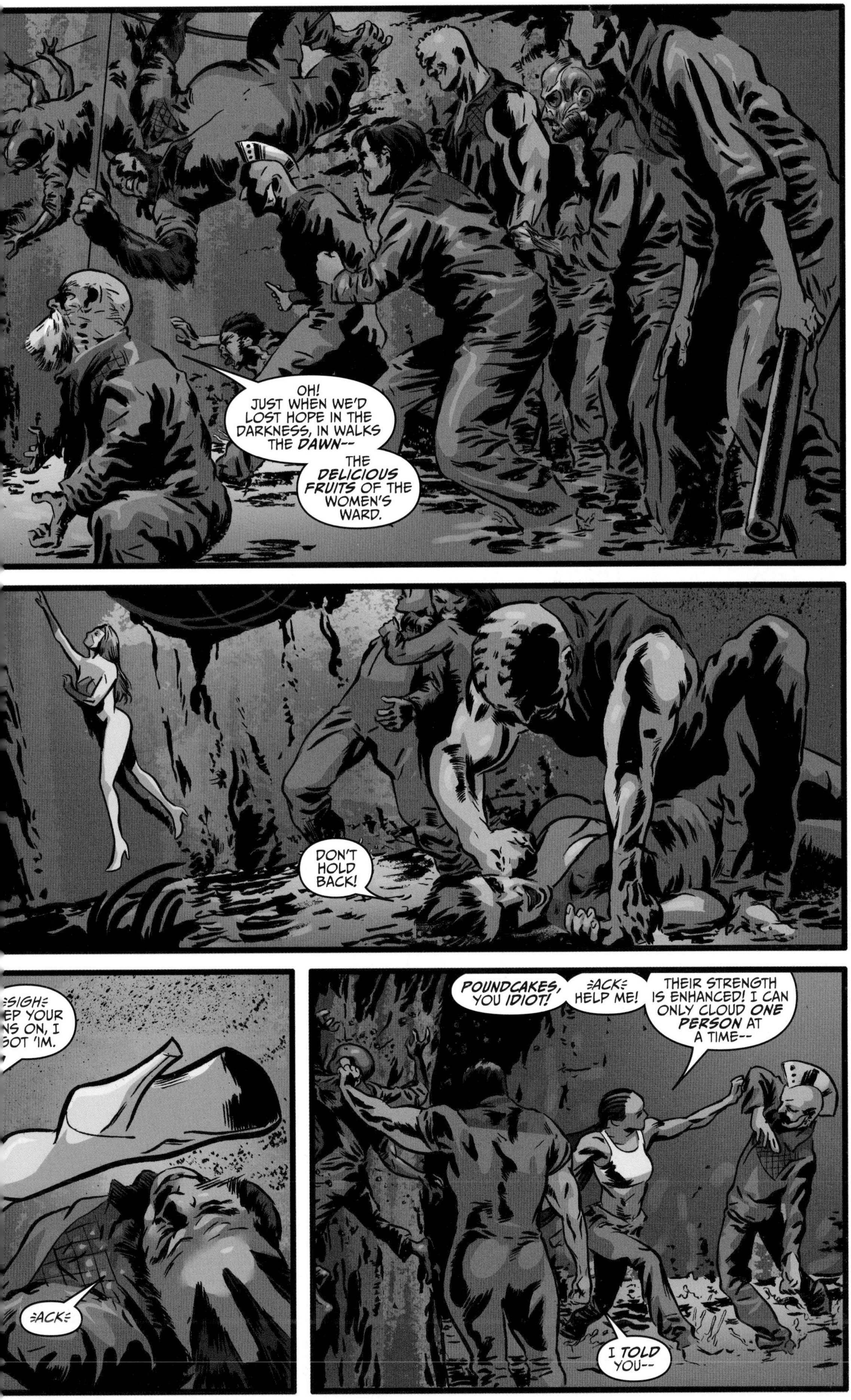
OH! JUST WHEN WE'D LOST HOPE IN THE DARKNESS, IN WALKS THE DAWN--
THE DELICIOUS FRUITS OF THE WOMEN'S WARD.
DON'T HOLD BACK!
=SIGH= EP YOUR NS ON, I GOT 'IM.
=ACK=
POUNDCAKES, YOU IDIOT!
=ACK= HELP ME!
THEIR STRENGTH IS ENHANCED! I CAN ONLY CLOUD ONE PERSON AT A TIME--
I TOLD YOU--

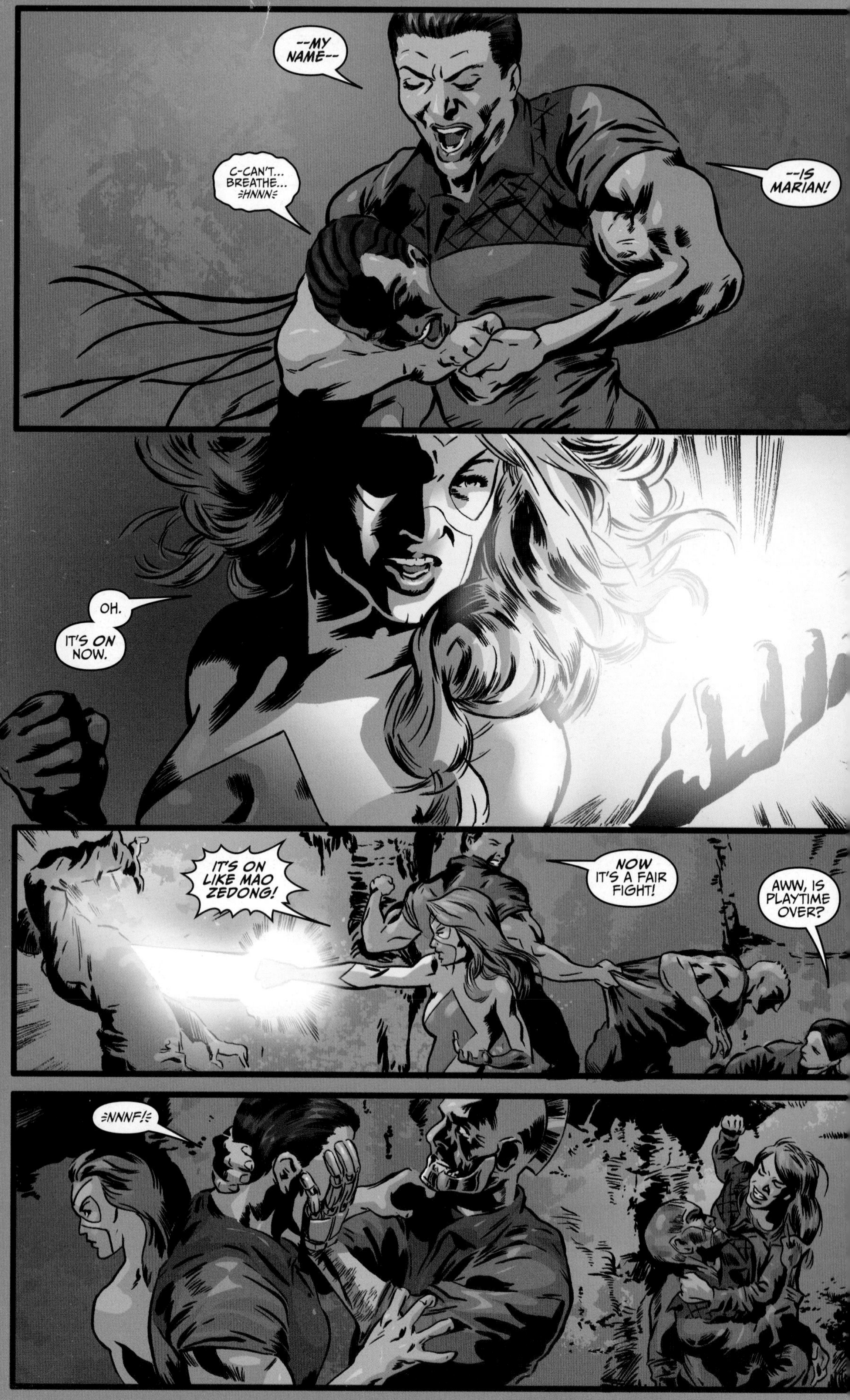
--MY NAME--
C-CAN'T... BREATHE... HNNN
--IS MARIAN!
OH.
IT'S ON NOW.
IT'S ON LIKE MAO ZEDONG!
NOW IT'S A FAIR FIGHT!
AWW, IS PLAYTIME OVER?
NNNF!

KLAMM

SQUEEEE!

SHRPPP

SO...

DON'T WORRY...

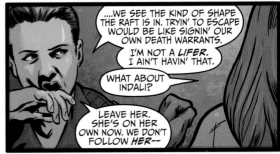

....WE SEE THE KIND OF SHAPE THE RAFT IS IN. TRYIN' TO ESCAPE WOULD BE LIKE SIGNIN' OUR OWN DEATH WARRANTS.

I'M NOT A *LIFER.* I AIN'T HAVIN' THAT.

WHAT ABOUT INDALI?

LEAVE HER. SHE'S ON HER OWN NOW. WE DON'T FOLLOW *HER*--

--WE FOLLOW YOU.

WE'RE COOL, SOFEN. FOR NOW.

UNDERSTOOD. MARIAN.

THE END

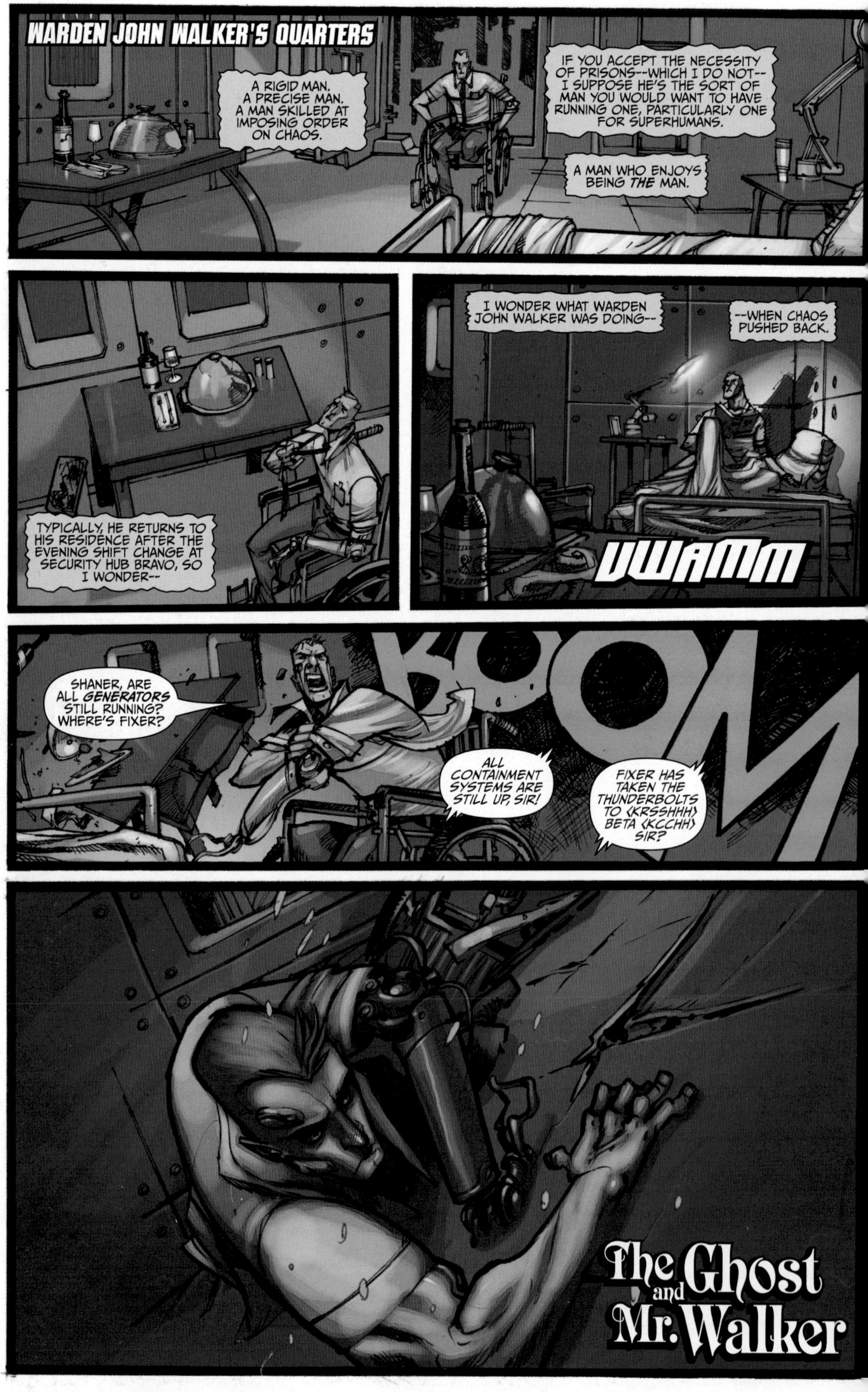
WARDEN JOHN WALKER'S QUARTERS
A RIGID MAN. A PRECISE MAN. A MAN SKILLED AT IMPOSING ORDER ON CHAOS.
IF YOU ACCEPT THE NECESSITY OF PRISONS--WHICH I DO NOT--I SUPPOSE HE'S THE SORT OF MAN YOU WOULD WANT TO HAVE RUNNING ONE, PARTICULARLY ONE FOR SUPERHUMANS.
A MAN WHO ENJOYS BEING THE MAN.
TYPICALLY, HE RETURNS TO HIS RESIDENCE AFTER THE EVENING SHIFT CHANGE AT SECURITY HUB BRAVO, SO I WONDER--
I WONDER WHAT WARDEN JOHN WALKER WAS DOING--
--WHEN CHAOS PUSHED BACK.
VWAMM
BOOM
SHANER, ARE ALL GENERATORS STILL RUNNING? WHERE'S FIXER?
ALL CONTAINMENT SYSTEMS ARE STILL UP, SIR!
FIXER HAS TAKEN THE THUNDERBOLTS TO ‹KRSSHHH› BETA ‹KCCHH› SIR?
The Ghost and Mr. Walker

SONGBIRD SENT ME TO FIND HIM.

IF HE WAS IN HIS **RESIDENCE**, HE *MAY* STILL BE ALIVE.

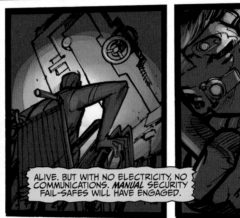

ALIVE. BUT WITH NO ELECTRICITY, NO COMMUNICATIONS. *MANUAL* SECURITY FAIL-SAFES WILL HAVE ENGAGED.

HE MIGHT AS WELL BE IN A *CELL*.

GREETINGS, WARDEN. THE RAMPS TO THE MEDICAL WING'S HELIPAD ARE LARGELY INTACT BACK *THIS WAY.*

IF WE CAN FIND A WAY TO GET YOU *ACROSS*, I CAN LEAD YOU SAFELY TO THE ROOF, TO *REGROUP* WITH THE OTHERS.

NO TIME... THIS IS AS *GROUP* AS IT *GETS* FOR NOW.

ANY OF THE SECURITY HUBS STILL HAVE POWER?

HUB *DELTA* APPEARS STRUCTURALLY SOUND BUT IS NOT COMMUNICATING.

WHAT ARE YOU DOING?

ONLY *ONE* WAY TO DELTA FROM *HERE.*

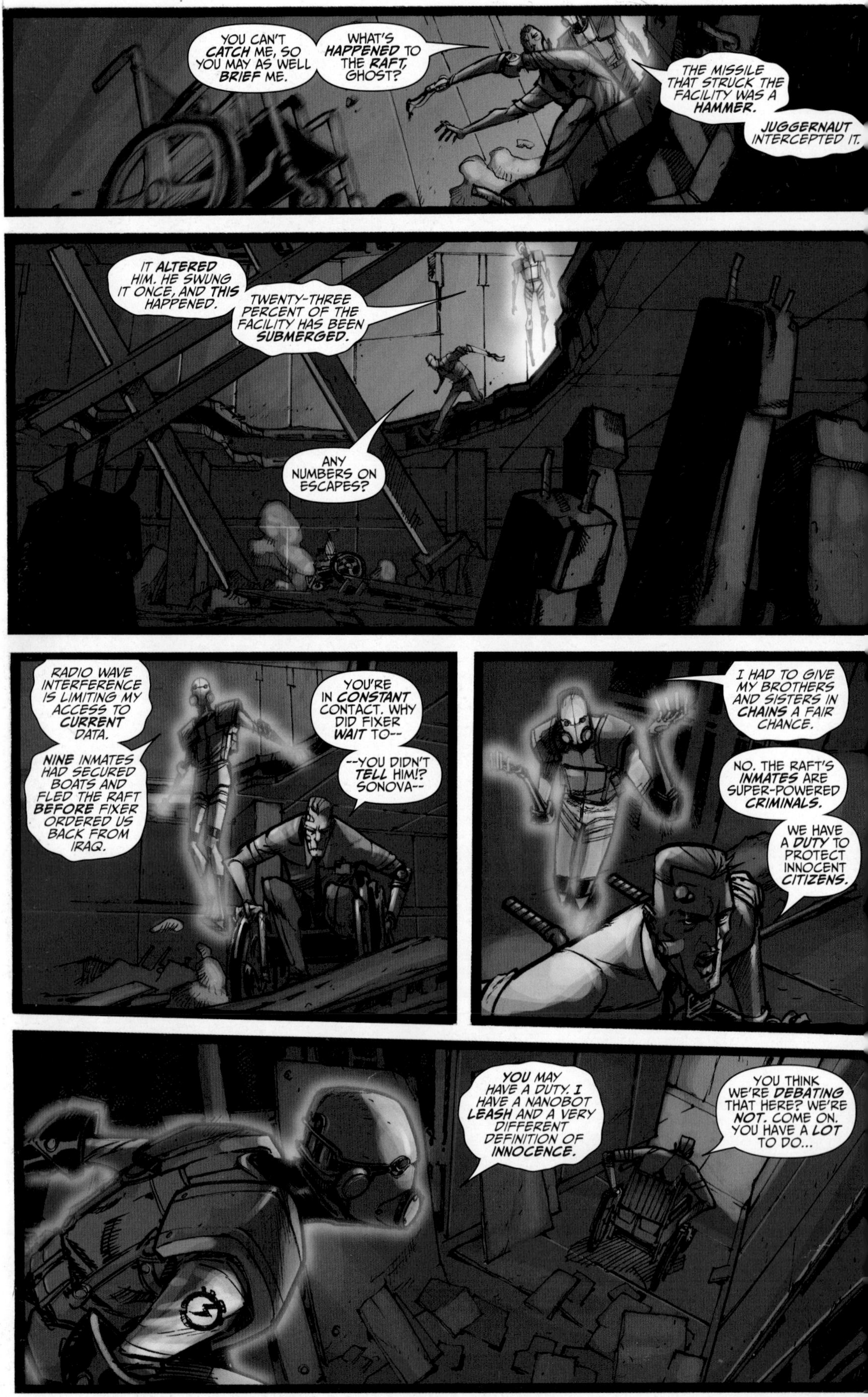
YOU CAN'T CATCH ME, SO YOU MAY AS WELL BRIEF ME.
WHAT'S HAPPENED TO THE RAFT, GHOST?
THE MISSILE THAT STRUCK THE FACILITY WAS A HAMMER.
JUGGERNAUT INTERCEPTED IT.
IT ALTERED HIM. HE SWUNG IT ONCE, AND THIS HAPPENED.
TWENTY-THREE PERCENT OF THE FACILITY HAS BEEN SUBMERGED.
ANY NUMBERS ON ESCAPES?
RADIO WAVE INTERFERENCE IS LIMITING MY ACCESS TO CURRENT DATA.
NINE INMATES HAD SECURED BOATS AND FLED THE RAFT BEFORE FIXER ORDERED US BACK FROM IRAQ.
YOU'RE IN CONSTANT CONTACT. WHY DID FIXER WAIT TO--
--YOU DIDN'T TELL HIM!? SONOVA--
I HAD TO GIVE MY BROTHERS AND SISTERS IN CHAINS A FAIR CHANCE.
NO. THE RAFT'S INMATES ARE SUPER-POWERED CRIMINALS.
WE HAVE A DUTY TO PROTECT INNOCENT CITIZENS.
YOU MAY HAVE A DUTY. I HAVE A NANOBOT LEASH AND A VERY DIFFERENT DEFINITION OF INNOCENCE.
YOU THINK WE'RE DEBATING THAT HERE? WE'RE NOT. COME ON. YOU HAVE A LOT TO DO...

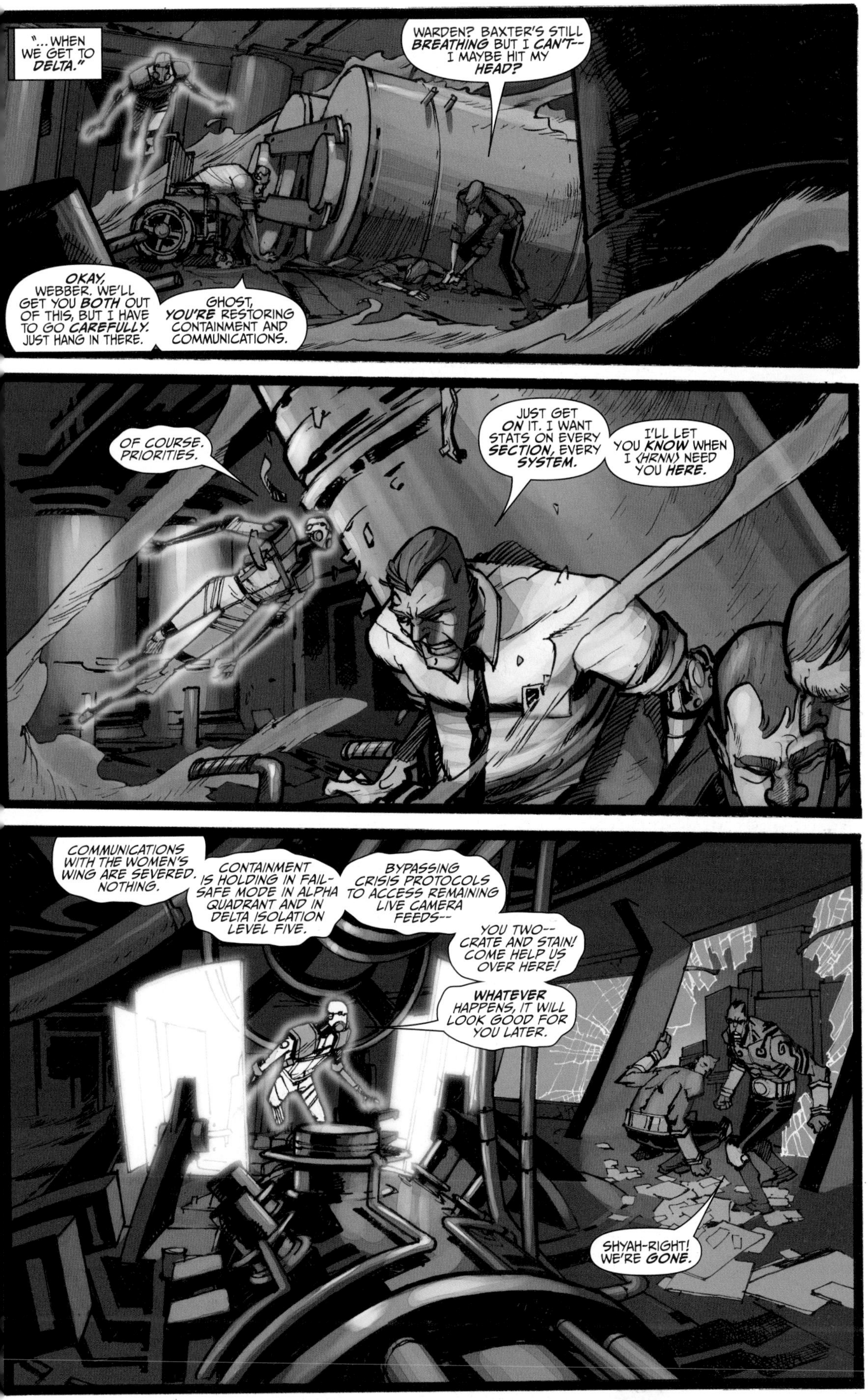
"...WHEN WE GET TO DELTA."
WARDEN? BAXTER'S STILL BREATHING BUT I CAN'T-- I MAYBE HIT MY HEAD?
OKAY, WEBBER. WE'LL GET YOU BOTH OUT OF THIS, BUT I HAVE TO GO CAREFULLY. JUST HANG IN THERE.
GHOST, YOU'RE RESTORING CONTAINMENT AND COMMUNICATIONS.
OF COURSE. PRIORITIES.
JUST GET ON IT. I WANT STATS ON EVERY SECTION, EVERY SYSTEM.
I'LL LET YOU KNOW WHEN I ‹HRNN› NEED YOU HERE.
COMMUNICATIONS WITH THE WOMEN'S WING ARE SEVERED. NOTHING.
CONTAINMENT IS HOLDING IN FAIL-SAFE MODE IN ALPHA QUADRANT AND IN DELTA ISOLATION LEVEL FIVE.
BYPASSING CRISIS PROTOCOLS TO ACCESS REMAINING LIVE CAMERA FEEDS--
YOU TWO-- CRATE AND STAIN! COME HELP US OVER HERE!
WHATEVER HAPPENS, IT WILL LOOK GOOD FOR YOU LATER.
SHYAH-RIGHT! WE'RE GONE.

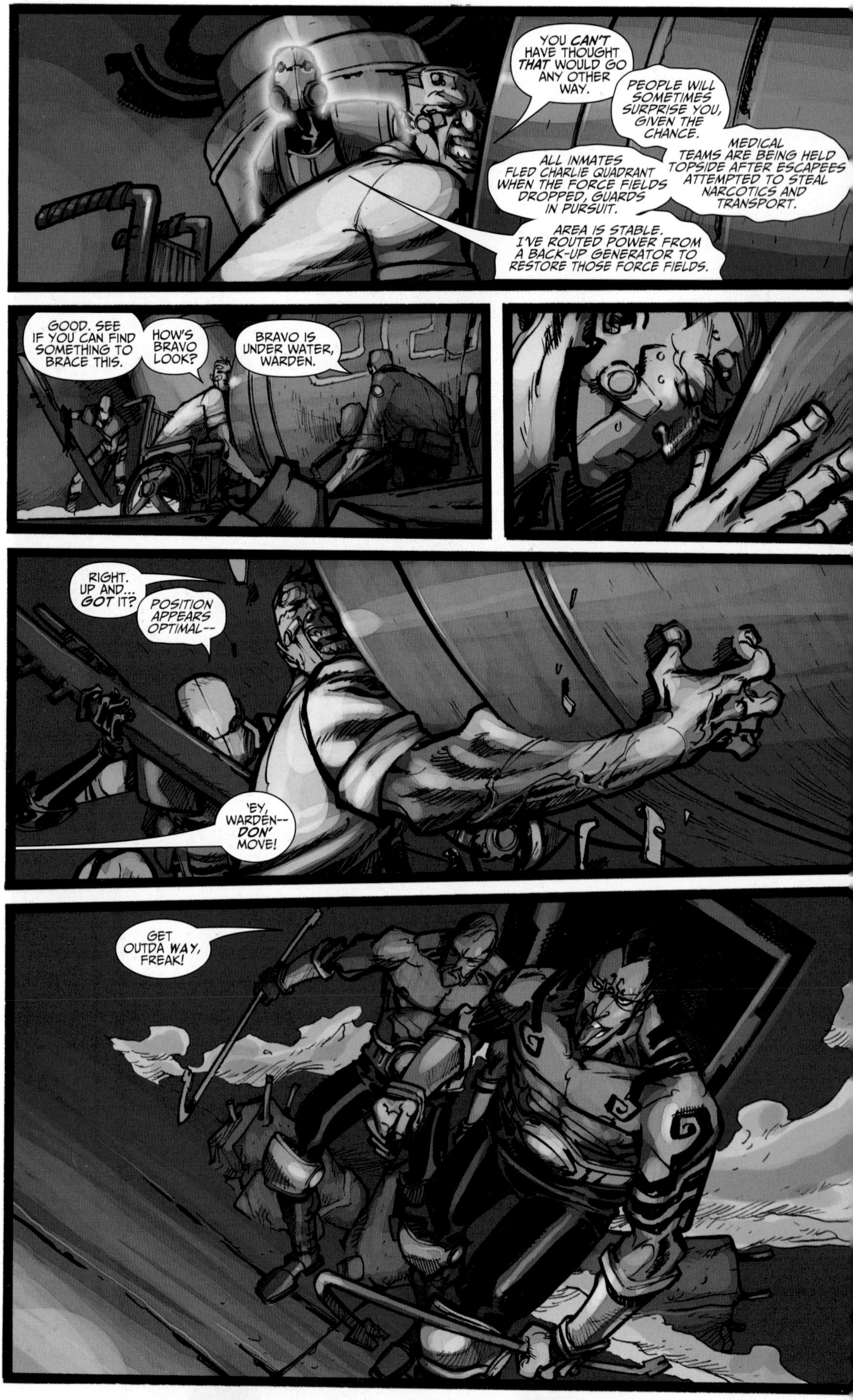
YOU CAN'T HAVE THOUGHT THAT WOULD GO ANY OTHER WAY.
PEOPLE WILL SOMETIMES SURPRISE YOU, GIVEN THE CHANCE.
MEDICAL TEAMS ARE BEING HELD TOPSIDE AFTER ESCAPEES ATTEMPTED TO STEAL NARCOTICS AND TRANSPORT.
ALL INMATES FLED CHARLIE QUADRANT WHEN THE FORCE FIELDS DROPPED, GUARDS IN PURSUIT.
AREA IS STABLE. I'VE ROUTED POWER FROM A BACK-UP GENERATOR TO RESTORE THOSE FORCE FIELDS.
GOOD. SEE IF YOU CAN FIND SOMETHING TO BRACE THIS.
HOW'S BRAVO LOOK?
BRAVO IS UNDER WATER, WARDEN.
RIGHT. UP AND... GOT IT?
POSITION APPEARS OPTIMAL--
'EY, WARDEN-- DON' MOVE!
GET OUTDA WAY, FREAK!

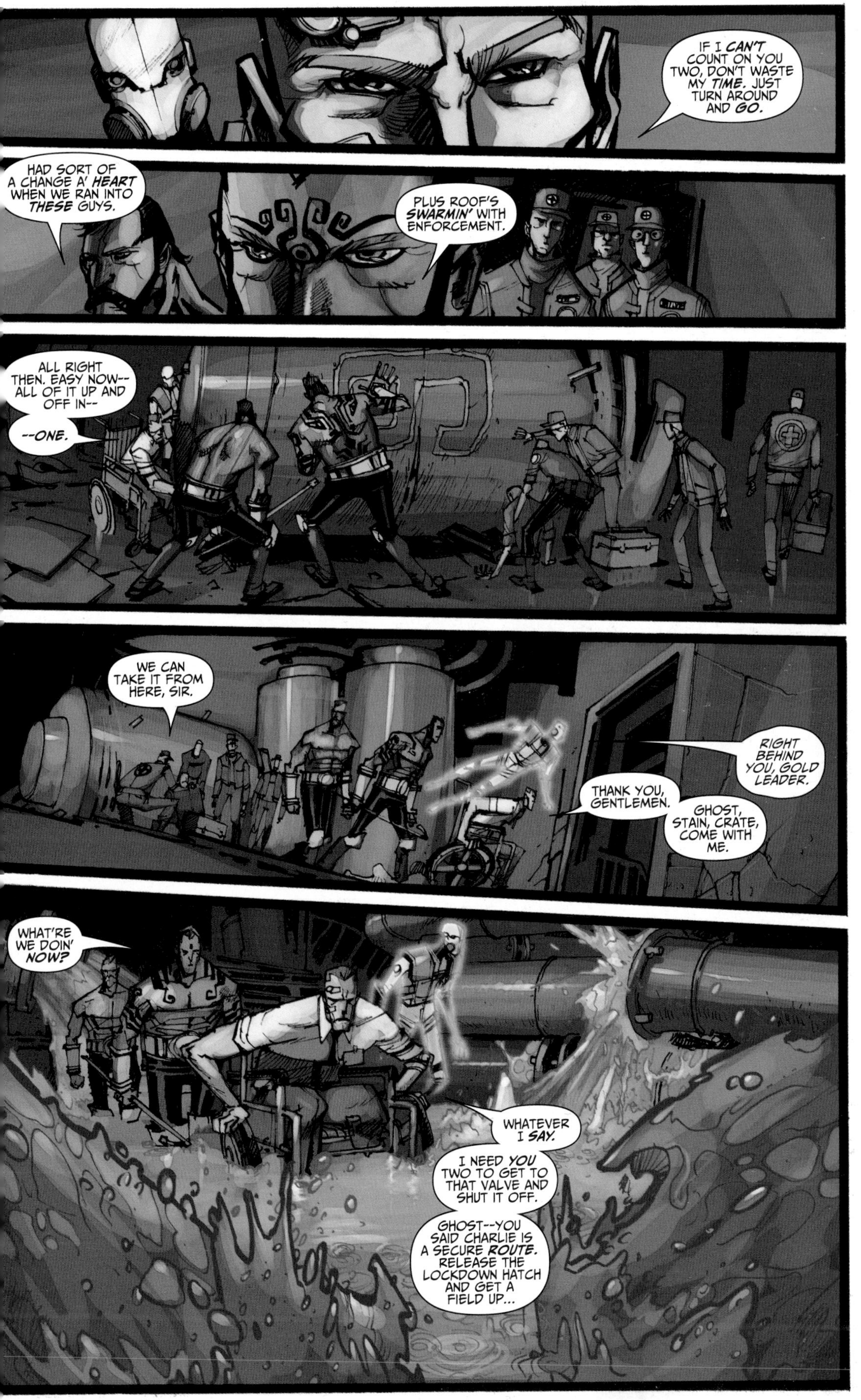
IF I CAN'T COUNT ON YOU TWO, DON'T WASTE MY TIME. JUST TURN AROUND AND GO.
HAD SORT OF A CHANGE A' HEART WHEN WE RAN INTO THESE GUYS.
PLUS ROOF'S SWARMIN' WITH ENFORCEMENT.
ALL RIGHT THEN. EASY NOW-- ALL OF IT UP AND OFF IN--
--ONE.
WE CAN TAKE IT FROM HERE, SIR.
RIGHT BEHIND YOU, GOLD LEADER.
THANK YOU, GENTLEMEN.
GHOST, STAIN, CRATE, COME WITH ME.
WHAT'RE WE DOIN' NOW?
WHATEVER I SAY.
I NEED YOU TWO TO GET TO THAT VALVE AND SHUT IT OFF.
GHOST--YOU SAID CHARLIE IS A SECURE ROUTE. RELEASE THE LOCKDOWN HATCH AND GET A FIELD UP...

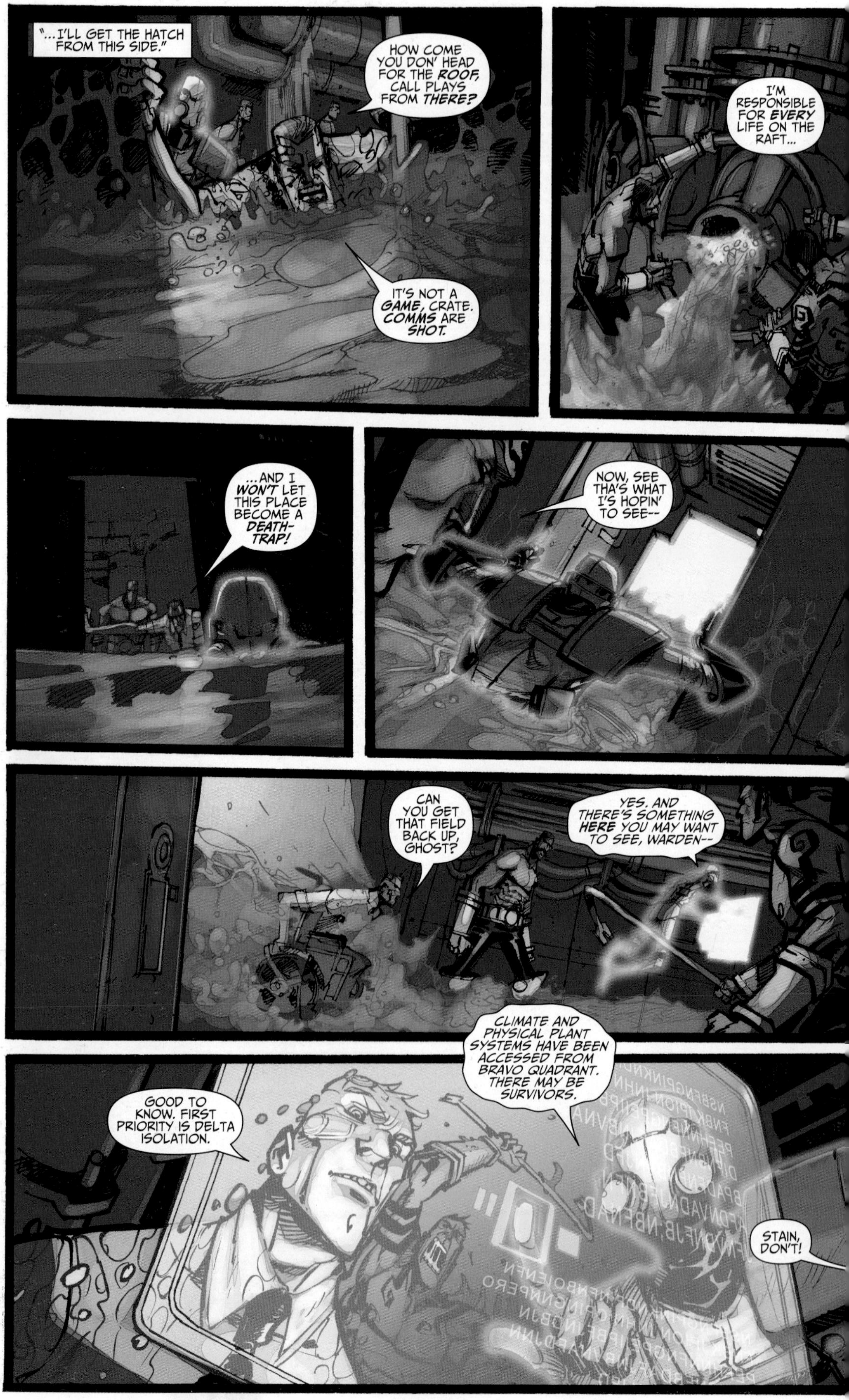
"...I'LL GET THE HATCH FROM THIS SIDE."
HOW COME YOU DON' HEAD FOR THE ROOF, CALL PLAYS FROM THERE?
IT'S NOT A GAME, CRATE. COMMS ARE SHOT.
I'M RESPONSIBLE FOR EVERY LIFE ON THE RAFT...
...AND I WON'T LET THIS PLACE BECOME A DEATH-TRAP!
NOW, SEE THA'S WHAT I'S HOPIN' TO SEE--
CAN YOU GET THAT FIELD BACK UP, GHOST?
YES. AND THERE'S SOMETHING HERE YOU MAY WANT TO SEE, WARDEN--
CLIMATE AND PHYSICAL PLANT SYSTEMS HAVE BEEN ACCESSED FROM BRAVO QUADRANT. THERE MAY BE SURVIVORS.
GOOD TO KNOW. FIRST PRIORITY IS DELTA ISOLATION.
STAIN, DON'T!

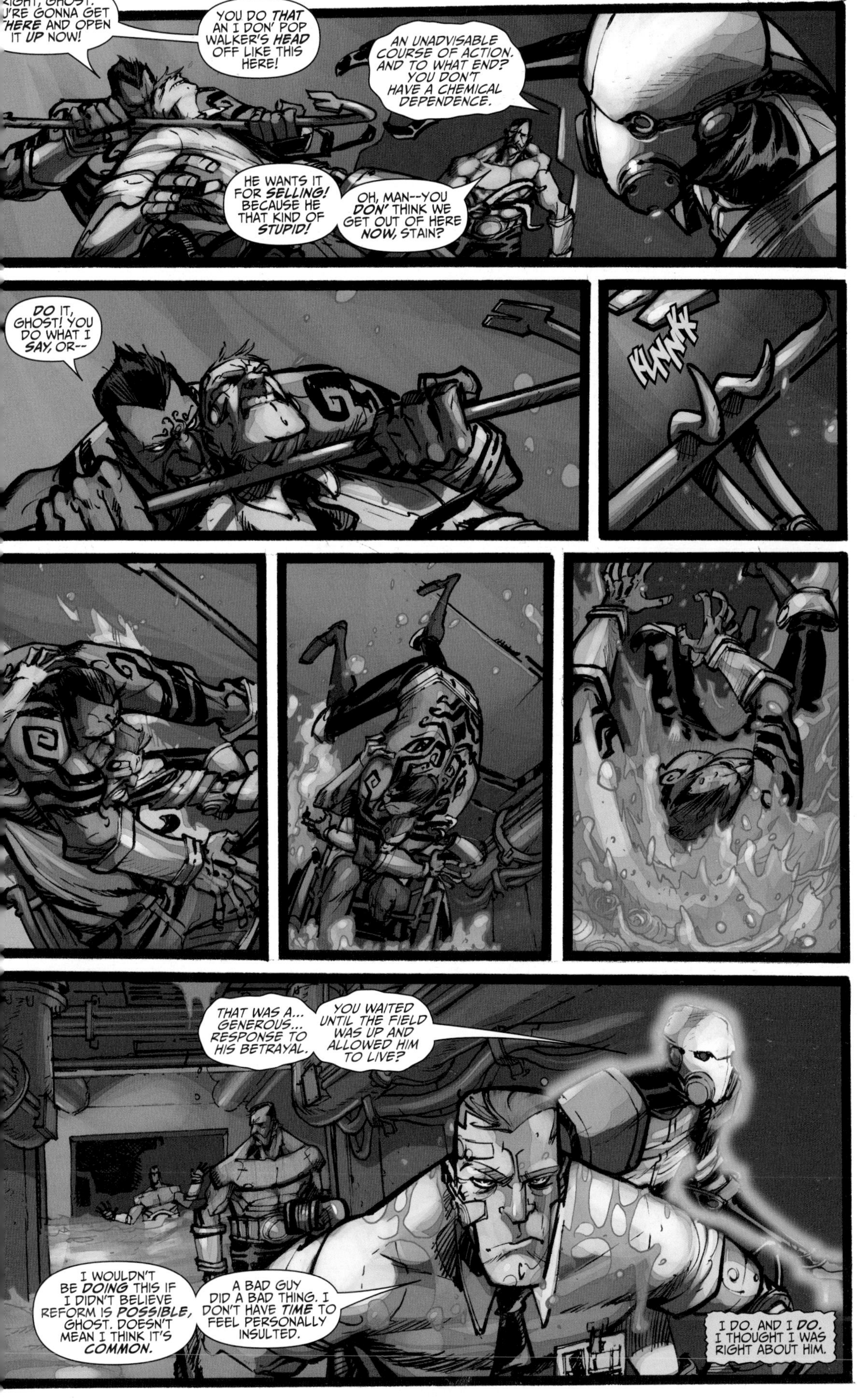

RIGHT, GHOST. U'RE GONNA GET THERE AND OPEN IT UP NOW!
YOU DO THAT AN I DON' POP WALKER'S HEAD OFF LIKE THIS HERE!
AN UNADVISABLE COURSE OF ACTION. AND TO WHAT END? YOU DON'T HAVE A CHEMICAL DEPENDENCE.
HE WANTS IT FOR SELLING! BECAUSE HE THAT KIND OF STUPID!
OH, MAN--YOU DON' THINK WE GET OUT OF HERE NOW, STAIN?
DO IT, GHOST! YOU DO WHAT I SAY, OR--
KLNNK
THAT WAS A... GENEROUS... RESPONSE TO HIS BETRAYAL.
YOU WAITED UNTIL THE FIELD WAS UP AND ALLOWED HIM TO LIVE?
I WOULDN'T BE DOING THIS IF I DIDN'T BELIEVE REFORM IS POSSIBLE, GHOST. DOESN'T MEAN I THINK IT'S COMMON.
A BAD GUY DID A BAD THING. I DON'T HAVE TIME TO FEEL PERSONALLY INSULTED.
I DO. AND I DO. I THOUGHT I WAS RIGHT ABOUT HIM.

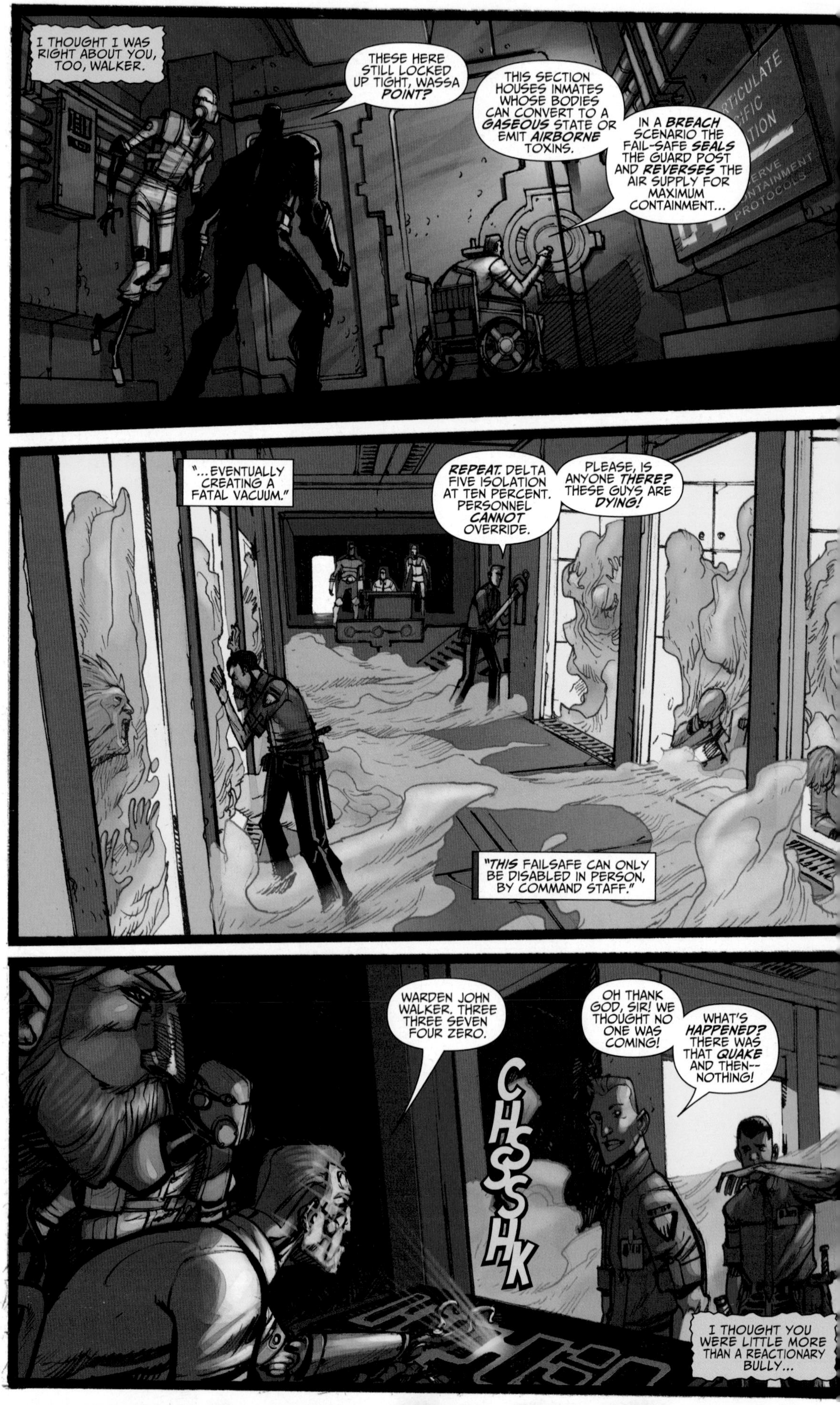
I THOUGHT I WAS RIGHT ABOUT YOU, TOO, WALKER.
THESE HERE STILL LOCKED UP TIGHT, WASSA POINT?
THIS SECTION HOUSES INMATES WHOSE BODIES CAN CONVERT TO A GASEOUS STATE OR EMIT AIRBORNE TOXINS.
IN A BREACH SCENARIO THE FAIL-SAFE SEALS THE GUARD POST AND REVERSES THE AIR SUPPLY FOR MAXIMUM CONTAINMENT...
"...EVENTUALLY CREATING A FATAL VACUUM."
REPEAT. DELTA FIVE ISOLATION AT TEN PERCENT. PERSONNEL CANNOT OVERRIDE.
PLEASE, IS ANYONE THERE? THESE GUYS ARE DYING!
"THIS FAILSAFE CAN ONLY BE DISABLED IN PERSON, BY COMMAND STAFF."
WARDEN JOHN WALKER. THREE THREE SEVEN FOUR ZERO.
CHSSSHK
OH THANK GOD, SIR! WE THOUGHT NO ONE WAS COMING!
WHAT'S HAPPENED? THERE WAS THAT QUAKE AND THEN--NOTHING!
I THOUGHT YOU WERE LITTLE MORE THAN A REACTIONARY BULLY...

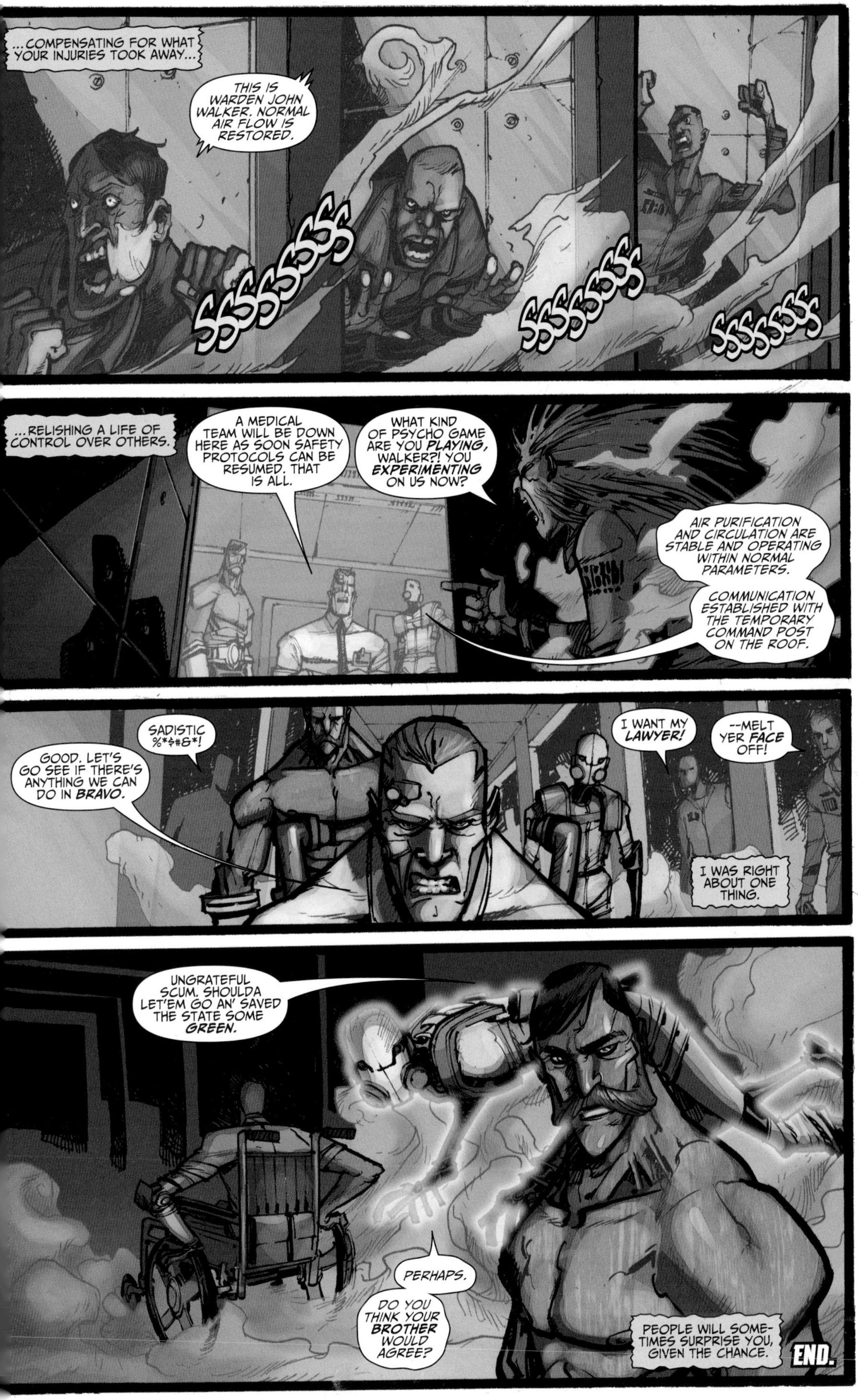
...COMPENSATING FOR WHAT YOUR INJURIES TOOK AWAY...
THIS IS WARDEN JOHN WALKER. NORMAL AIR FLOW IS RESTORED.
SSSSSSSSS
SSSSSSSS
SSSSSSSS
...RELISHING A LIFE OF CONTROL OVER OTHERS.
A MEDICAL TEAM WILL BE DOWN HERE AS SOON SAFETY PROTOCOLS CAN BE RESUMED. THAT IS ALL.
WHAT KIND OF PSYCHO GAME ARE YOU PLAYING, WALKER?! YOU EXPERIMENTING ON US NOW?
AIR PURIFICATION AND CIRCULATION ARE STABLE AND OPERATING WITHIN NORMAL PARAMETERS.
COMMUNICATION ESTABLISHED WITH THE TEMPORARY COMMAND POST ON THE ROOF.
SADISTIC %*$#&*!
GOOD. LET'S GO SEE IF THERE'S ANYTHING WE CAN DO IN BRAVO.
I WANT MY LAWYER!
--MELT YER FACE OFF!
I WAS RIGHT ABOUT ONE THING.
UNGRATEFUL SCUM. SHOULDA LET'EM GO AN' SAVED THE STATE SOME GREEN.
PERHAPS.
DO YOU THINK YOUR BROTHER WOULD AGREE?
PEOPLE WILL SOME-TIMES SURPRISE YOU, GIVEN THE CHANCE.
END.

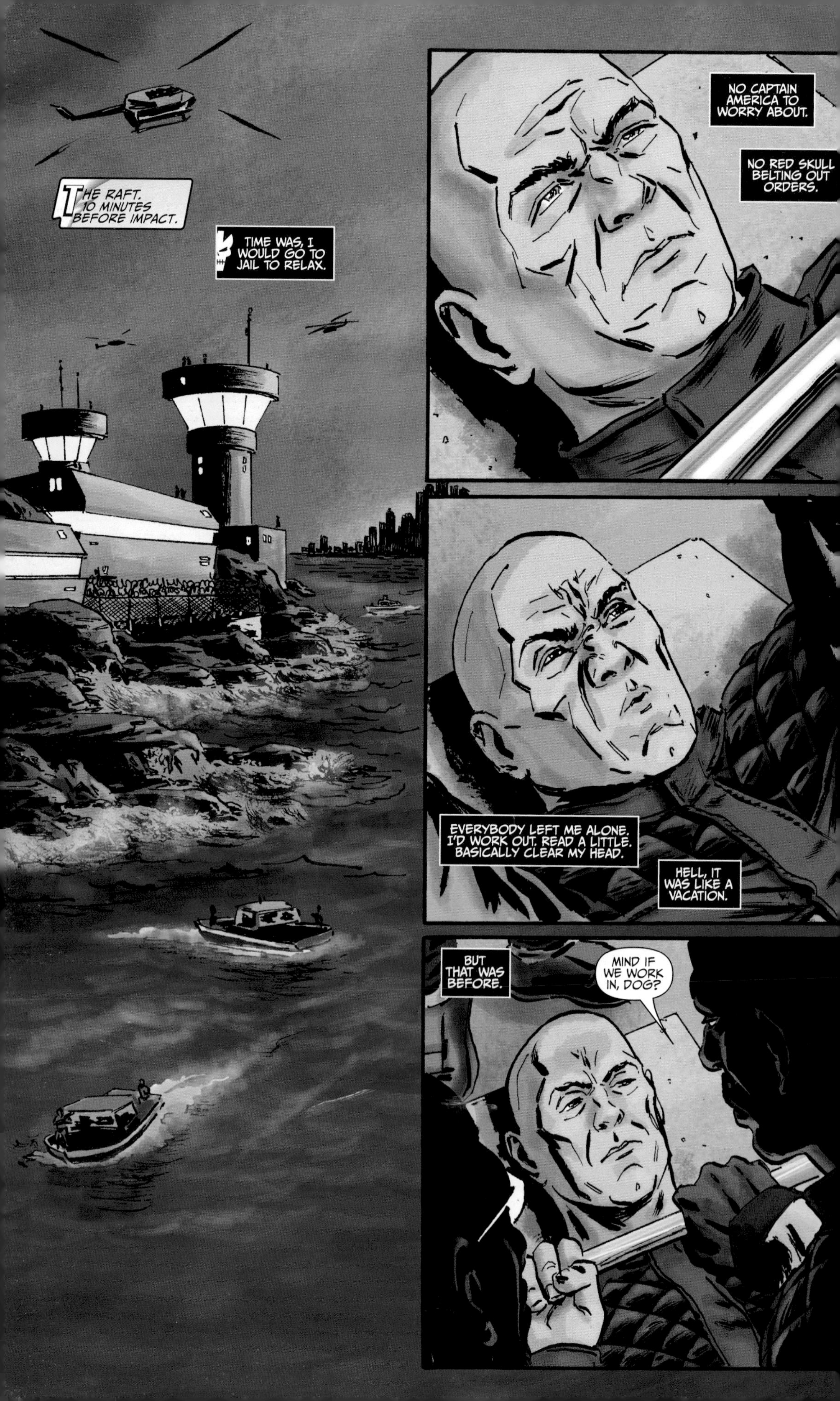
THE RAFT. 10 MINUTES BEFORE IMPACT.
TIME WAS, I WOULD GO TO JAIL TO RELAX.
NO CAPTAIN AMERICA TO WORRY ABOUT.
NO RED SKULL BELTING OUT ORDERS.
EVERYBODY LEFT ME ALONE. I'D WORK OUT. READ A LITTLE. BASICALLY CLEAR MY HEAD.
HELL, IT WAS LIKE A VACATION.
BUT THAT WAS BEFORE.
MIND IF WE WORK IN, DOG?

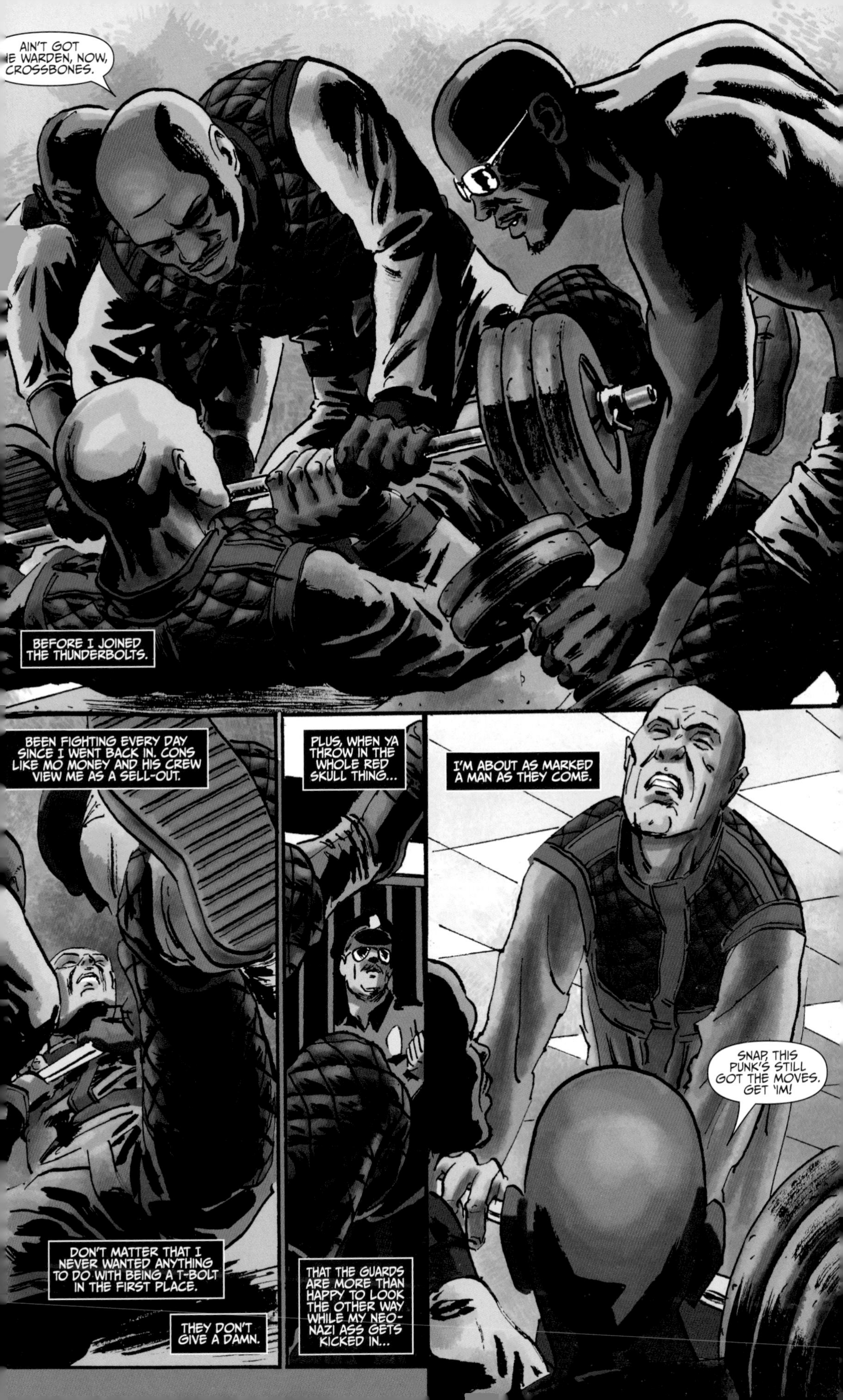

AIN'T GOT
E WARDEN, NOW,
CROSSBONES.
BEFORE I JOINED THE THUNDERBOLTS.
BEEN FIGHTING EVERY DAY SINCE I WENT BACK IN. CONS LIKE MO MONEY AND HIS CREW VIEW ME AS A SELL-OUT.
DON'T MATTER THAT I NEVER WANTED ANYTHING TO DO WITH BEING A T-BOLT IN THE FIRST PLACE.
THEY DON'T GIVE A DAMN.
PLUS, WHEN YA THROW IN THE WHOLE RED SKULL THING...
THAT THE GUARDS ARE MORE THAN HAPPY TO LOOK THE OTHER WAY WHILE MY NEO-NAZI ASS GETS KICKED IN...
I'M ABOUT AS MARKED A MAN AS THEY COME.
SNAP, THIS PUNK'S STILL GOT THE MOVES. GET 'IM!

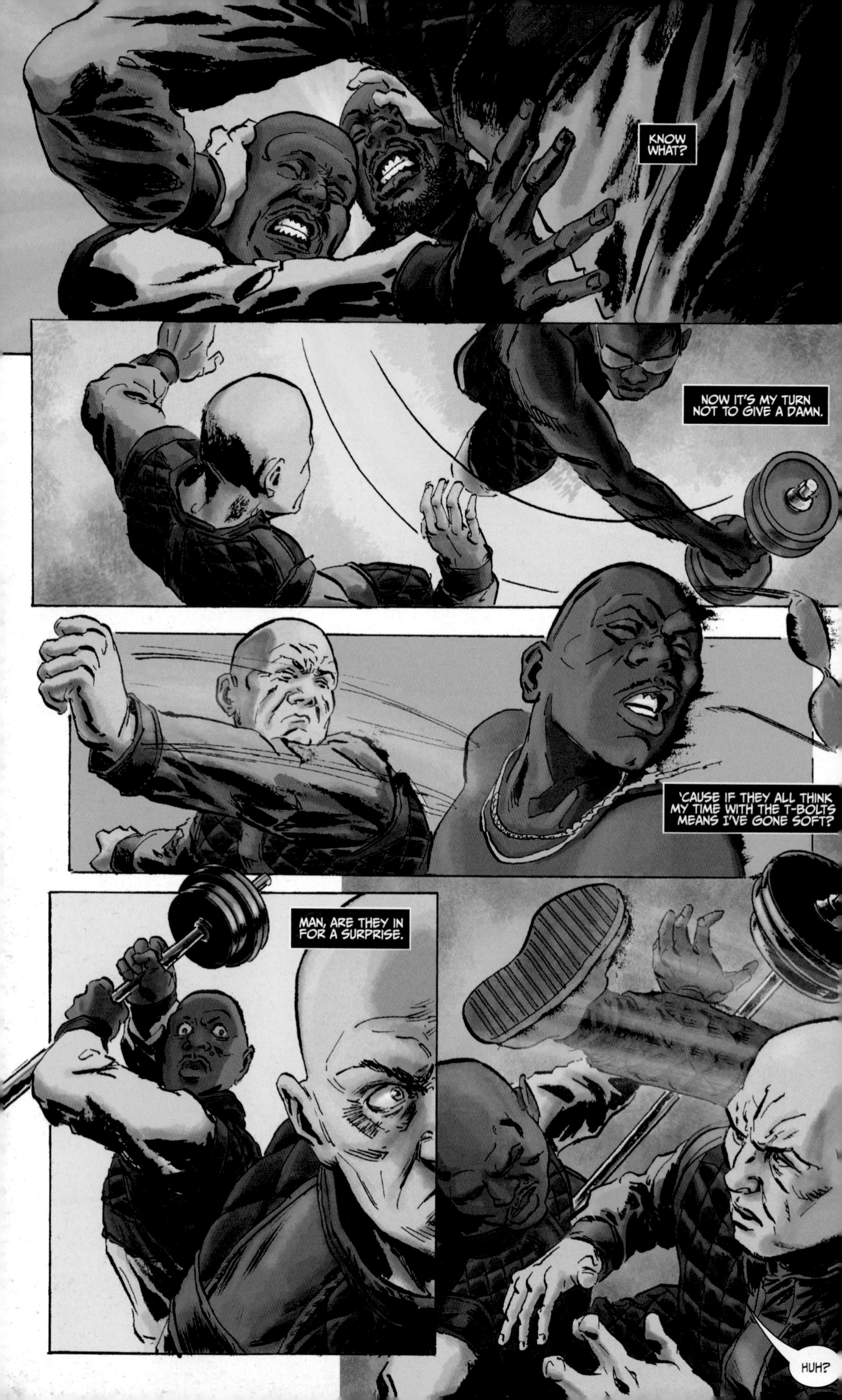
KNOW WHAT?
NOW IT'S MY TURN NOT TO GIVE A DAMN.
'CAUSE IF THEY ALL THINK MY TIME WITH THE T-BOLTS MEANS I'VE GONE SOFT?
MAN, ARE THEY IN FOR A SURPRISE.
HUH?

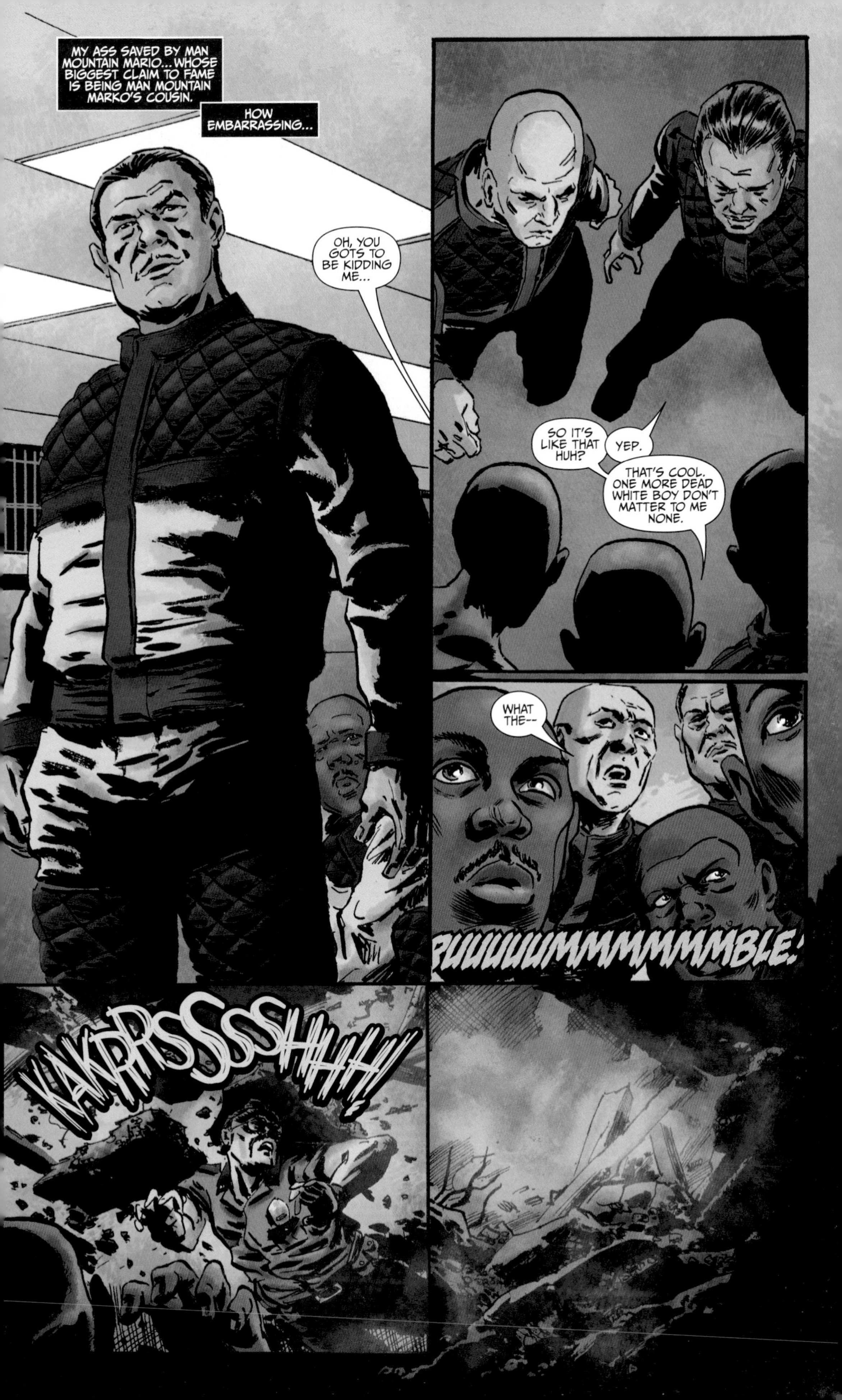
MY ASS SAVED BY MAN MOUNTAIN MARIO... WHOSE BIGGEST CLAIM TO FAME IS BEING MAN MOUNTAIN MARKO'S COUSIN.
HOW EMBARRASSING...
OH, YOU GOTS TO BE KIDDING ME...
SO IT'S LIKE THAT HUH?
YEP.
THAT'S COOL. ONE MORE DEAD WHITE BOY DON'T MATTER TO ME NONE.
WHAT THE--
RUUUUUMMMMMMMBLE!
KAKRRSSSSHHHH!

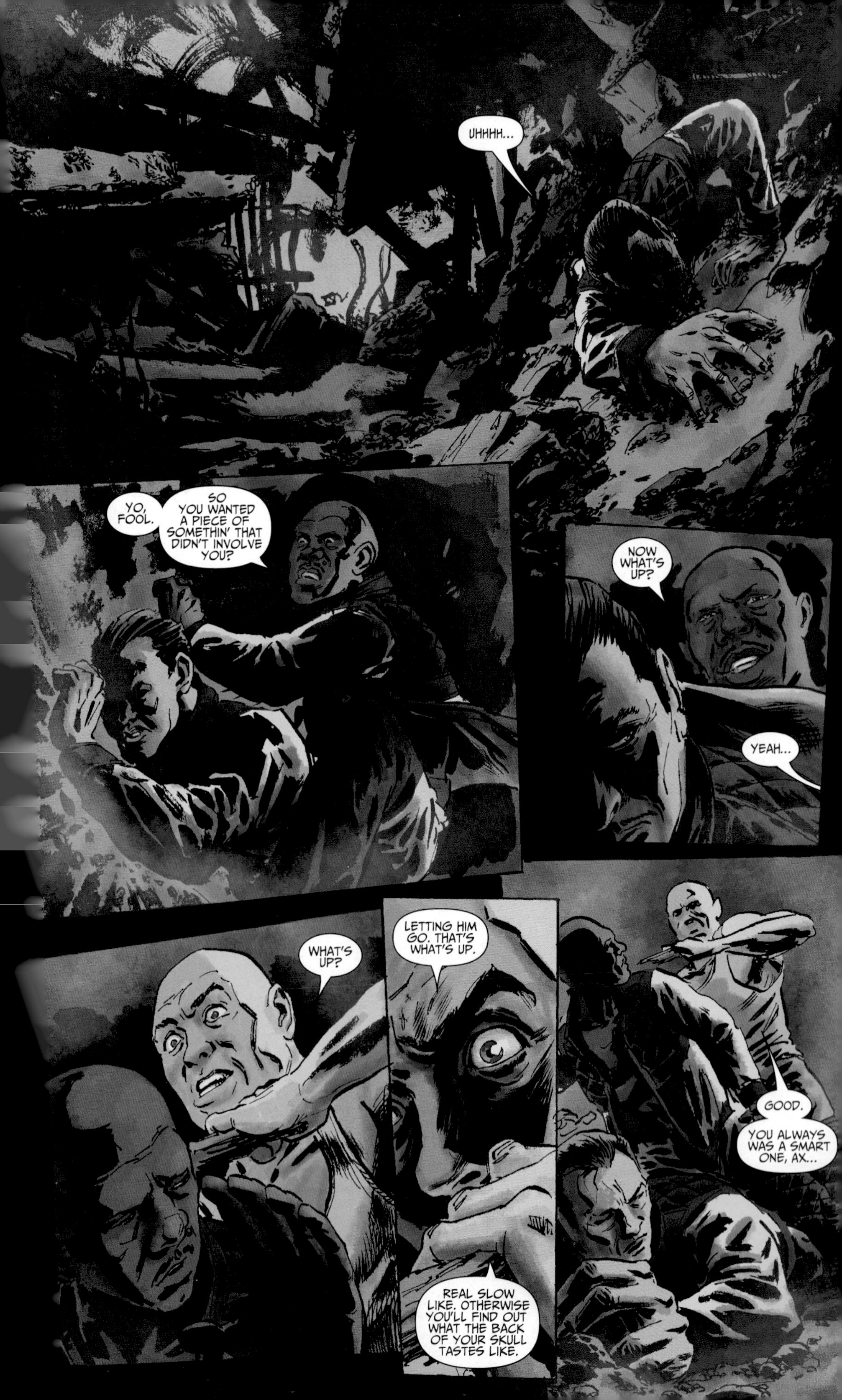
UHHHH...
YO, FOOL.
SO YOU WANTED A PIECE OF SOMETHIN' THAT DIDN'T INVOLVE YOU?
NOW WHAT'S UP?
YEAH...
WHAT'S UP?
LETTING HIM GO. THAT'S WHAT'S UP.
REAL SLOW LIKE. OTHERWISE YOU'LL FIND OUT WHAT THE BACK OF YOUR SKULL TASTES LIKE.
GOOD.
YOU ALWAYS WAS A SMART ONE, AX...

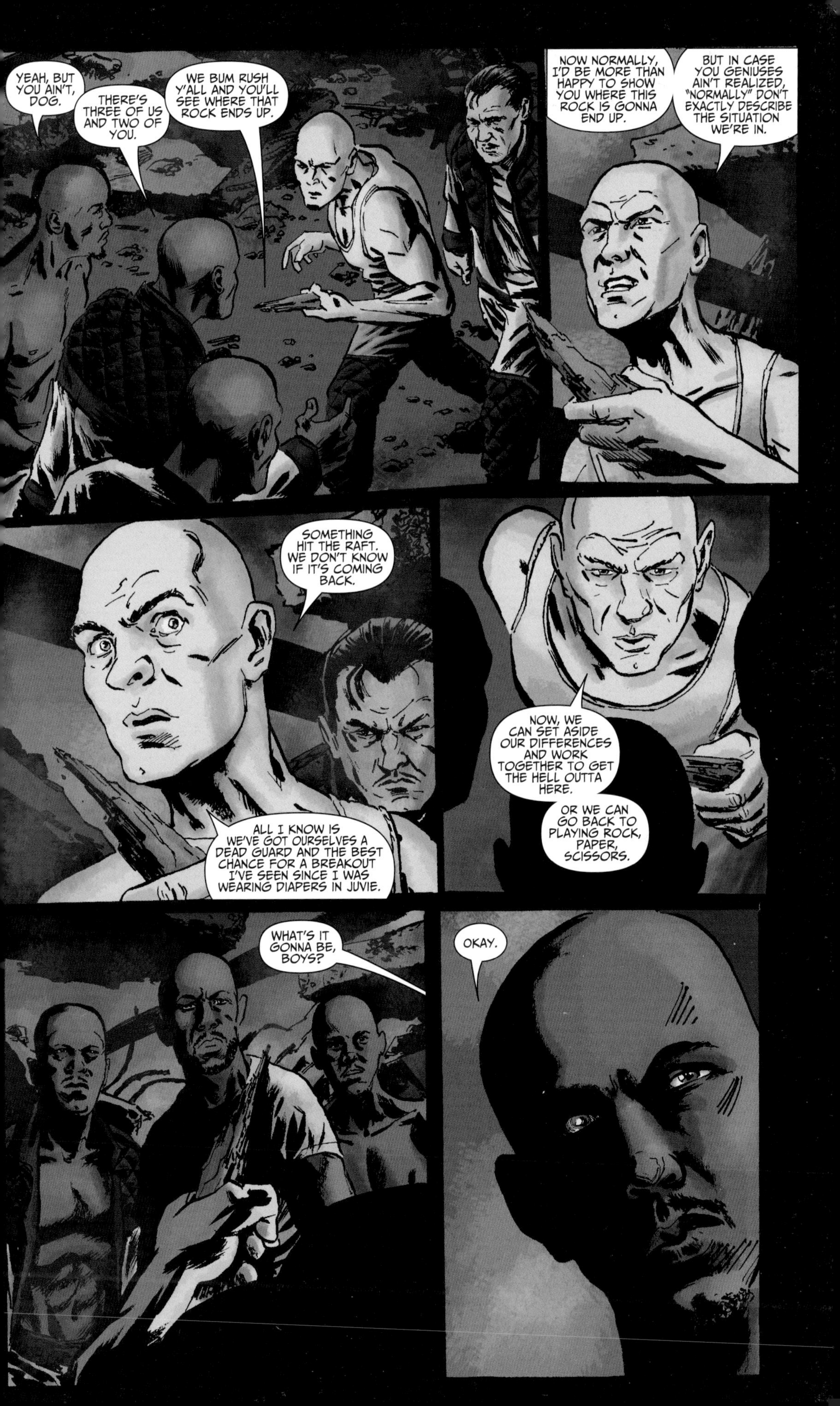
YEAH, BUT YOU AIN'T, DOG.
THERE'S THREE OF US AND TWO OF YOU.
WE BUM RUSH Y'ALL AND YOU'LL SEE WHERE THAT ROCK ENDS UP.
NOW NORMALLY, I'D BE MORE THAN HAPPY TO SHOW YOU WHERE THIS ROCK IS GONNA END UP.
BUT IN CASE YOU GENIUSES AIN'T REALIZED, "NORMALLY" DON'T EXACTLY DESCRIBE THE SITUATION WE'RE IN.
SOMETHING HIT THE RAFT. WE DON'T KNOW IF IT'S COMING BACK.
ALL I KNOW IS WE'VE GOT OURSELVES A DEAD GUARD AND THE BEST CHANCE FOR A BREAKOUT I'VE SEEN SINCE I WAS WEARING DIAPERS IN JUVIE.
NOW, WE CAN SET ASIDE OUR DIFFERENCES AND WORK TOGETHER TO GET THE HELL OUTTA HERE.
OR WE CAN GO BACK TO PLAYING ROCK, PAPER, SCISSORS.
WHAT'S IT GONNA BE, BOYS?
OKAY.

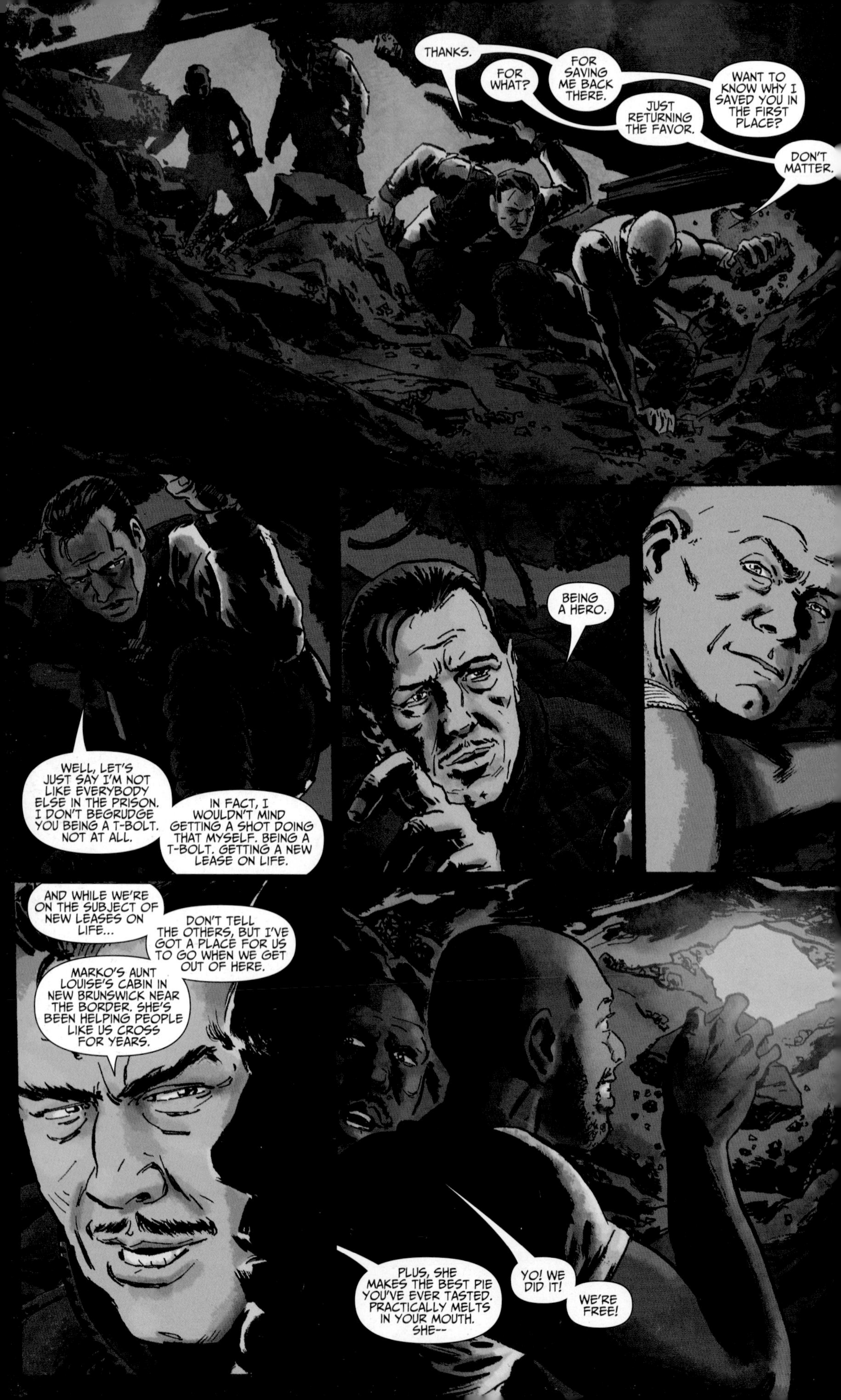
THANKS.
FOR WHAT?
FOR SAVING ME BACK THERE.
JUST RETURNING THE FAVOR.
WANT TO KNOW WHY I SAVED YOU IN THE FIRST PLACE?
DON'T MATTER.
WELL, LET'S JUST SAY I'M NOT LIKE EVERYBODY ELSE IN THE PRISON. I DON'T BEGRUDGE YOU BEING A T-BOLT. NOT AT ALL.
IN FACT, I WOULDN'T MIND GETTING A SHOT DOING THAT MYSELF. BEING A T-BOLT. GETTING A NEW LEASE ON LIFE.
BEING A HERO.
AND WHILE WE'RE ON THE SUBJECT OF NEW LEASES ON LIFE...
DON'T TELL THE OTHERS, BUT I'VE GOT A PLACE FOR US TO GO WHEN WE GET OUT OF HERE.
MARKO'S AUNT LOUISE'S CABIN IN NEW BRUNSWICK NEAR THE BORDER. SHE'S BEEN HELPING PEOPLE LIKE US CROSS FOR YEARS.
PLUS, SHE MAKES THE BEST PIE YOU'VE EVER TASTED. PRACTICALLY MELTS IN YOUR MOUTH. SHE--
YO! WE DID IT!
WE'RE FREE!

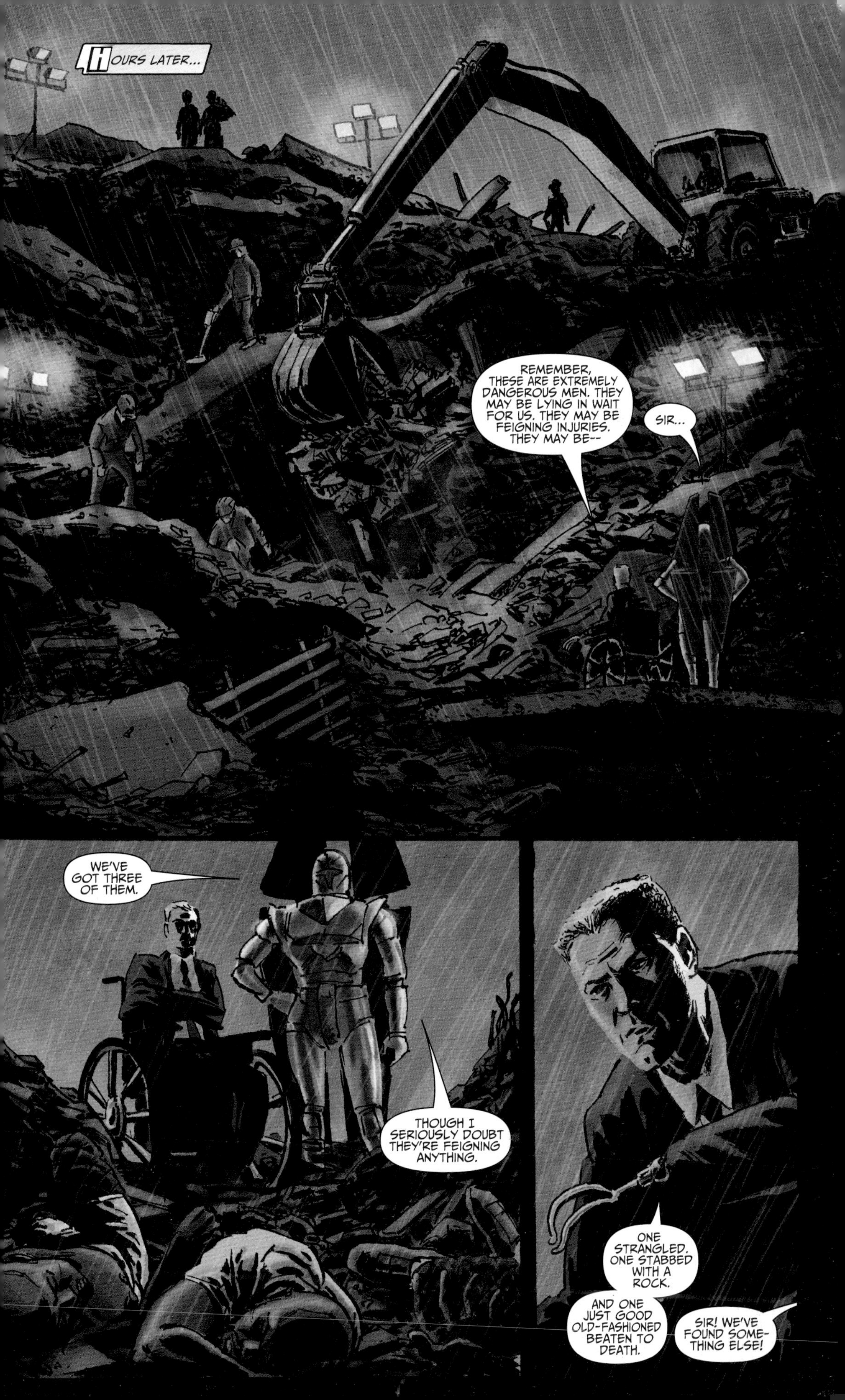
HOURS LATER...
REMEMBER, THESE ARE EXTREMELY DANGEROUS MEN. THEY MAY BE LYING IN WAIT FOR US. THEY MAY BE FEIGNING INJURIES. THEY MAY BE--
SIR...
WE'VE GOT THREE OF THEM.
THOUGH I SERIOUSLY DOUBT THEY'RE FEIGNING ANYTHING.
ONE STRANGLED. ONE STABBED WITH A ROCK.
AND ONE JUST GOOD OLD-FASHIONED BEATEN TO DEATH.
SIR! WE'VE FOUND SOME-THING ELSE!

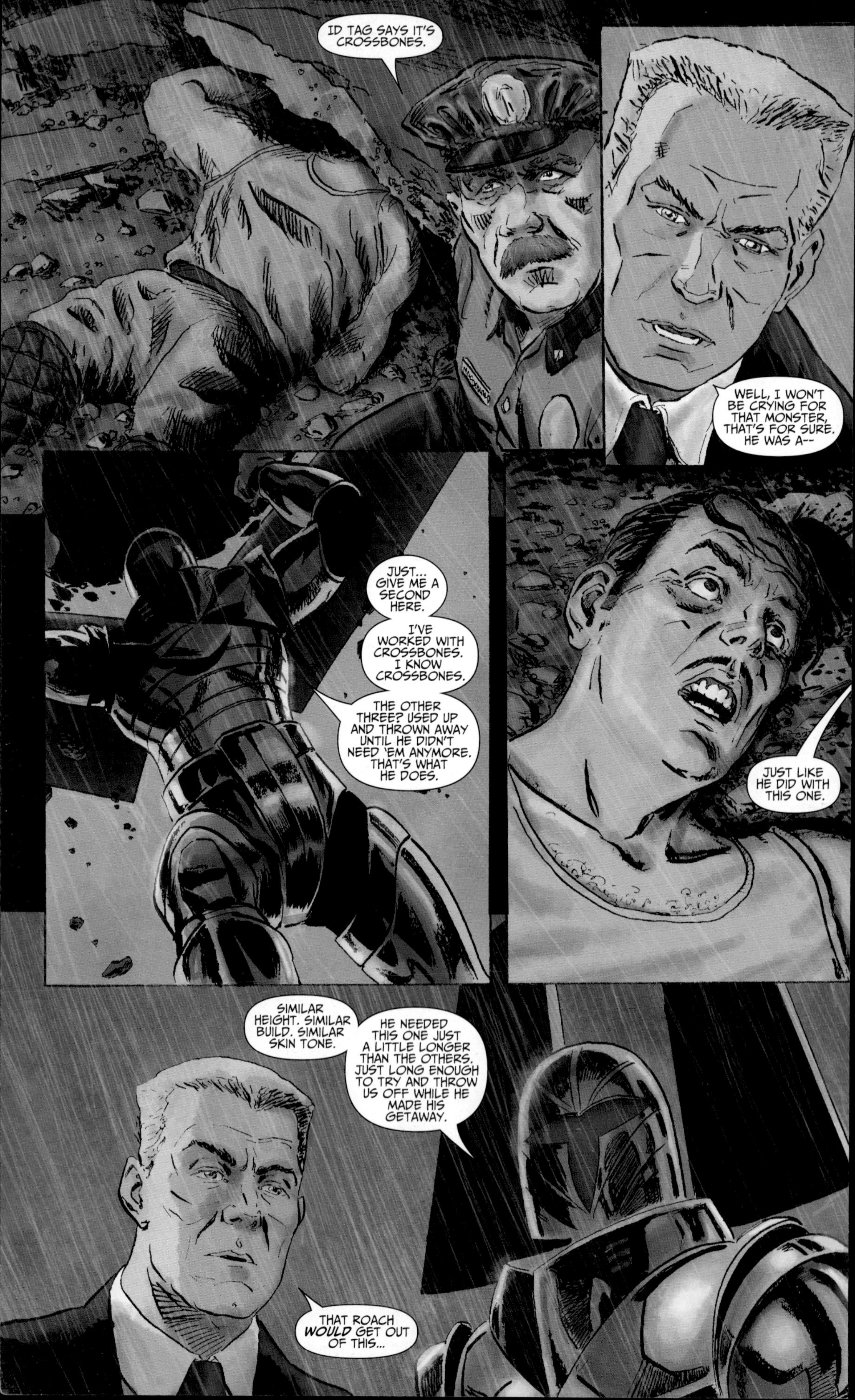
ID TAG SAYS IT'S CROSSBONES.
WELL, I WON'T BE CRYING FOR THAT MONSTER, THAT'S FOR SURE. HE WAS A--
JUST... GIVE ME A SECOND HERE.
I'VE WORKED WITH CROSSBONES. I KNOW CROSSBONES.
THE OTHER THREE? USED UP AND THROWN AWAY UNTIL HE DIDN'T NEED 'EM ANYMORE. THAT'S WHAT HE DOES.
JUST LIKE HE DID WITH THIS ONE.
SIMILAR HEIGHT. SIMILAR BUILD. SIMILAR SKIN TONE.
HE NEEDED THIS ONE JUST A LITTLE LONGER THAN THE OTHERS. JUST LONG ENOUGH TO TRY AND THROW US OFF WHILE HE MADE HIS GETAWAY.
THAT ROACH ***WOULD*** GET OUT OF THIS...

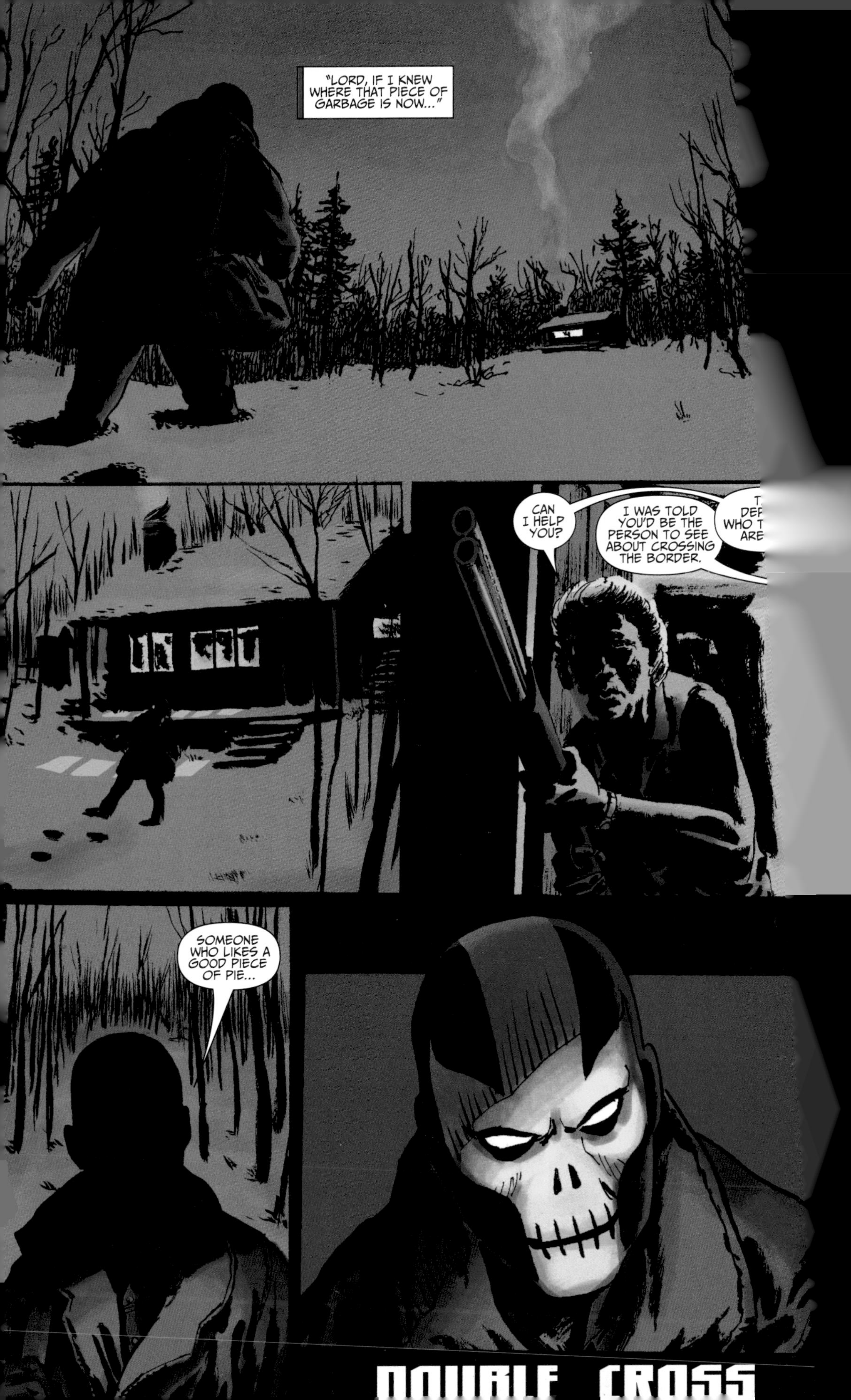
"LORD, IF I KNEW WHERE THAT PIECE OF GARBAGE IS NOW..."
CAN I HELP YOU?
I WAS TOLD YOU'D BE THE PERSON TO SEE ABOUT CROSSING THE BORDER.
SOMEONE WHO LIKES A GOOD PIECE OF PIE...
DOUBLE CROSS

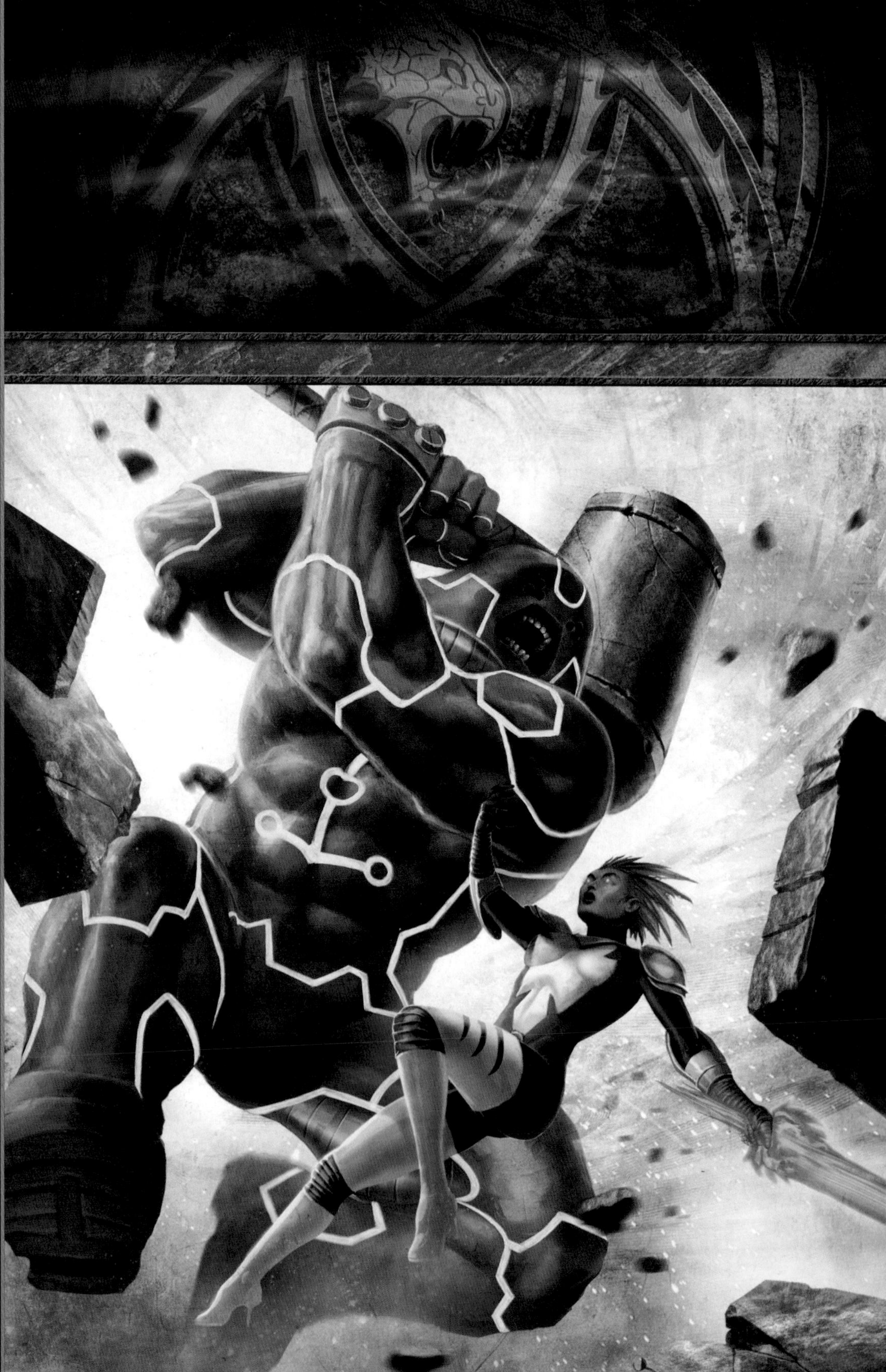

THUNDERBOLTS #160

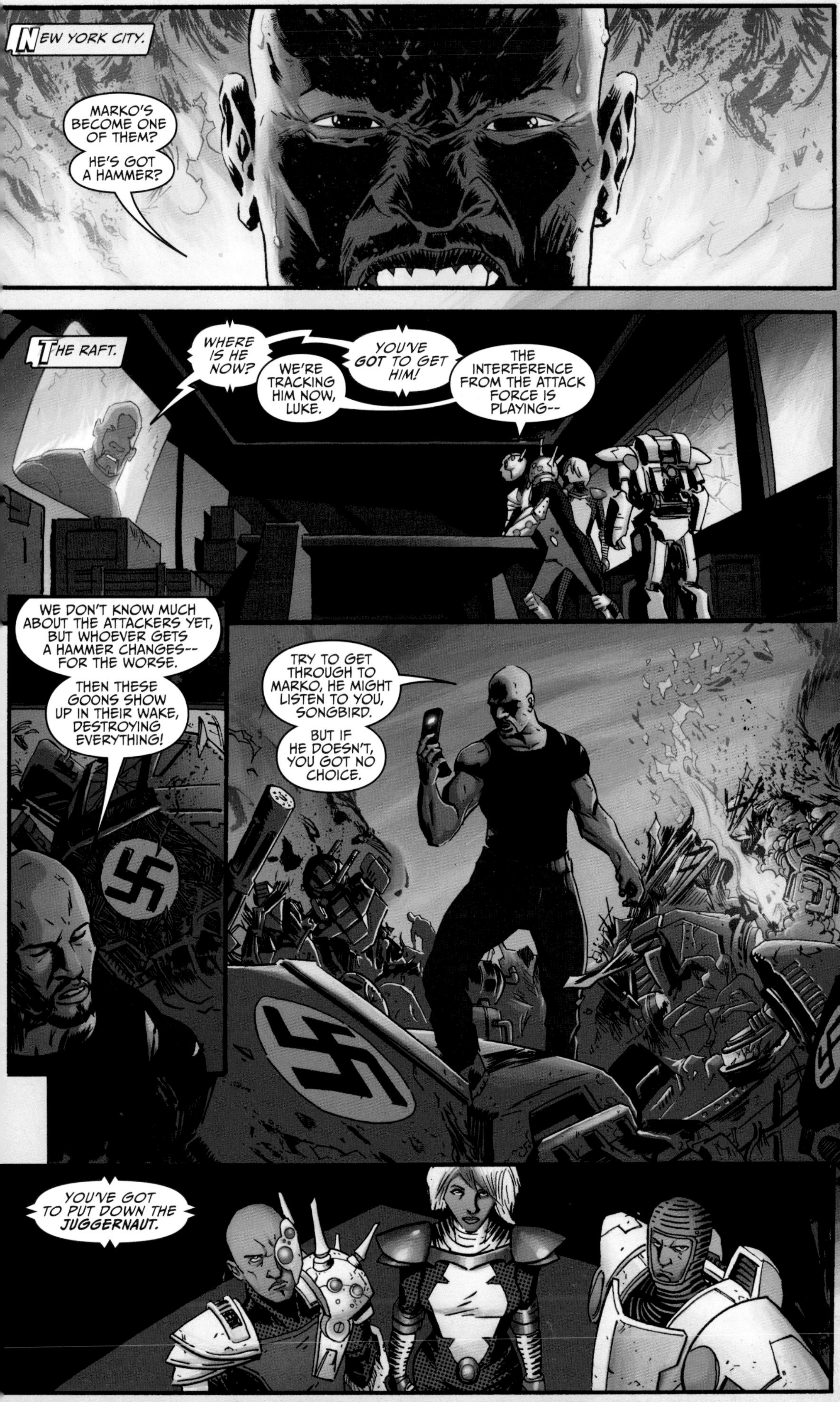

NEW YORK CITY.
MARKO'S BECOME ONE OF THEM?
HE'S GOT A HAMMER?
THE RAFT.
WHERE IS HE NOW?
WE'RE TRACKING HIM NOW, LUKE.
YOU'VE GOT TO GET HIM!
THE INTERFERENCE FROM THE ATTACK FORCE IS PLAYING--
WE DON'T KNOW MUCH ABOUT THE ATTACKERS YET, BUT WHOEVER GETS A HAMMER CHANGES-- FOR THE WORSE.
THEN THESE GOONS SHOW UP IN THEIR WAKE, DESTROYING EVERYTHING!
TRY TO GET THROUGH TO MARKO, HE MIGHT LISTEN TO YOU, SONGBIRD.
BUT IF HE DOESN'T, YOU GOT NO CHOICE.
YOU'VE GOT TO PUT DOWN THE JUGGERNAUT.

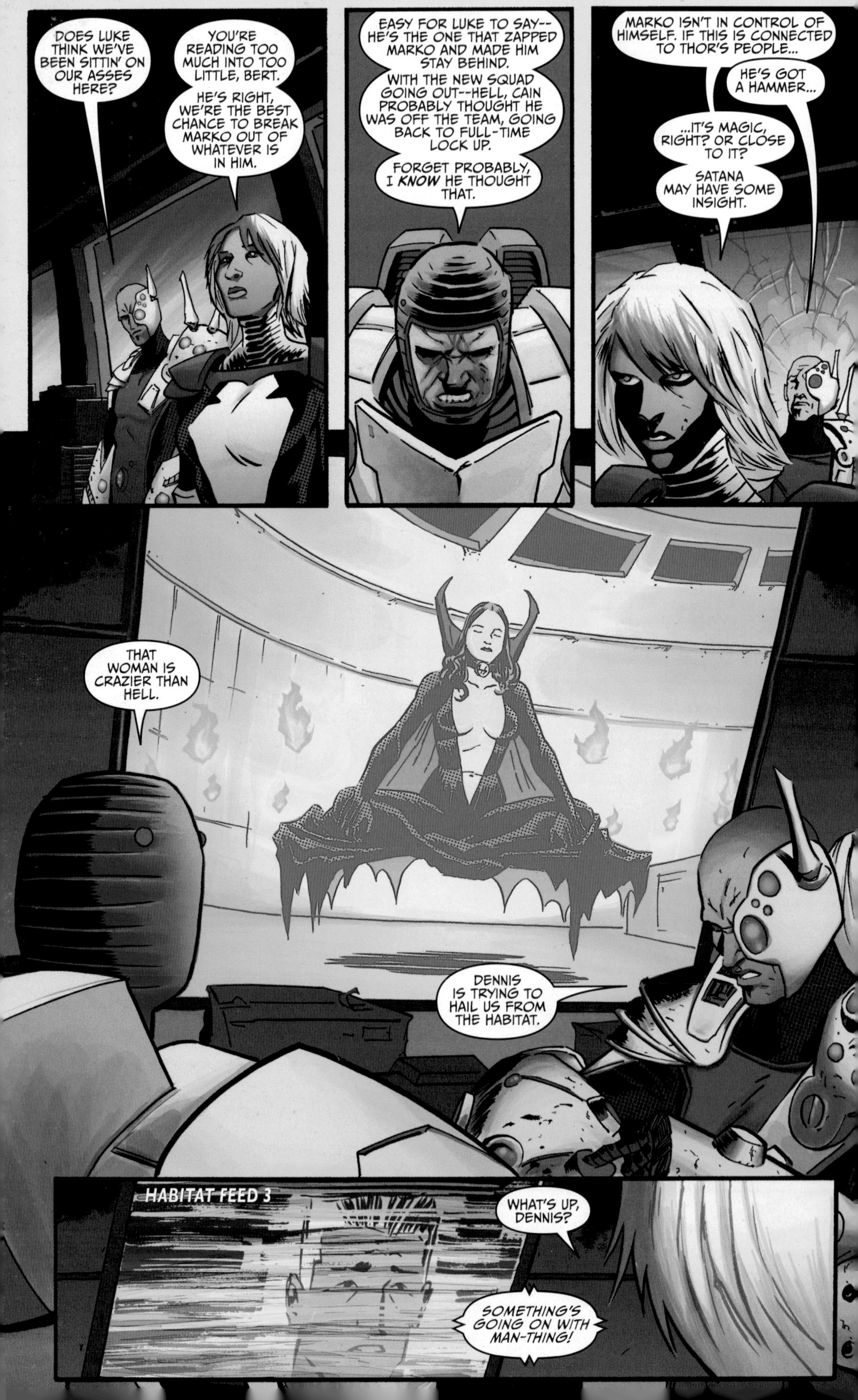
DOES LUKE THINK WE'VE BEEN SITTIN' ON OUR ASSES HERE?
YOU'RE READING TOO MUCH INTO TOO LITTLE, BERT.
HE'S RIGHT, WE'RE THE BEST CHANCE TO BREAK MARKO OUT OF WHATEVER IS IN HIM.
EASY FOR LUKE TO SAY-- HE'S THE ONE THAT ZAPPED MARKO AND MADE HIM STAY BEHIND.
WITH THE NEW SQUAD GOING OUT--HELL, CAIN PROBABLY THOUGHT HE WAS OFF THE TEAM, GOING BACK TO FULL-TIME LOCK UP.
FORGET PROBABLY, I KNOW HE THOUGHT THAT.
MARKO ISN'T IN CONTROL OF HIMSELF. IF THIS IS CONNECTED TO THOR'S PEOPLE...
HE'S GOT A HAMMER...
...IT'S MAGIC, RIGHT? OR CLOSE TO IT?
SATANA MAY HAVE SOME INSIGHT.
THAT WOMAN IS CRAZIER THAN HELL.
DENNIS IS TRYING TO HAIL US FROM THE HABITAT.
HABITAT FEED 3
WHAT'S UP, DENNIS?
SOMETHING'S GOING ON WITH MAN-THING!

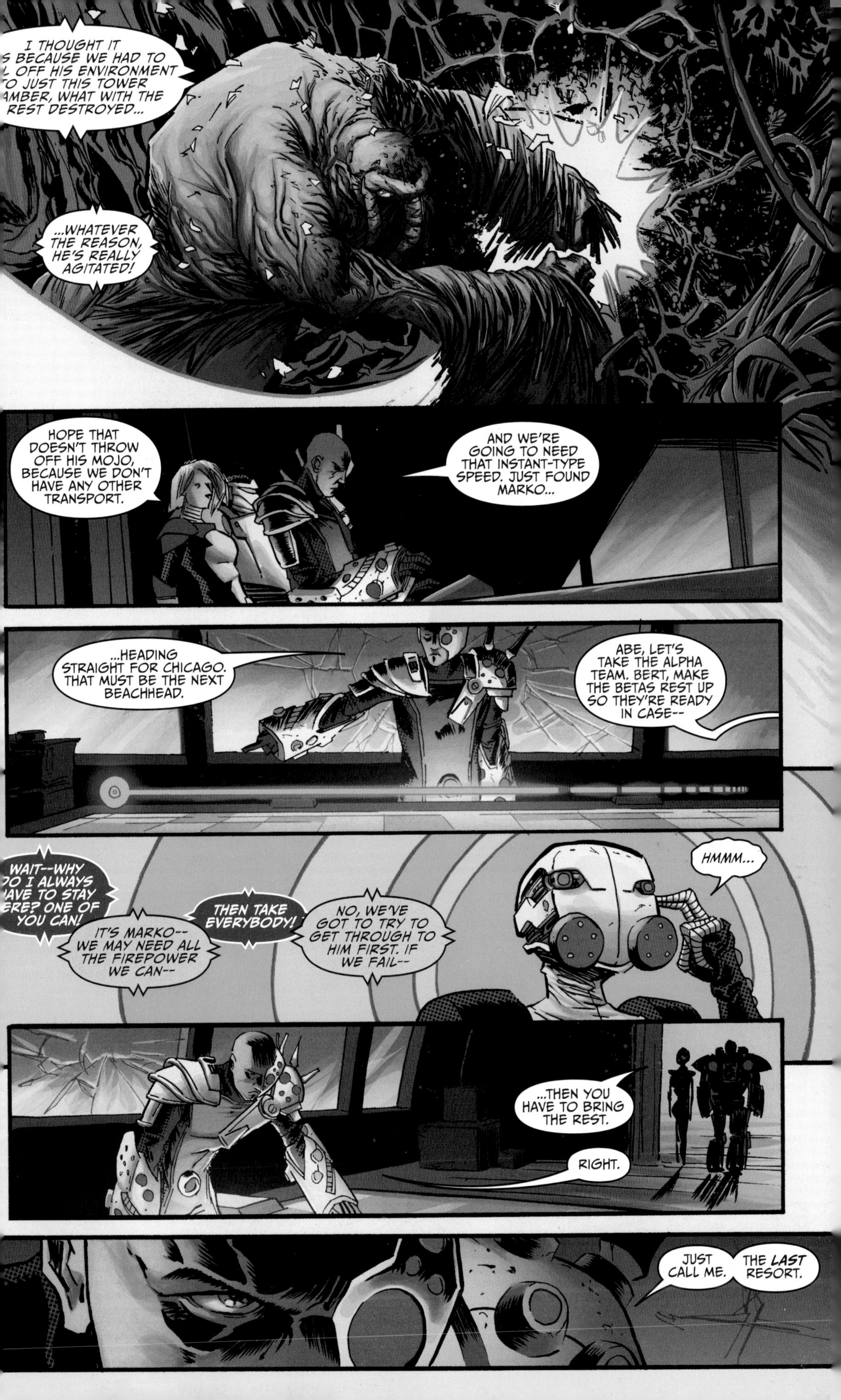

I THOUGHT IT S BECAUSE WE HAD TO L OFF HIS ENVIRONMENT TO JUST THIS TOWER AMBER, WHAT WITH THE REST DESTROYED...
...WHATEVER THE REASON, HE'S REALLY AGITATED!
HOPE THAT DOESN'T THROW OFF HIS MOJO, BECAUSE WE DON'T HAVE ANY OTHER TRANSPORT.
AND WE'RE GOING TO NEED THAT INSTANT-TYPE SPEED. JUST FOUND MARKO...
...HEADING STRAIGHT FOR CHICAGO. THAT MUST BE THE NEXT BEACHHEAD.
ABE, LET'S TAKE THE ALPHA TEAM. BERT, MAKE THE BETAS REST UP SO THEY'RE READY IN CASE--
WAIT--WHY DO I ALWAYS HAVE TO STAY ERE? ONE OF YOU CAN!
IT'S MARKO-- WE MAY NEED ALL THE FIREPOWER WE CAN--
THEN TAKE EVERYBODY!
NO, WE'VE GOT TO TRY TO GET THROUGH TO HIM FIRST. IF WE FAIL--
HMMM...
...THEN YOU HAVE TO BRING THE REST.
RIGHT.
JUST CALL ME.
THE LAST RESORT.

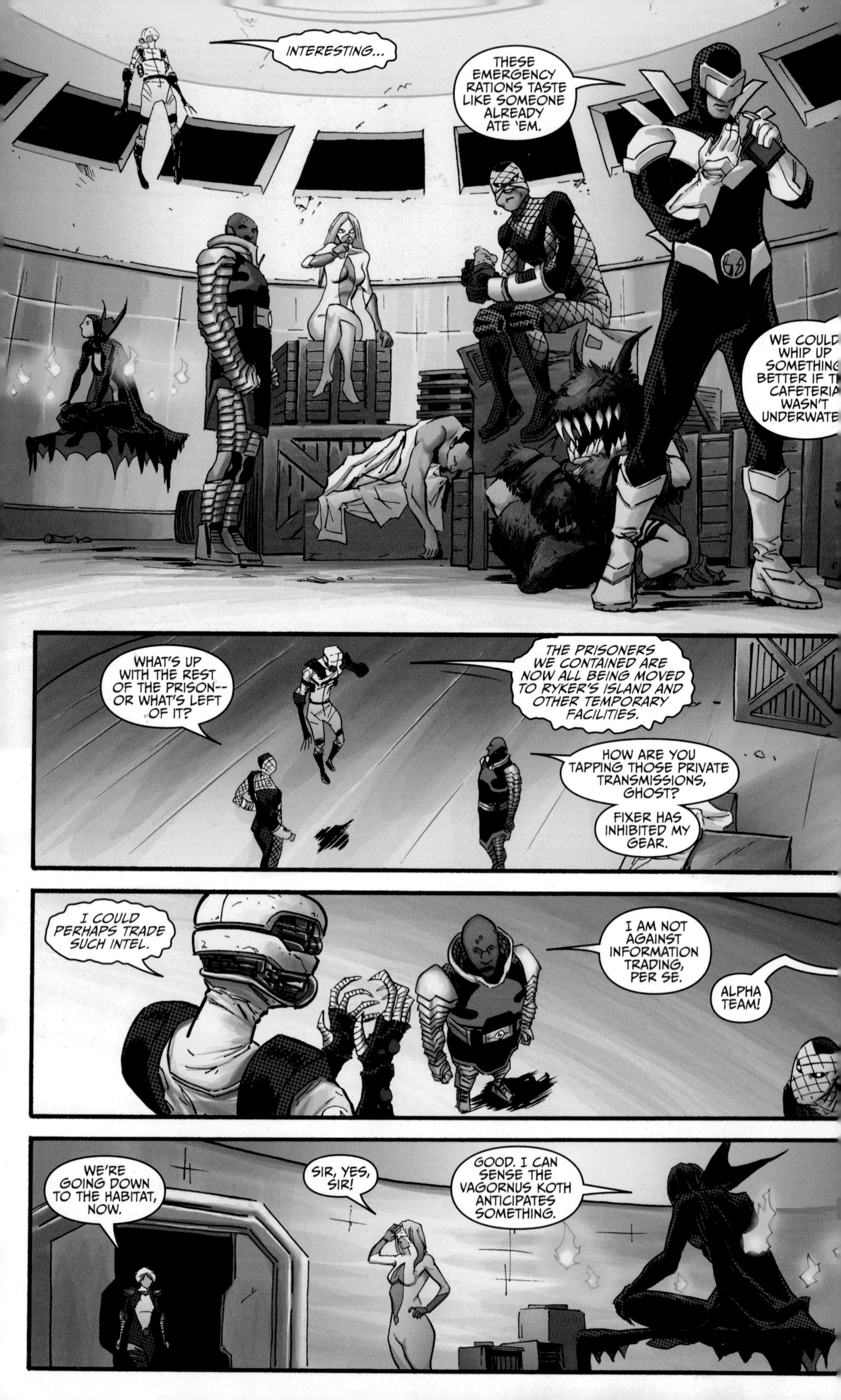

INTERESTING...
THESE EMERGENCY RATIONS TASTE LIKE SOMEONE ALREADY ATE 'EM.
WE COULD WHIP UP SOMETHING BETTER IF THE CAFETERIA WASN'T UNDERWATER
WHAT'S UP WITH THE REST OF THE PRISON-- OR WHAT'S LEFT OF IT?
THE PRISONERS WE CONTAINED ARE NOW ALL BEING MOVED TO RYKER'S ISLAND AND OTHER TEMPORARY FACILITIES.
HOW ARE YOU TAPPING THOSE PRIVATE TRANSMISSIONS, GHOST?
FIXER HAS INHIBITED MY GEAR.
I COULD PERHAPS TRADE SUCH INTEL.
I AM NOT AGAINST INFORMATION TRADING, PER SE.
ALPHA TEAM!
WE'RE GOING DOWN TO THE HABITAT, NOW.
SIR, YES, SIR!
GOOD. I CAN SENSE THE VAGORNUS KOTH ANTICIPATES SOMETHING.

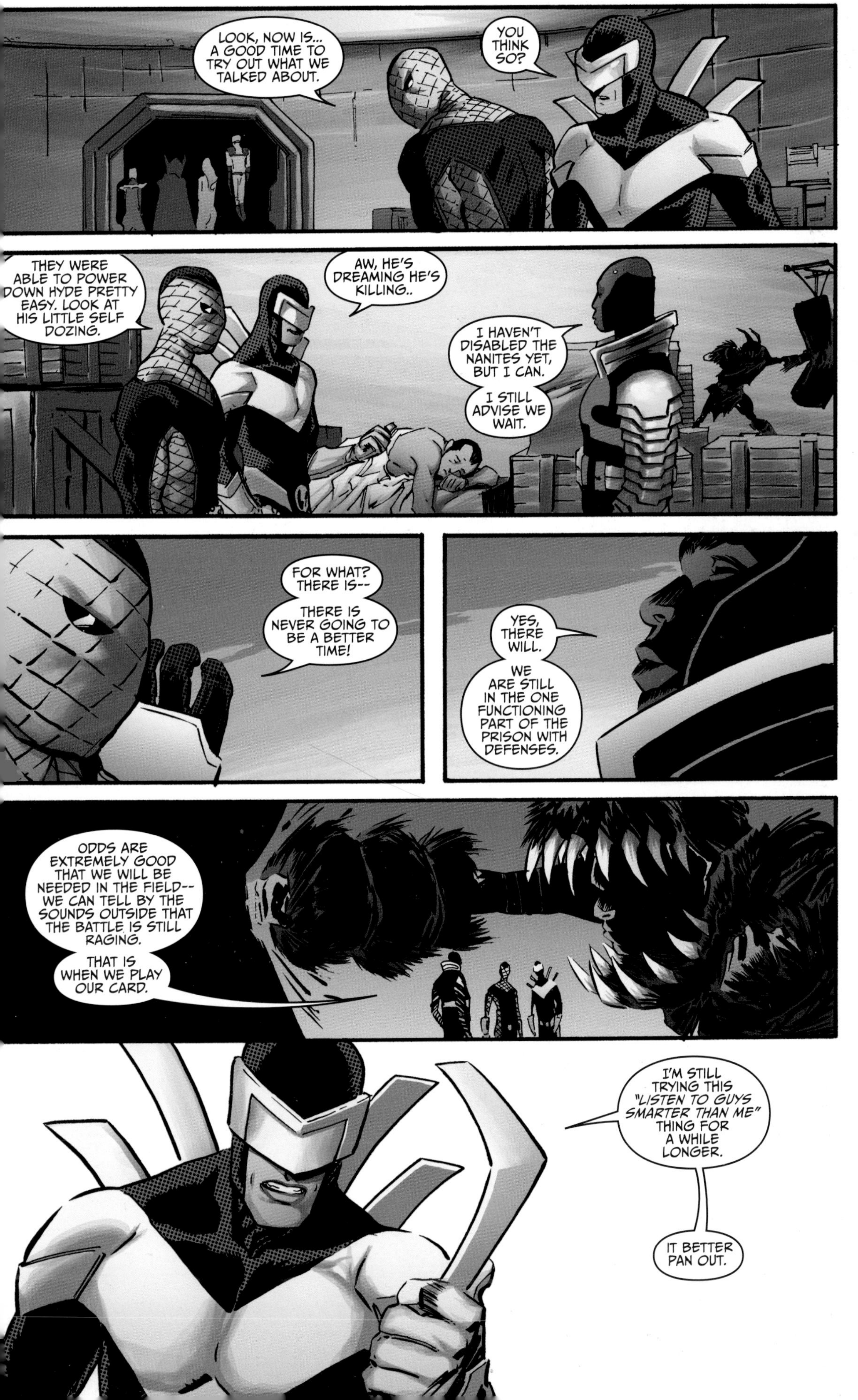
LOOK, NOW IS... A GOOD TIME TO TRY OUT WHAT WE TALKED ABOUT.
YOU THINK SO?
THEY WERE ABLE TO POWER DOWN HYDE PRETTY EASY. LOOK AT HIS LITTLE SELF DOZING.
AW, HE'S DREAMING HE'S KILLING..
I HAVEN'T DISABLED THE NANITES YET, BUT I CAN.
I STILL ADVISE WE WAIT.
FOR WHAT? THERE IS--
THERE IS NEVER GOING TO BE A BETTER TIME!
YES, THERE WILL.
WE ARE STILL IN THE ONE FUNCTIONING PART OF THE PRISON WITH DEFENSES.
ODDS ARE EXTREMELY GOOD THAT WE WILL BE NEEDED IN THE FIELD-- WE CAN TELL BY THE SOUNDS OUTSIDE THAT THE BATTLE IS STILL RAGING.
THAT IS WHEN WE PLAY OUR CARD.
I'M STILL TRYING THIS *"LISTEN TO GUYS SMARTER THAN ME"* THING FOR A WHILE LONGER.
IT BETTER PAN OUT.

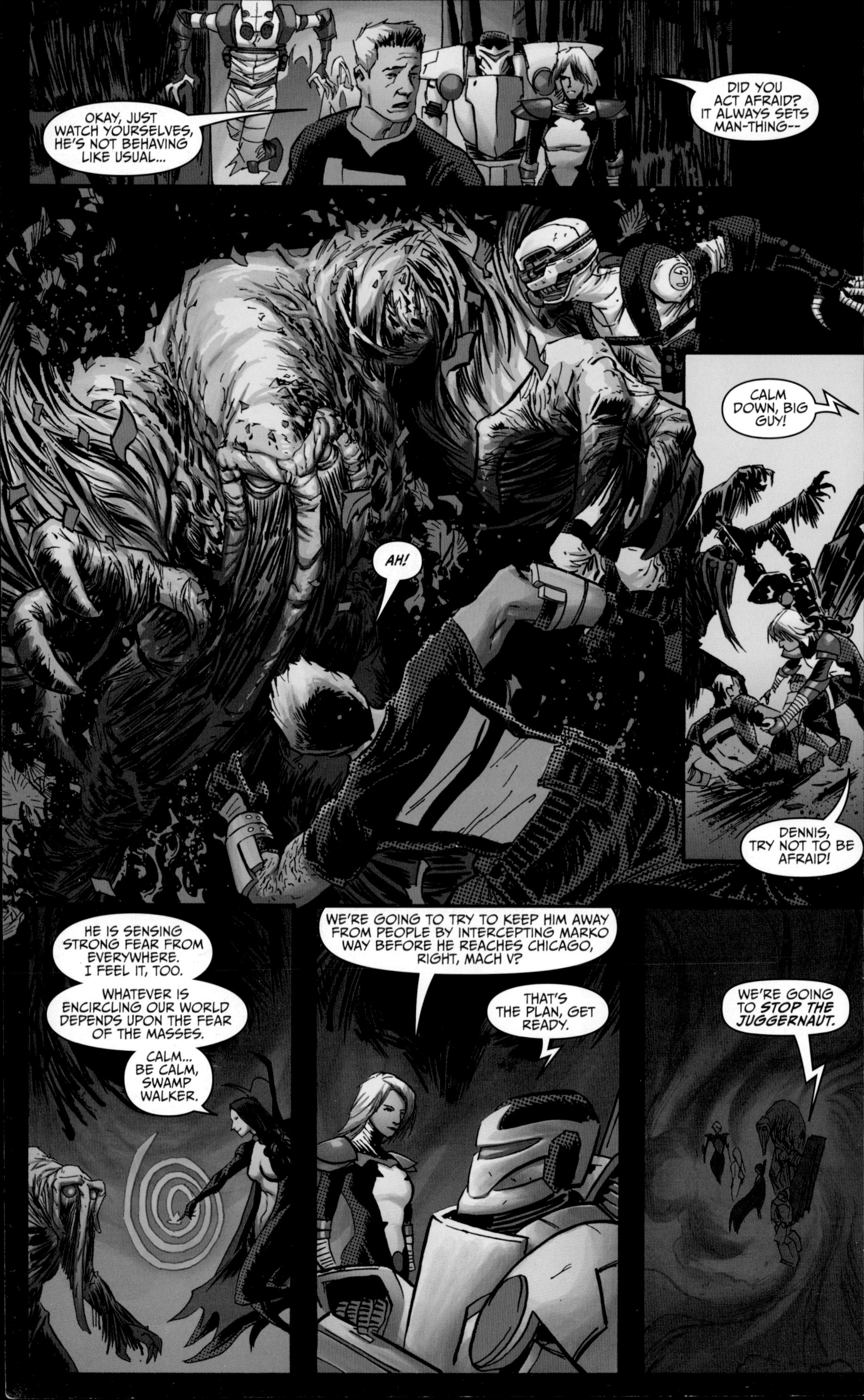
OKAY, JUST WATCH YOURSELVES, HE'S NOT BEHAVING LIKE USUAL...
DID YOU ACT AFRAID? IT ALWAYS SETS MAN-THING--
AH!
CALM DOWN, BIG GUY!
DENNIS, TRY NOT TO BE AFRAID!
HE IS SENSING STRONG FEAR FROM EVERYWHERE. I FEEL IT, TOO.
WHATEVER IS ENCIRCLING OUR WORLD DEPENDS UPON THE FEAR OF THE MASSES.
CALM... BE CALM, SWAMP WALKER.
WE'RE GOING TO TRY TO KEEP HIM AWAY FROM PEOPLE BY INTERCEPTING MARKO WAY BEFORE HE REACHES CHICAGO, RIGHT, MACH V?
THAT'S THE PLAN, GET READY.
WE'RE GOING TO STOP THE JUGGERNAUT.

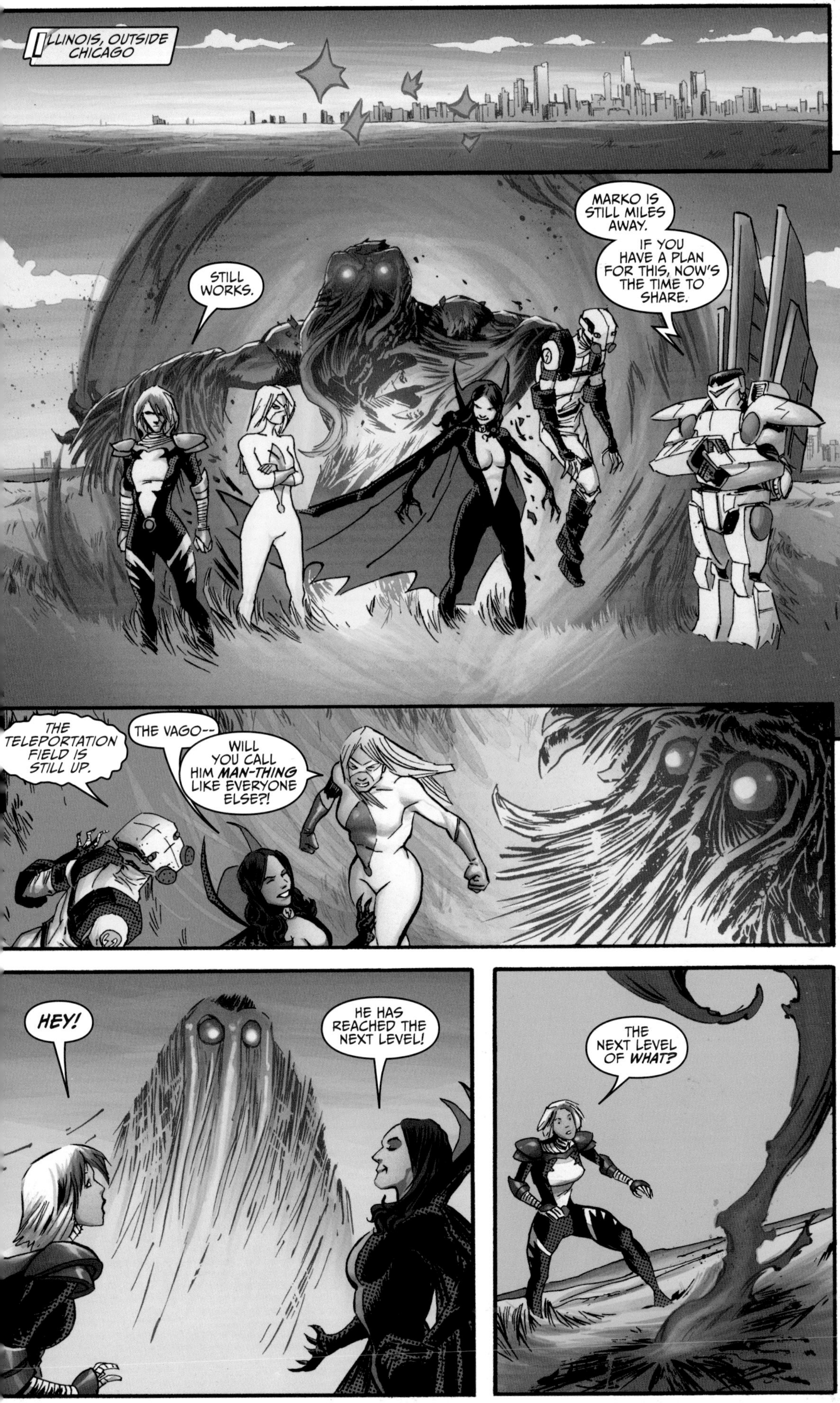
ILLINOIS, OUTSIDE CHICAGO
STILL WORKS.
MARKO IS STILL MILES AWAY.
IF YOU HAVE A PLAN FOR THIS, NOW'S THE TIME TO SHARE.
THE TELEPORTATION FIELD IS STILL UP.
THE VAGO--
WILL YOU CALL HIM MAN-THING LIKE EVERYONE ELSE?!
HEY!
HE HAS REACHED THE NEXT LEVEL!
THE NEXT LEVEL OF WHAT?

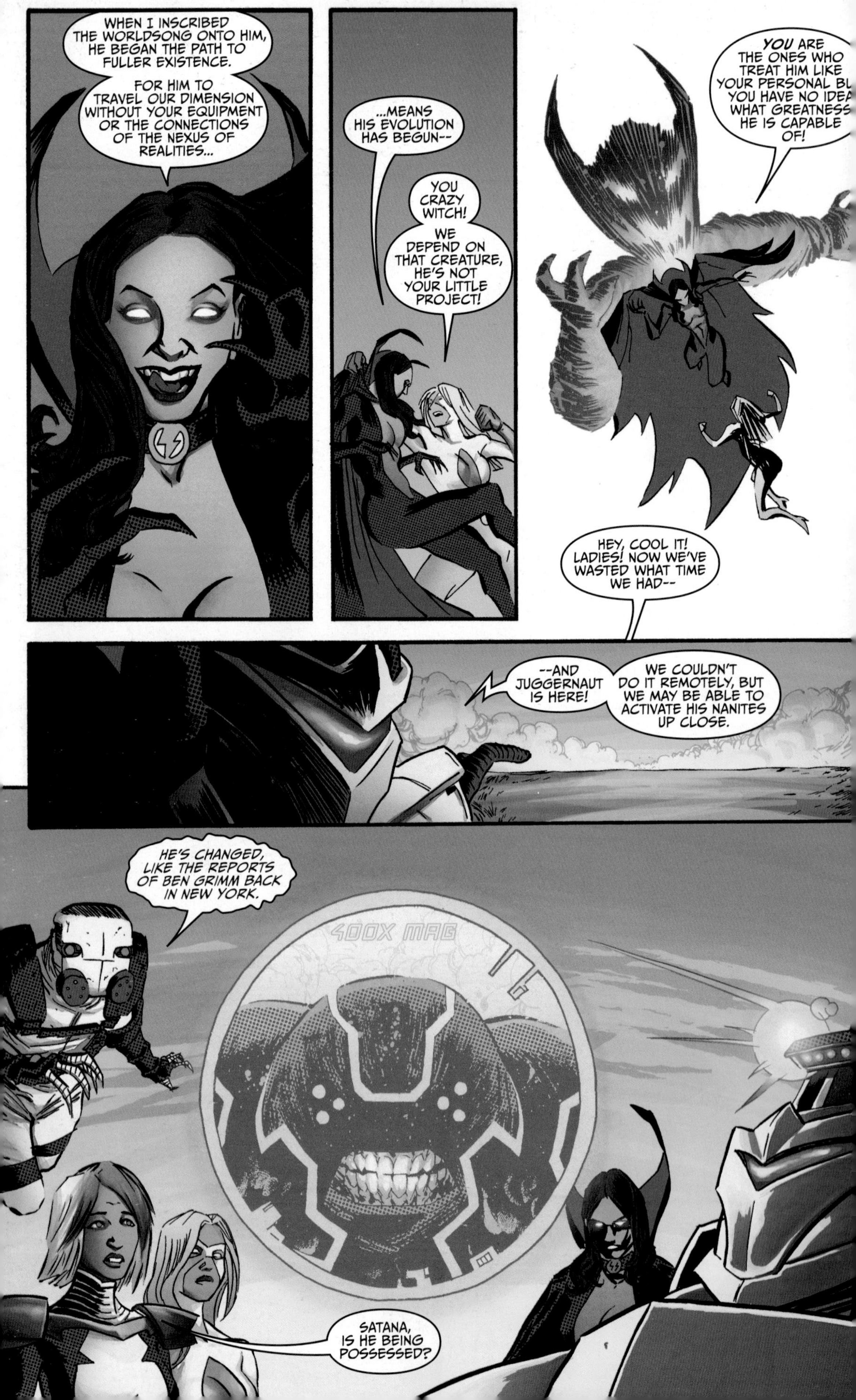
WHEN I INSCRIBED THE WORLDSONG ONTO HIM, HE BEGAN THE PATH TO FULLER EXISTENCE.
FOR HIM TO TRAVEL OUR DIMENSION WITHOUT YOUR EQUIPMENT OR THE CONNECTIONS OF THE NEXUS OF REALITIES...
...MEANS HIS EVOLUTION HAS BEGUN--
YOU CRAZY WITCH!
WE DEPEND ON THAT CREATURE, HE'S NOT YOUR LITTLE PROJECT!
YOU ARE THE ONES WHO TREAT HIM LIKE YOUR PERSONAL BL
YOU HAVE NO IDEA WHAT GREATNESS HE IS CAPABLE OF!
HEY, COOL IT! LADIES! NOW WE'VE WASTED WHAT TIME WE HAD--
--AND JUGGERNAUT IS HERE!
WE COULDN'T DO IT REMOTELY, BUT WE MAY BE ABLE TO ACTIVATE HIS NANITES UP CLOSE.
HE'S CHANGED, LIKE THE REPORTS OF BEN GRIMM BACK IN NEW YORK.
400X MAG
SATANA, IS HE BEING POSSESSED?

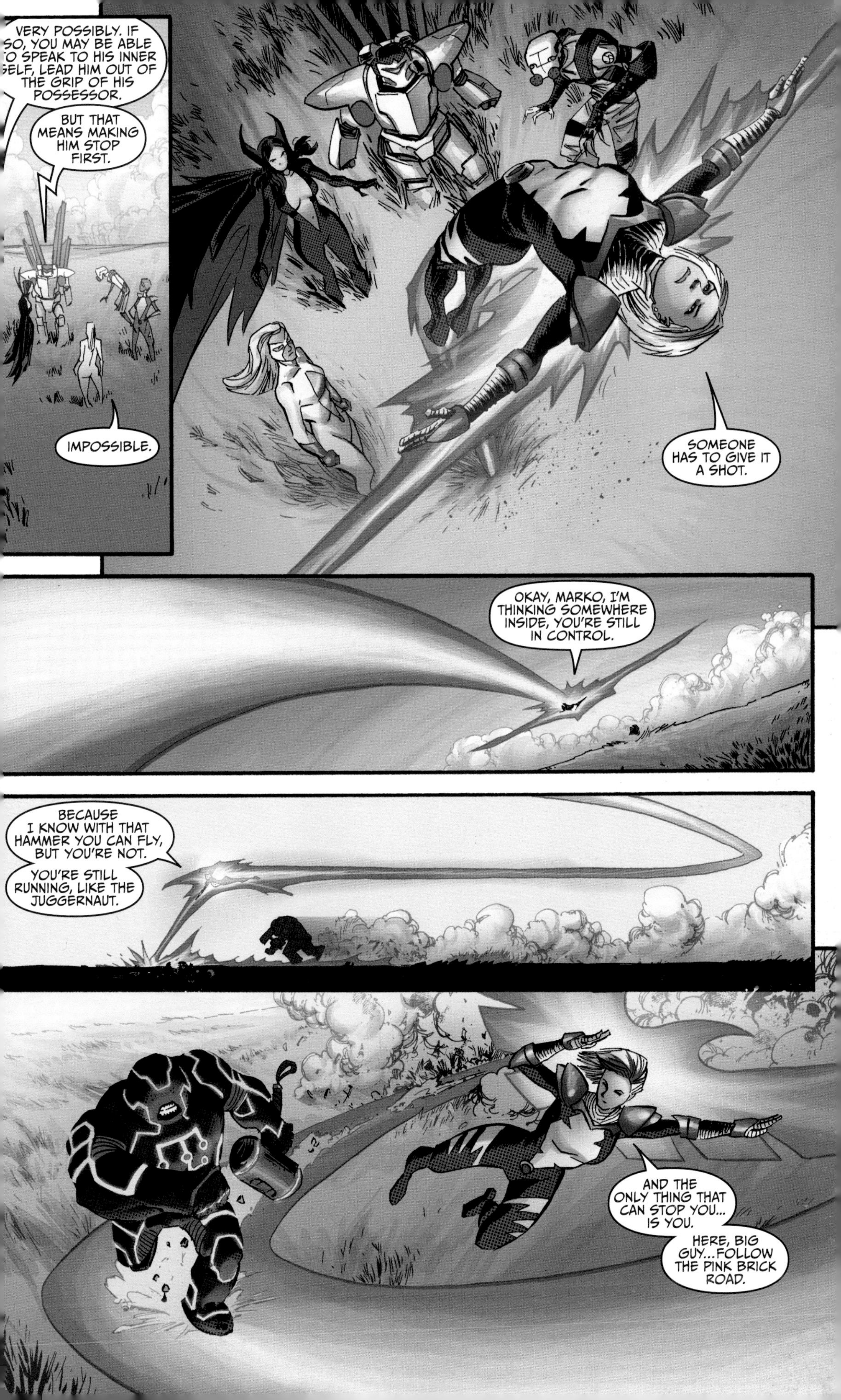
VERY POSSIBLY. IF SO, YOU MAY BE ABLE TO SPEAK TO HIS INNER SELF, LEAD HIM OUT OF THE GRIP OF HIS POSSESSOR.
BUT THAT MEANS MAKING HIM STOP FIRST.
IMPOSSIBLE.
SOMEONE HAS TO GIVE IT A SHOT.
OKAY, MARKO, I'M THINKING SOMEWHERE INSIDE, YOU'RE STILL IN CONTROL.
BECAUSE I KNOW WITH THAT HAMMER YOU CAN FLY, BUT YOU'RE NOT.
YOU'RE STILL RUNNING, LIKE THE JUGGERNAUT.
AND THE ONLY THING THAT CAN STOP YOU... IS YOU.
HERE, BIG GUY...FOLLOW THE PINK BRICK ROAD.

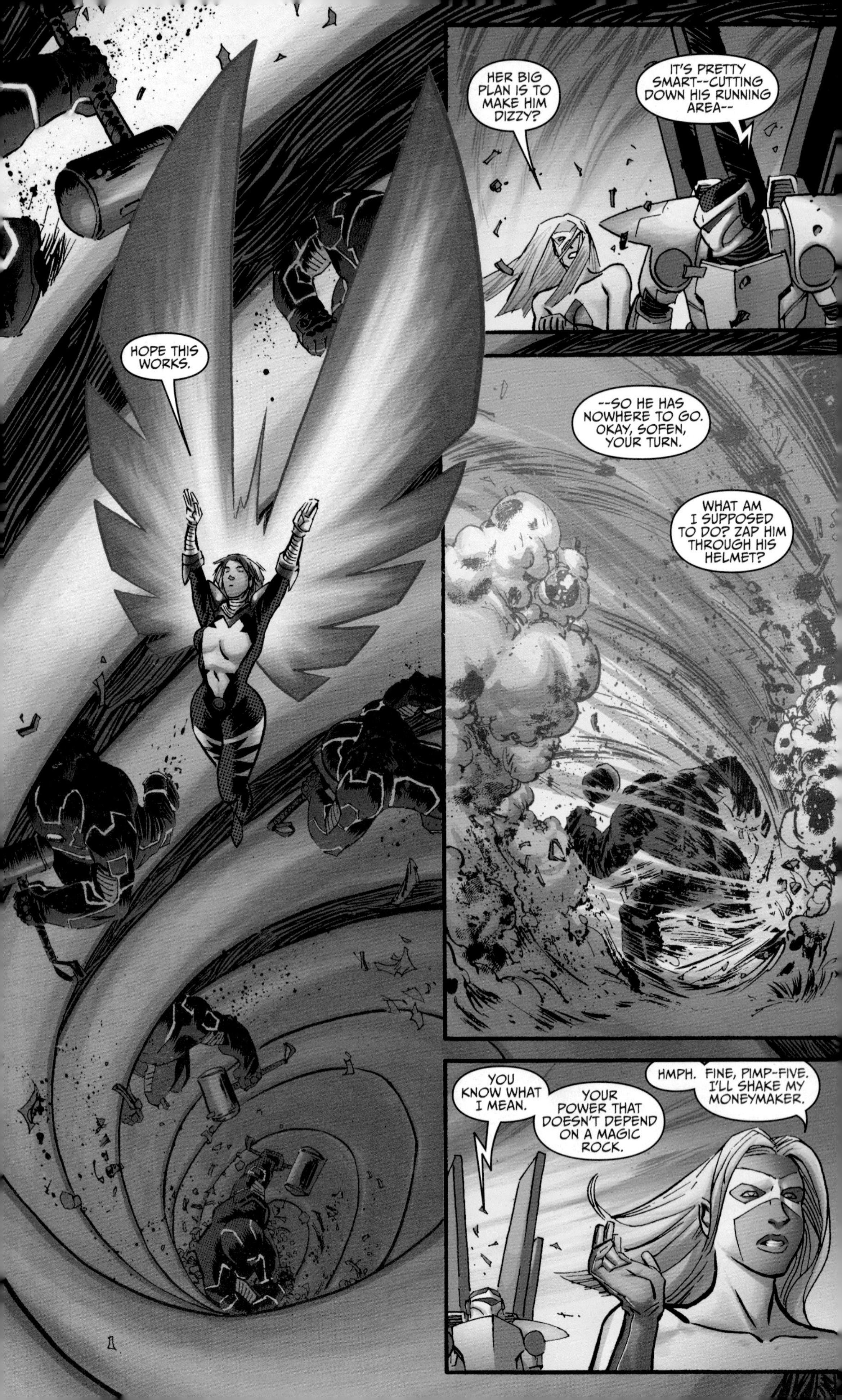

HOPE THIS WORKS.
HER BIG PLAN IS TO MAKE HIM DIZZY?
IT'S PRETTY SMART--CUTTING DOWN HIS RUNNING AREA--
--SO HE HAS NOWHERE TO GO. OKAY, SOFEN, YOUR TURN.
WHAT AM I SUPPOSED TO DO? ZAP HIM THROUGH HIS HELMET?
YOU KNOW WHAT I MEAN.
YOUR POWER THAT DOESN'T DEPEND ON A MAGIC ROCK.
HMPH. FINE, PIMP-FIVE. I'LL SHAKE MY MONEYMAKER.

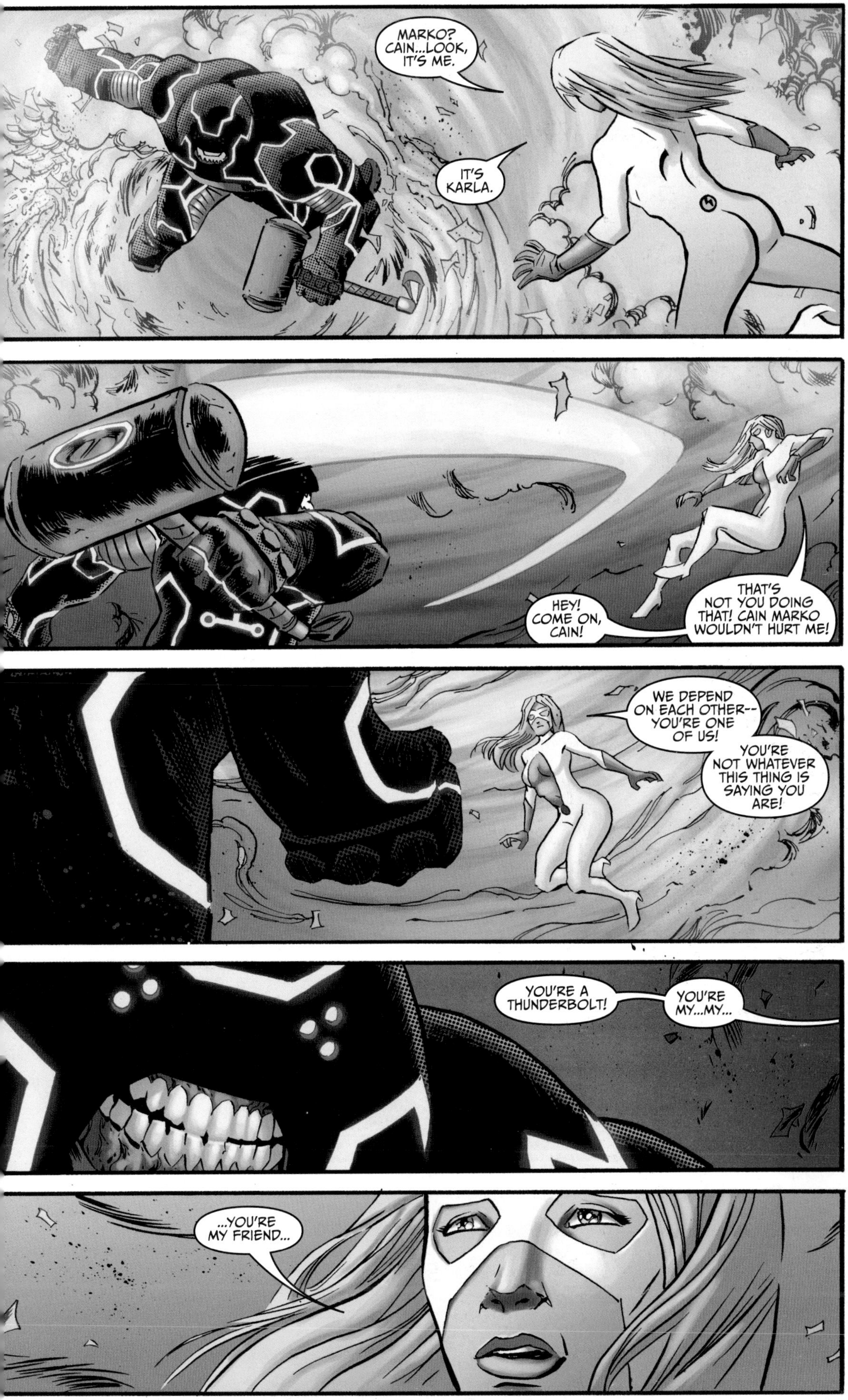
MARKO? CAIN...LOOK, IT'S ME.
IT'S KARLA.
HEY! COME ON, CAIN!
THAT'S NOT YOU DOING THAT! CAIN MARKO WOULDN'T HURT ME!
WE DEPEND ON EACH OTHER--YOU'RE ONE OF US!
YOU'RE NOT WHATEVER THIS THING IS SAYING YOU ARE!
YOU'RE A THUNDERBOLT!
YOU'RE MY...MY...
...YOU'RE MY FRIEND...

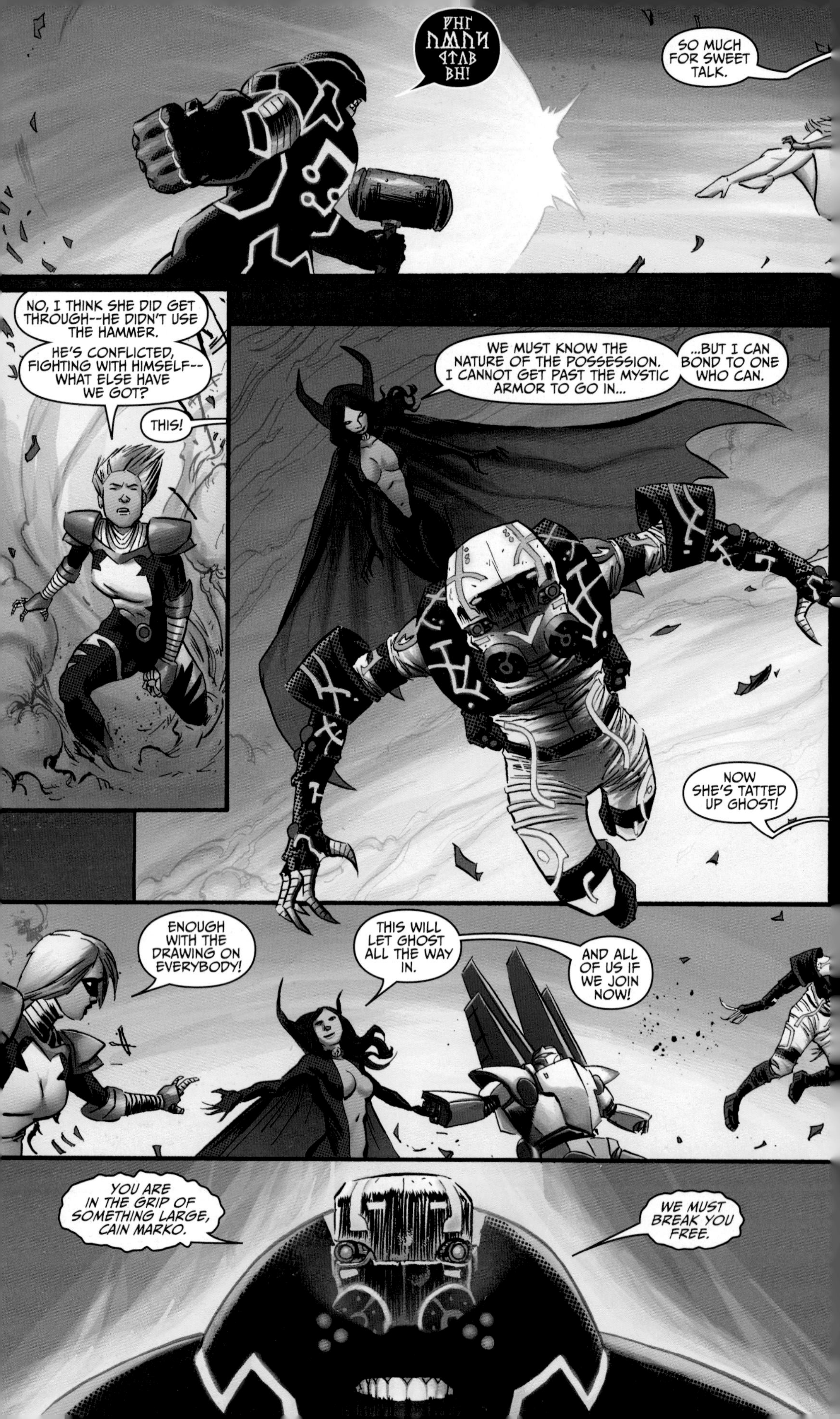
SO MUCH FOR SWEET TALK.
NO, I THINK SHE DID GET THROUGH--HE DIDN'T USE THE HAMMER.
HE'S CONFLICTED, FIGHTING WITH HIMSELF--WHAT ELSE HAVE WE GOT?
THIS!
WE MUST KNOW THE NATURE OF THE POSSESSION. I CANNOT GET PAST THE MYSTIC ARMOR TO GO IN...
...BUT I CAN BOND TO ONE WHO CAN.
NOW SHE'S TATTED UP GHOST!
ENOUGH WITH THE DRAWING ON EVERYBODY!
THIS WILL LET GHOST ALL THE WAY IN.
AND ALL OF US IF WE JOIN NOW!
YOU ARE IN THE GRIP OF SOMETHING LARGE, CAIN MARKO.
WE MUST BREAK YOU FREE.

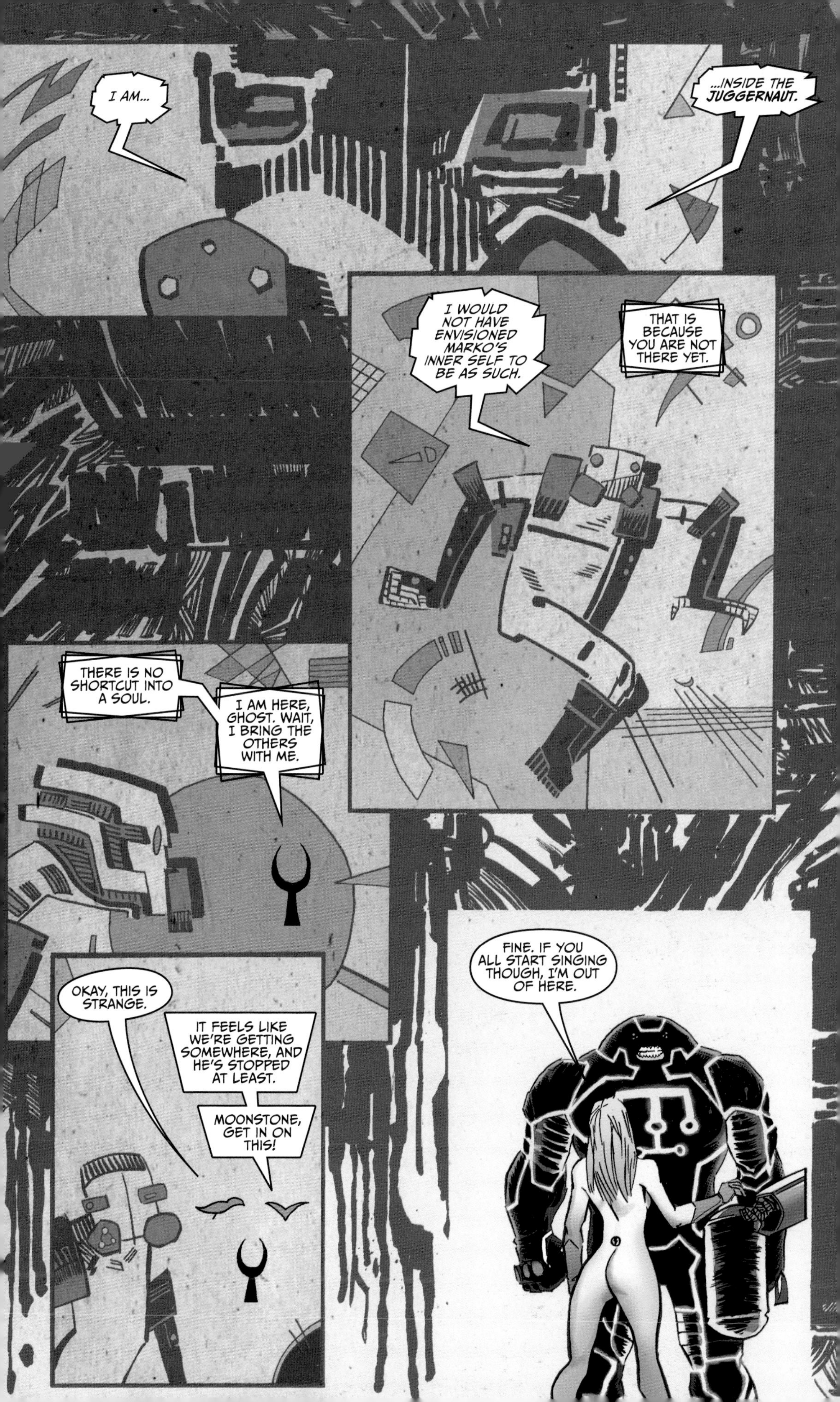

I AM...
...INSIDE THE JUGGERNAUT.
I WOULD NOT HAVE ENVISIONED MARKO'S INNER SELF TO BE AS SUCH.
THAT IS BECAUSE YOU ARE NOT THERE YET.
THERE IS NO SHORTCUT INTO A SOUL.
I AM HERE, GHOST. WAIT, I BRING THE OTHERS WITH ME.
OKAY, THIS IS STRANGE.
IT FEELS LIKE WE'RE GETTING SOMEWHERE, AND HE'S STOPPED AT LEAST.
MOONSTONE, GET IN ON THIS!
FINE. IF YOU ALL START SINGING THOUGH, I'M OUT OF HERE.

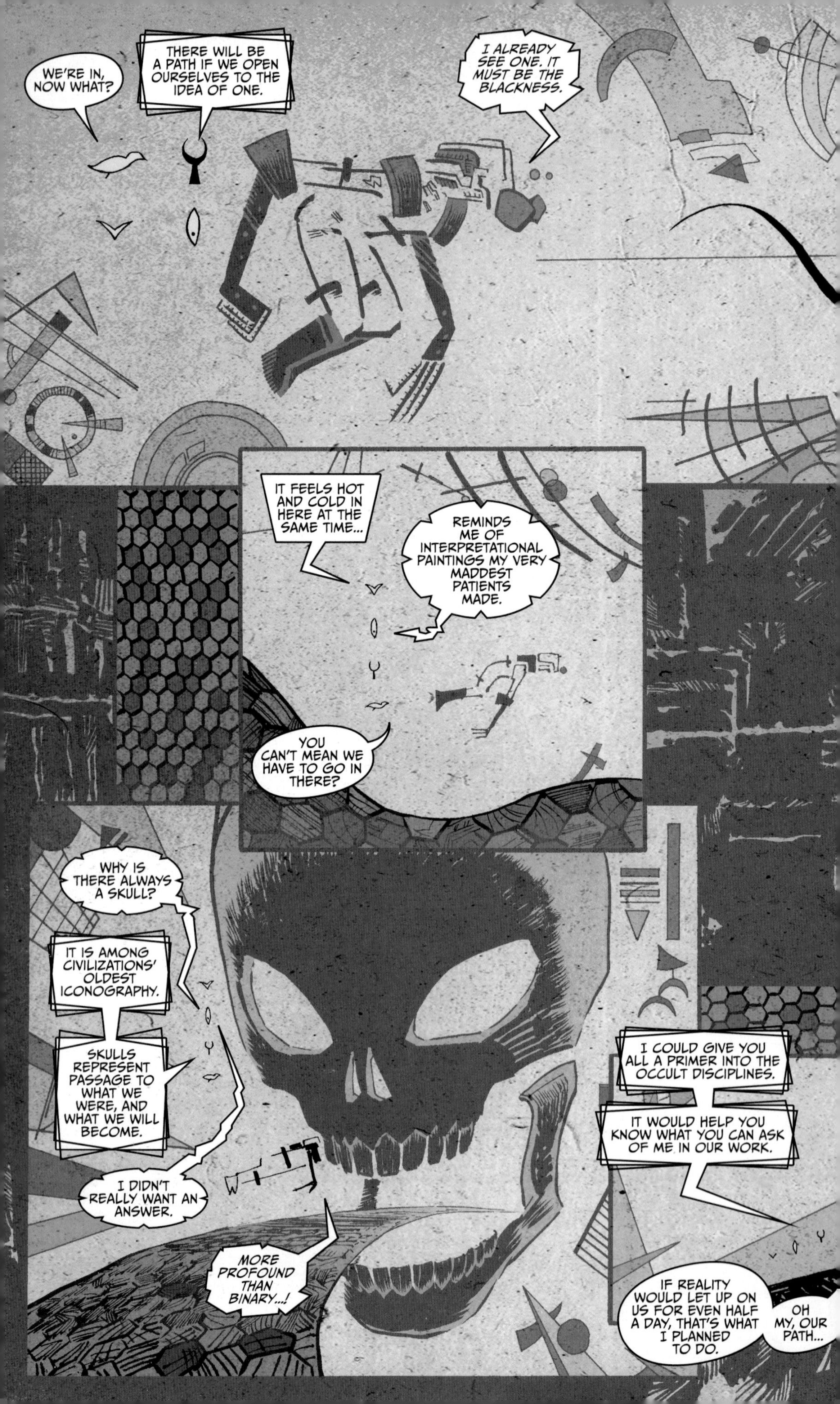
WE'RE IN, NOW WHAT?
THERE WILL BE A PATH IF WE OPEN OURSELVES TO THE IDEA OF ONE.
I ALREADY SEE ONE. IT MUST BE THE BLACKNESS.
IT FEELS HOT AND COLD IN HERE AT THE SAME TIME...
REMINDS ME OF INTERPRETATIONAL PAINTINGS MY VERY MADDEST PATIENTS MADE.
YOU CAN'T MEAN WE HAVE TO GO IN THERE?
WHY IS THERE ALWAYS A SKULL?
IT IS AMONG CIVILIZATIONS' OLDEST ICONOGRAPHY.
SKULLS REPRESENT PASSAGE TO WHAT WE WERE, AND WHAT WE WILL BECOME.
I DIDN'T REALLY WANT AN ANSWER.
MORE PROFOUND THAN BINARY...!
I COULD GIVE YOU ALL A PRIMER INTO THE OCCULT DISCIPLINES.
IT WOULD HELP YOU KNOW WHAT YOU CAN ASK OF ME IN OUR WORK.
IF REALITY WOULD LET UP ON US FOR EVEN HALF A DAY, THAT'S WHAT I PLANNED TO DO.
OH MY, OUR PATH...

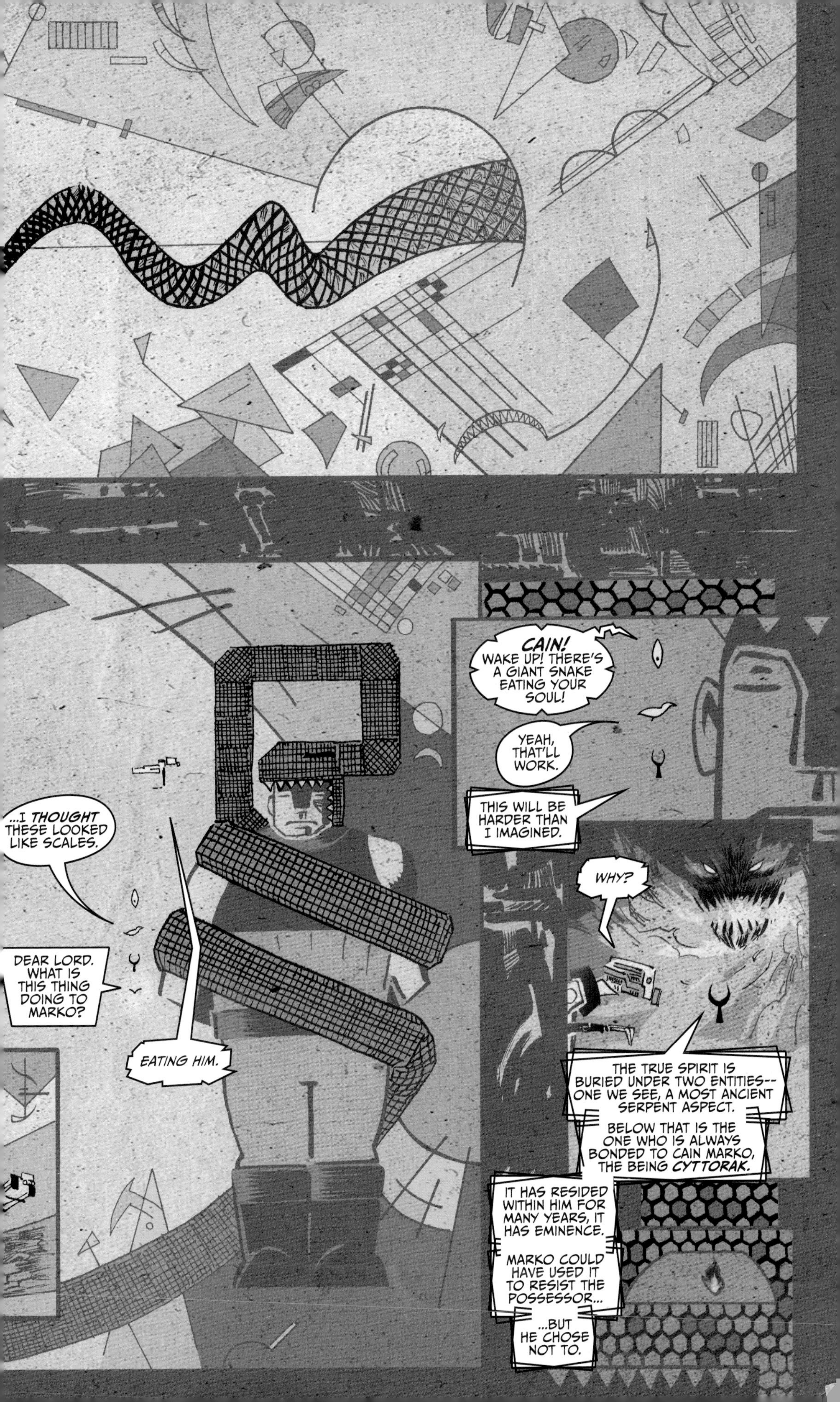

...I THOUGHT THESE LOOKED LIKE SCALES.
DEAR LORD. WHAT IS THIS THING DOING TO MARKO?
EATING HIM.
CAIN! WAKE UP! THERE'S A GIANT SNAKE EATING YOUR SOUL!
YEAH, THAT'LL WORK.
THIS WILL BE HARDER THAN I IMAGINED.
WHY?
THE TRUE SPIRIT IS BURIED UNDER TWO ENTITIES-- ONE WE SEE, A MOST ANCIENT SERPENT ASPECT.
BELOW THAT IS THE ONE WHO IS ALWAYS BONDED TO CAIN MARKO, THE BEING CYTTORAK.
IT HAS RESIDED WITHIN HIM FOR MANY YEARS, IT HAS EMINENCE.
MARKO COULD HAVE USED IT TO RESIST THE POSSESSOR...
...BUT HE CHOSE NOT TO.

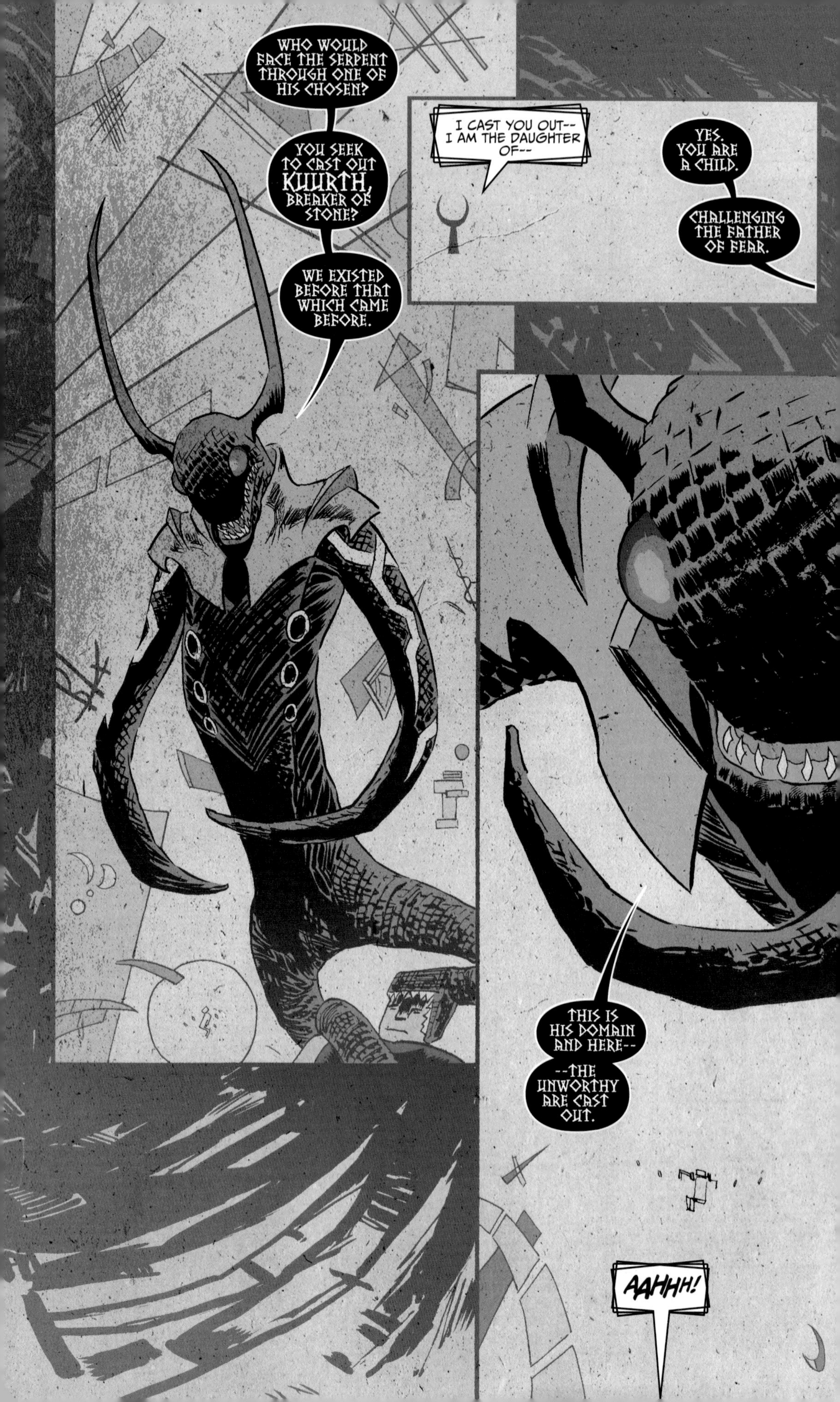
WHO WOULD FACE THE SERPENT THROUGH ONE OF HIS CHOSEN?
YOU SEEK TO CAST OUT KUURTH, BREAKER OF STONE?
WE EXISTED BEFORE THAT WHICH CAME BEFORE.
I CAST YOU OUT-- I AM THE DAUGHTER OF--
YES. YOU ARE A CHILD.
CHALLENGING THE FATHER OF FEAR.
THIS IS HIS DOMAIN AND HERE--
--THE UNWORTHY ARE CAST OUT.
AAHHH!

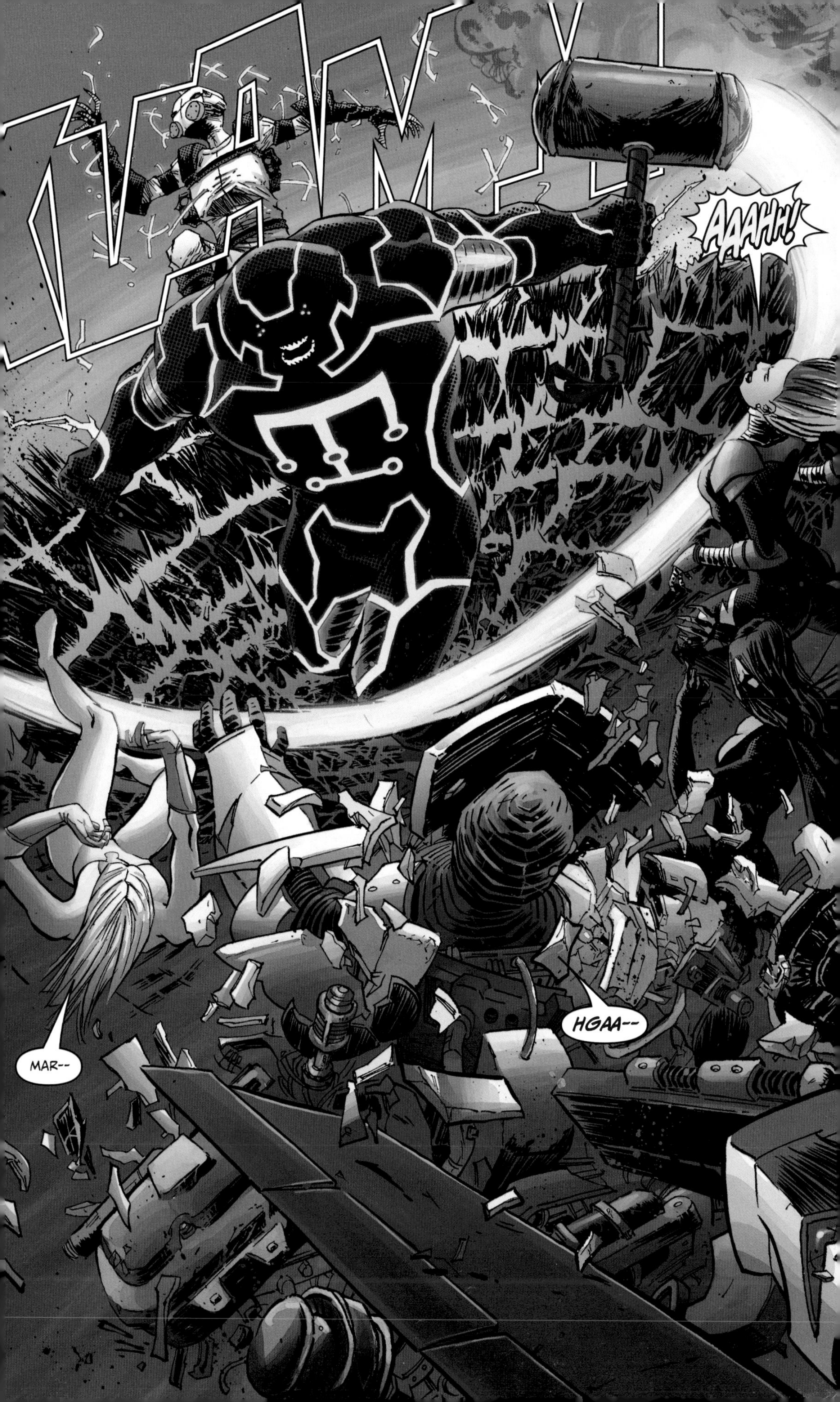
AAAHH!
HGAA--
MAR--

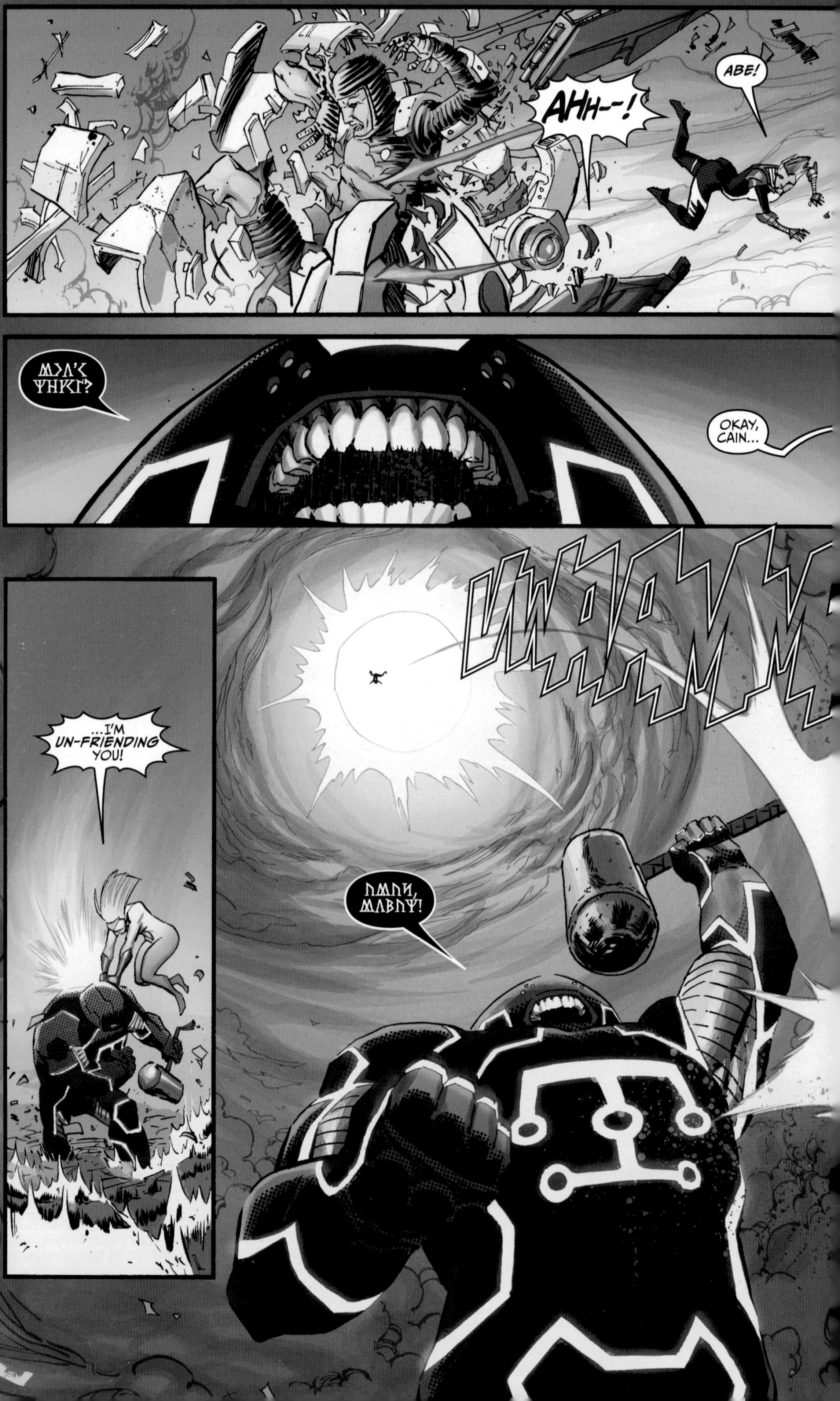
AHH--!
ABE!
OKAY, CAIN...
...I'M UN-FRIENDING YOU!

ENOUGH!

VEEP VEEP VEEP

ᚢᛏᚾᚹᚲ!

ᛏᚢᚹᚲ--

THE NANITES... HE'S BURNING THEM OUT!

ᚥᚤᛗ, ᚤᛚᚴ ᚾᚤᚤ ᚠᛁᚼ!

RUN... MOVE!

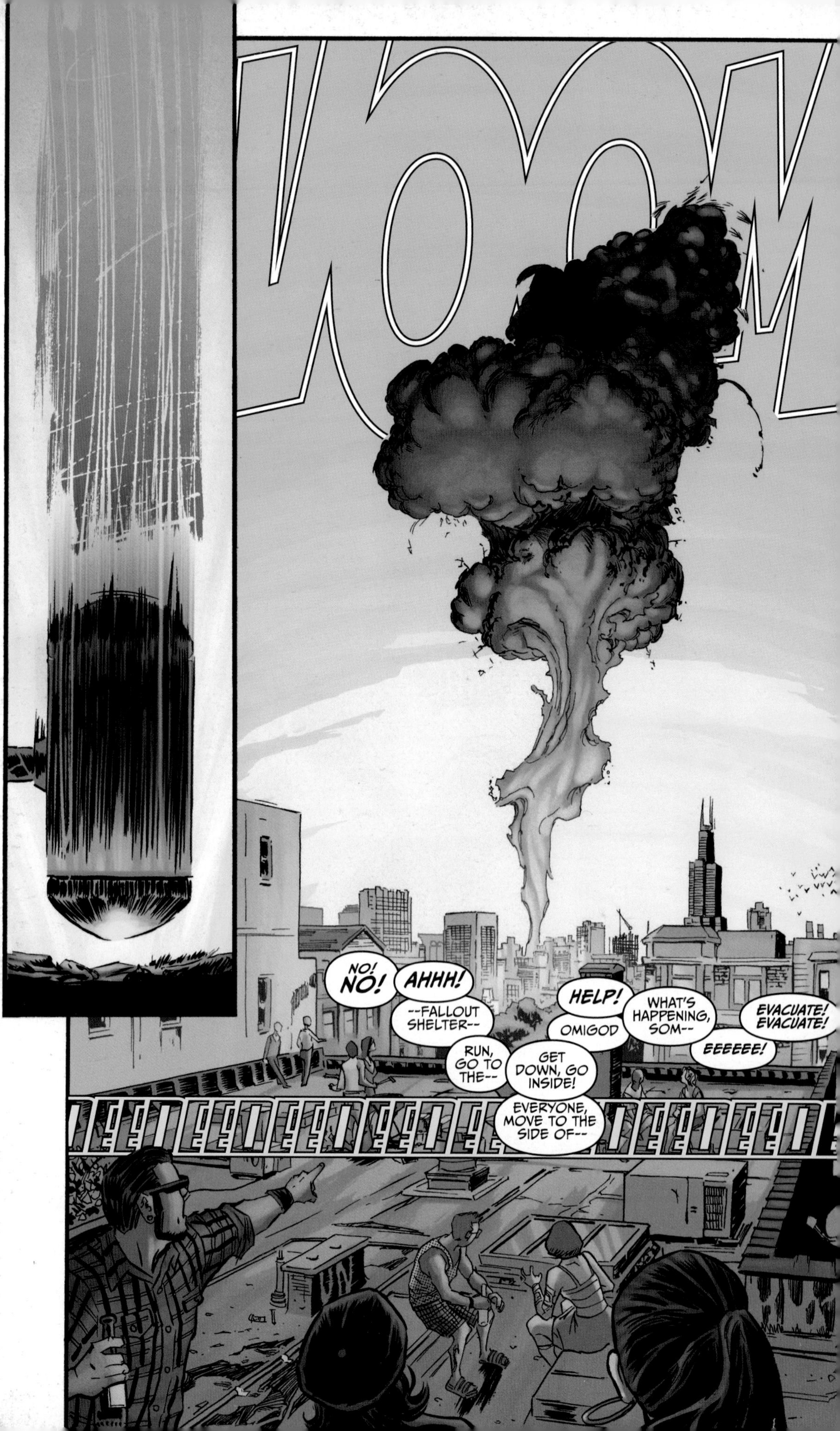
VOOM
NO! NO!
AHHH!
--FALLOUT SHELTER--
RUN, GO TO THE--
HELP!
OMIGOD
WHAT'S HAPPENING, SOM--
GET DOWN, GO INSIDE!
EVERYONE, MOVE TO THE SIDE OF--
EEEEEE!
EVACUATE! EVACUATE!

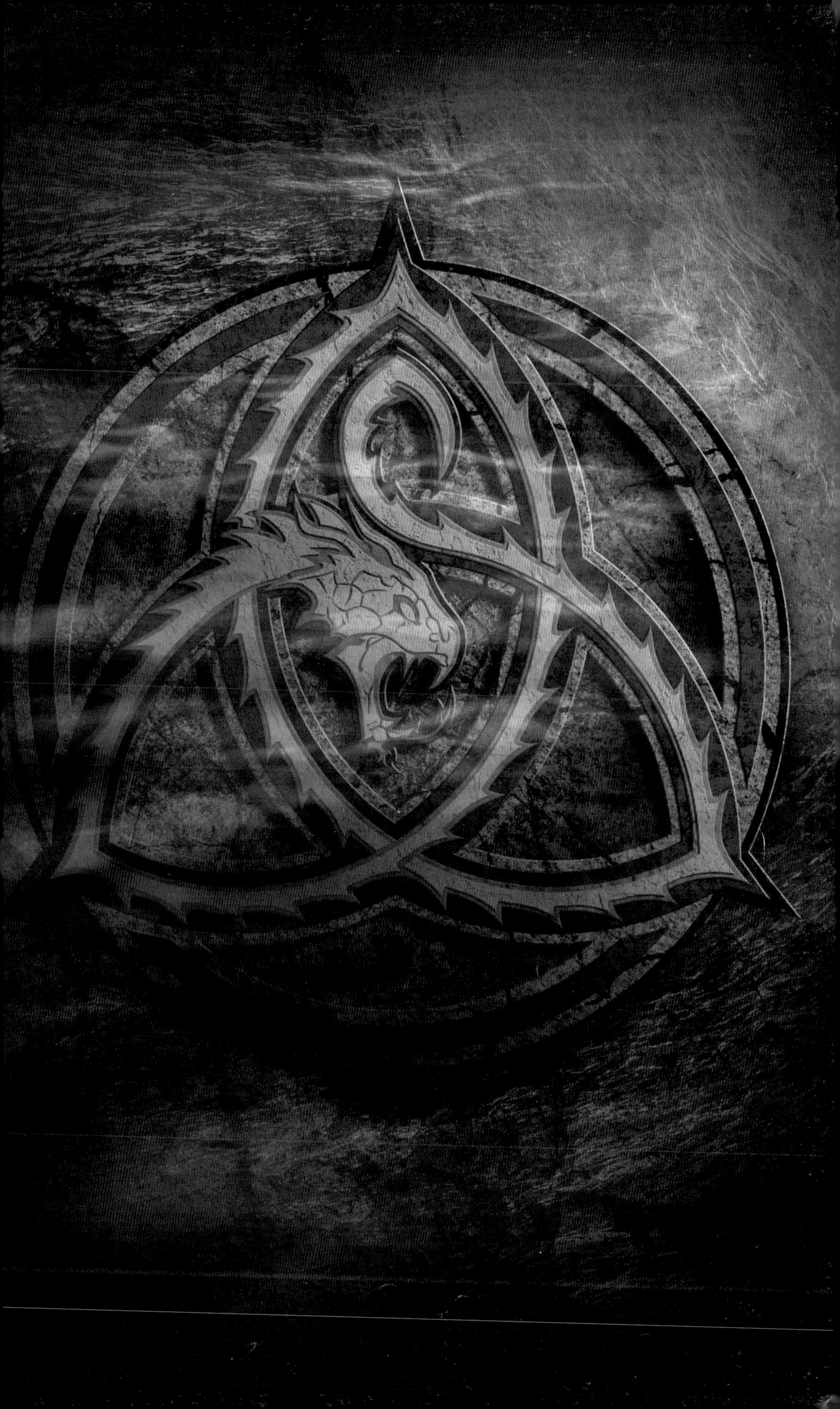

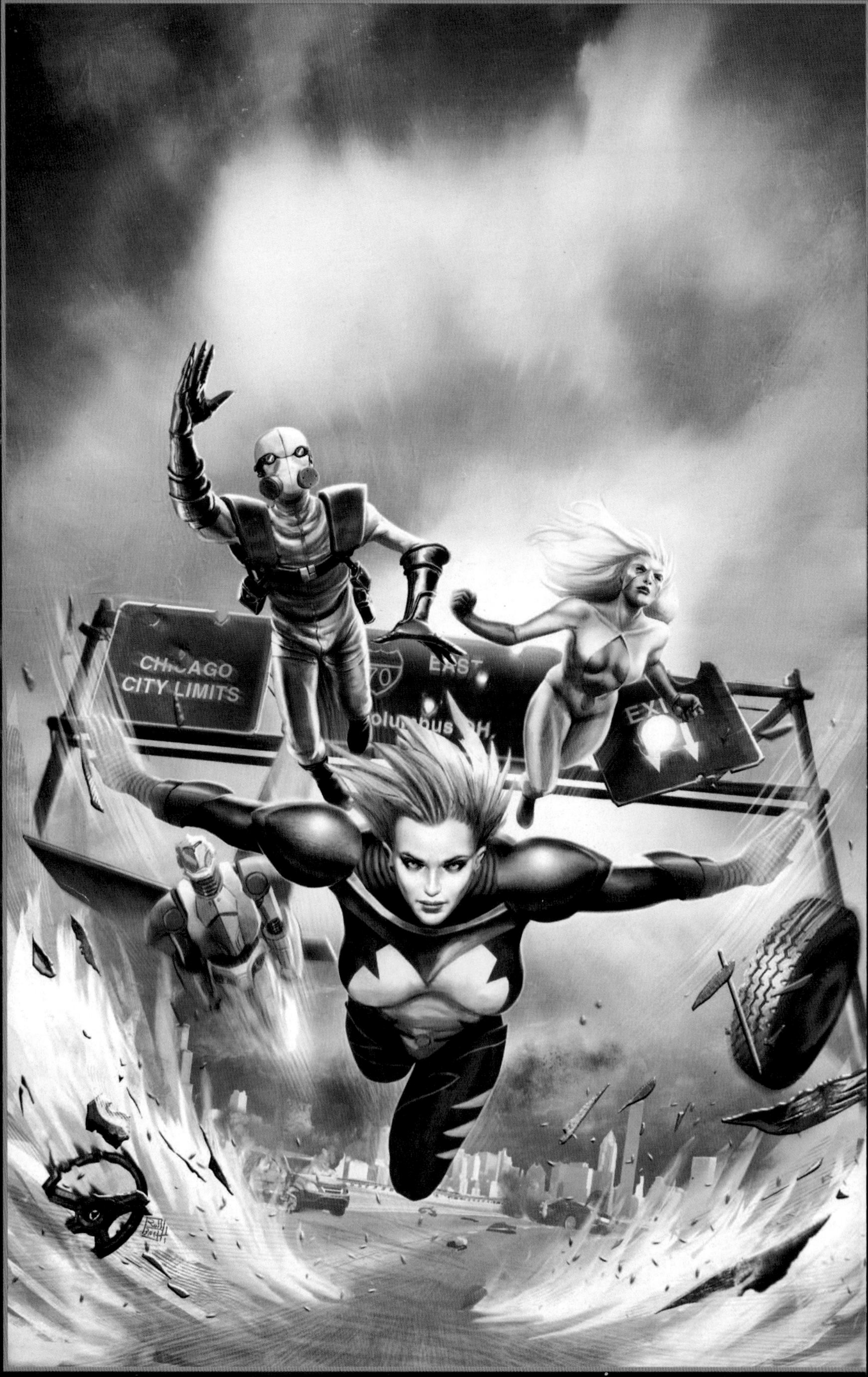
CHICAGO
CITY LIMITS
EAST

THUNDERBOLTS #161

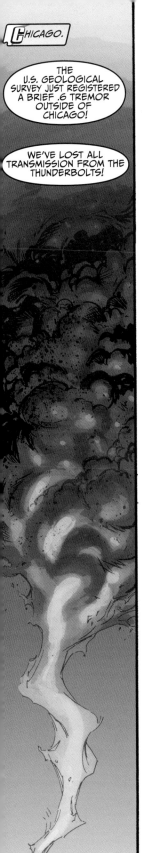

THE U.S. GEOLOGICAL SURVEY JUST REGISTERED A BRIEF .6 TREMOR OUTSIDE OF CHICAGO!

WE'VE LOST ALL TRANSMISSION FROM THE THUNDERBOLTS!

THE RAFT. NEW YORK CITY.

WHAT ABOUT MACH-V'S VIDEO FEED? OR GHOST?

THAT'S WHAT I MEAN, WARDEN, I'M GETTING NOTHING!

HANG ON, I'M GOING TO A SATELLITE VIEW.

THERE'S A MILITARY SATELLITE ON APPROACH AT THAT LATITUDE THAT SHOULD GIVE US A HIGH-DEF OVERVIEW.

WHAT? YOU DON'T HAVE CLEARANCE TO TAP DEPARTMENT OF DEFENSE SAT SYSTEMS, FIXER!

DO YOU WANT TO KNOW WHAT JUST HAPPENED TO THE TEAM OR NOT?!

I'M DOING WHAT I CAN!

IT'S AN EMERGENCY.

JUST MAKE IT QUICK.

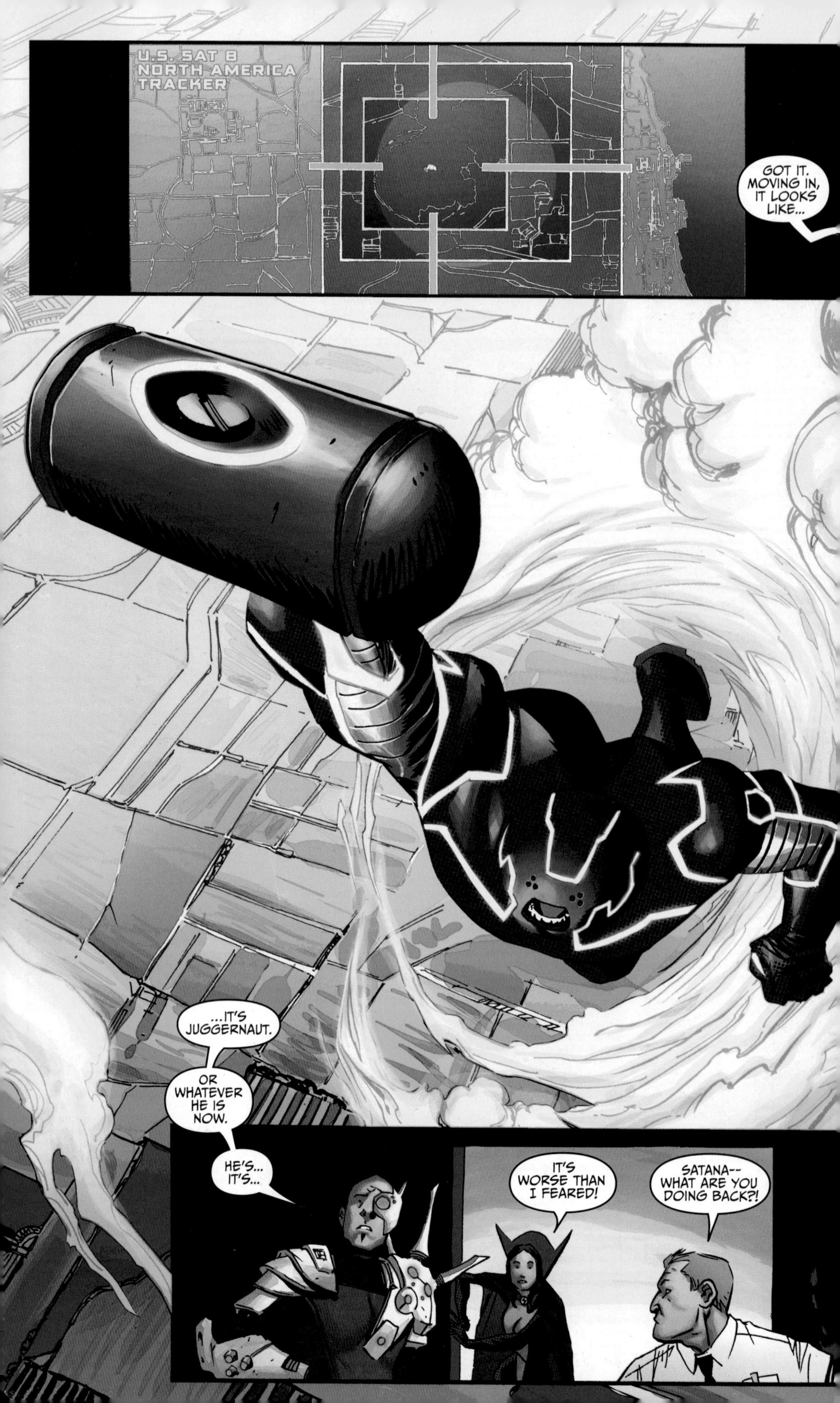
U.S. SAT 8
NORTH AMERICA
TRACKER
GOT IT. MOVING IN, IT LOOKS LIKE...
...IT'S JUGGERNAUT.
OR WHATEVER HE IS NOW.
HE'S... IT'S...
IT'S WORSE THAN I FEARED!
SATANA-- WHAT ARE YOU DOING BACK?!

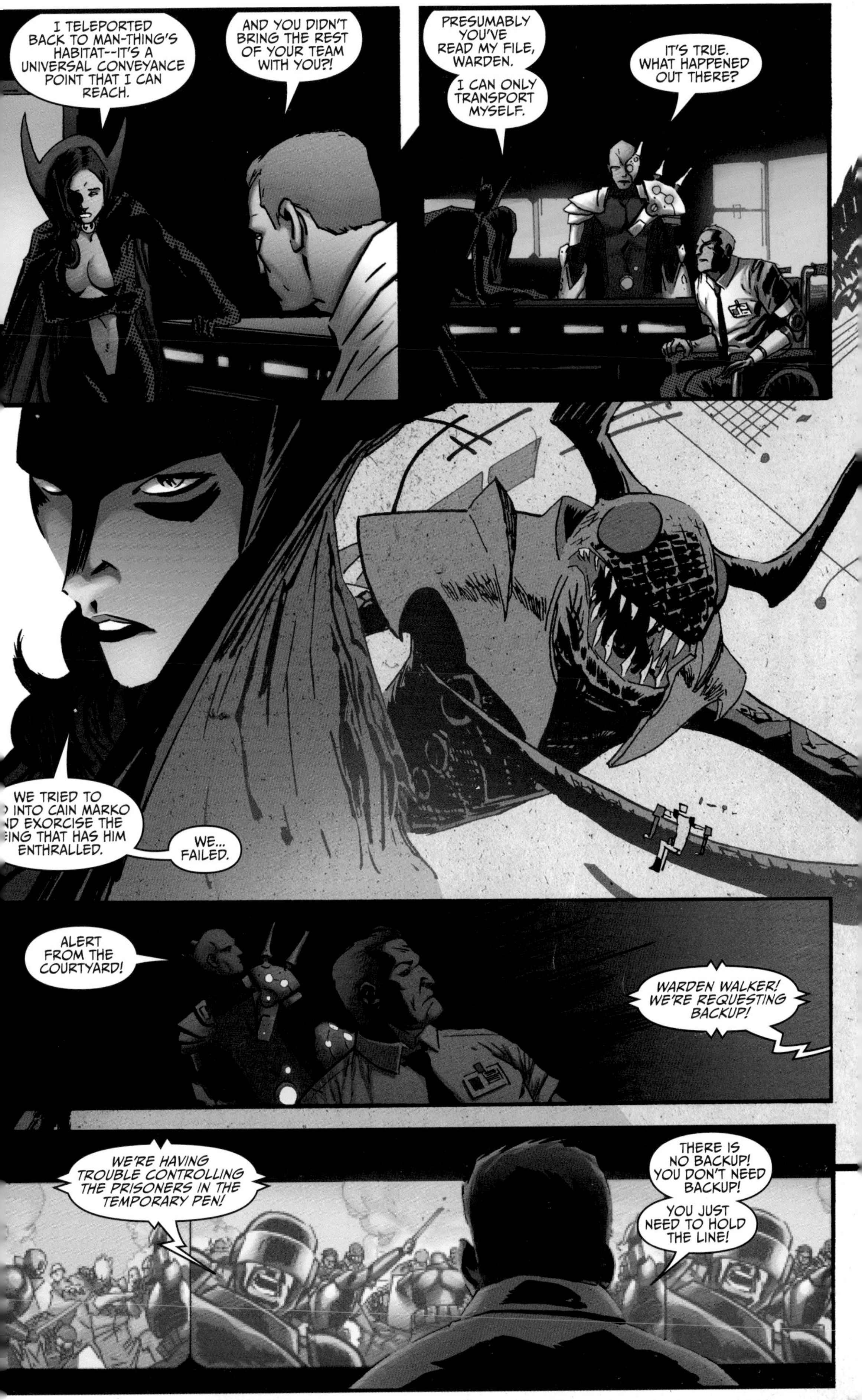
I TELEPORTED BACK TO MAN-THING'S HABITAT--IT'S A UNIVERSAL CONVEYANCE POINT THAT I CAN REACH.
AND YOU DIDN'T BRING THE REST OF YOUR TEAM WITH YOU?!
PRESUMABLY YOU'VE READ MY FILE, WARDEN.
I CAN ONLY TRANSPORT MYSELF.
IT'S TRUE. WHAT HAPPENED OUT THERE?
WE TRIED TO INTO CAIN MARKO ND EXORCISE THE EING THAT HAS HIM ENTHRALLED.
WE... FAILED.
ALERT FROM THE COURTYARD!
WARDEN WALKER! WE'RE REQUESTING BACKUP!
WE'RE HAVING TROUBLE CONTROLLING THE PRISONERS IN THE TEMPORARY PEN!
THERE IS NO BACKUP! YOU DON'T NEED BACKUP!
YOU JUST NEED TO HOLD THE LINE!

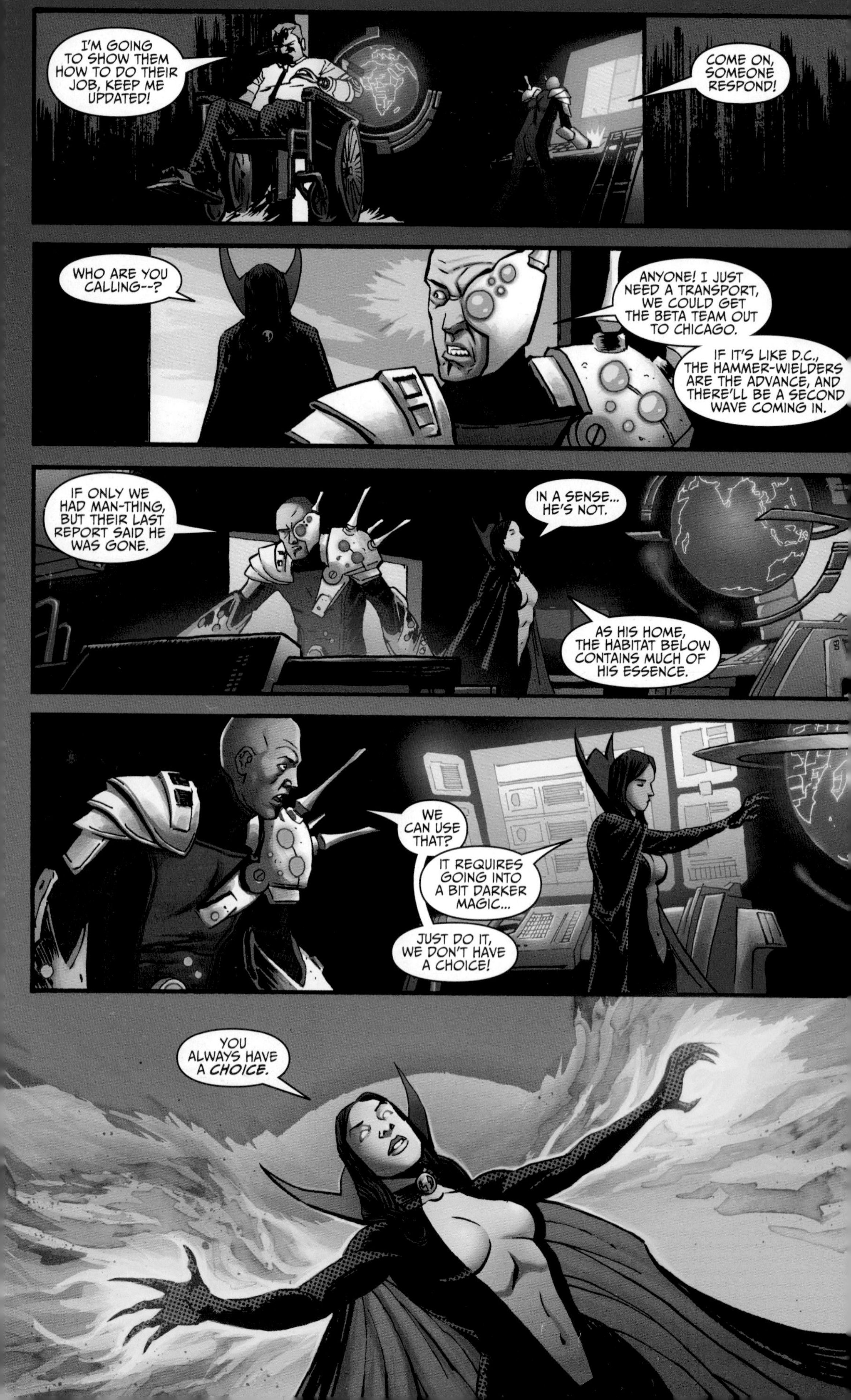
I'M GOING TO SHOW THEM HOW TO DO THEIR JOB, KEEP ME UPDATED!
COME ON, SOMEONE RESPOND!
WHO ARE YOU CALLING--?
ANYONE! I JUST NEED A TRANSPORT, WE COULD GET THE BETA TEAM OUT TO CHICAGO.
IF IT'S LIKE D.C., THE HAMMER-WIELDERS ARE THE ADVANCE, AND THERE'LL BE A SECOND WAVE COMING IN.
IF ONLY WE HAD MAN-THING, BUT THEIR LAST REPORT SAID HE WAS GONE.
IN A SENSE... HE'S NOT.
AS HIS HOME, THE HABITAT BELOW CONTAINS MUCH OF HIS ESSENCE.
WE CAN USE THAT?
IT REQUIRES GOING INTO A BIT DARKER MAGIC...
JUST DO IT, WE DON'T HAVE A CHOICE!
YOU ALWAYS HAVE A *CHOICE*.

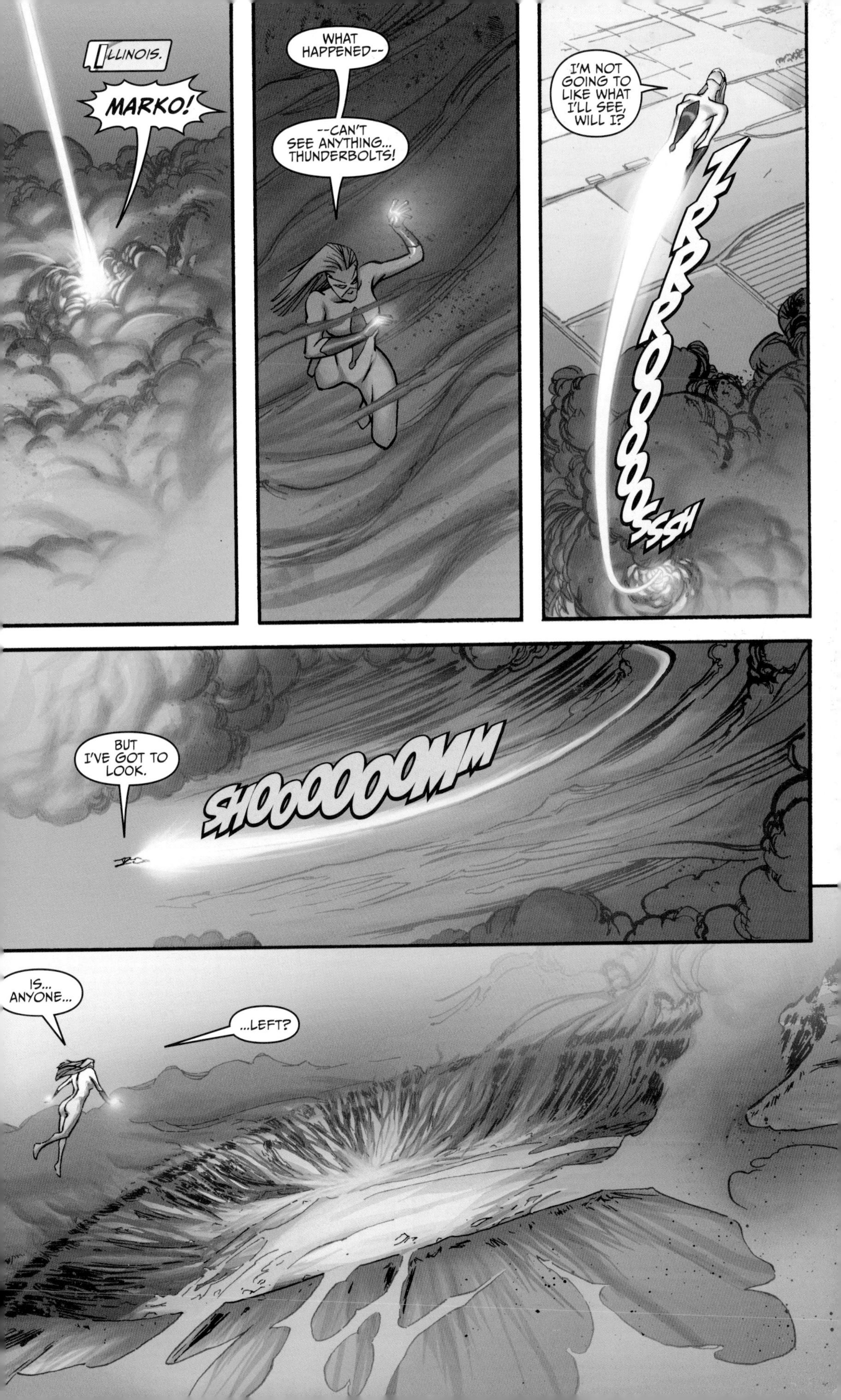
ILLINOIS.
MARKO!
WHAT HAPPENED--
--CAN'T SEE ANYTHING... THUNDERBOLTS!
I'M NOT GOING TO LIKE WHAT I'LL SEE, WILL I?
ZRRROOOOOOSSSH
BUT I'VE GOT TO LOOK.
SHOOOOOOMM
IS... ANYONE...
...LEFT?

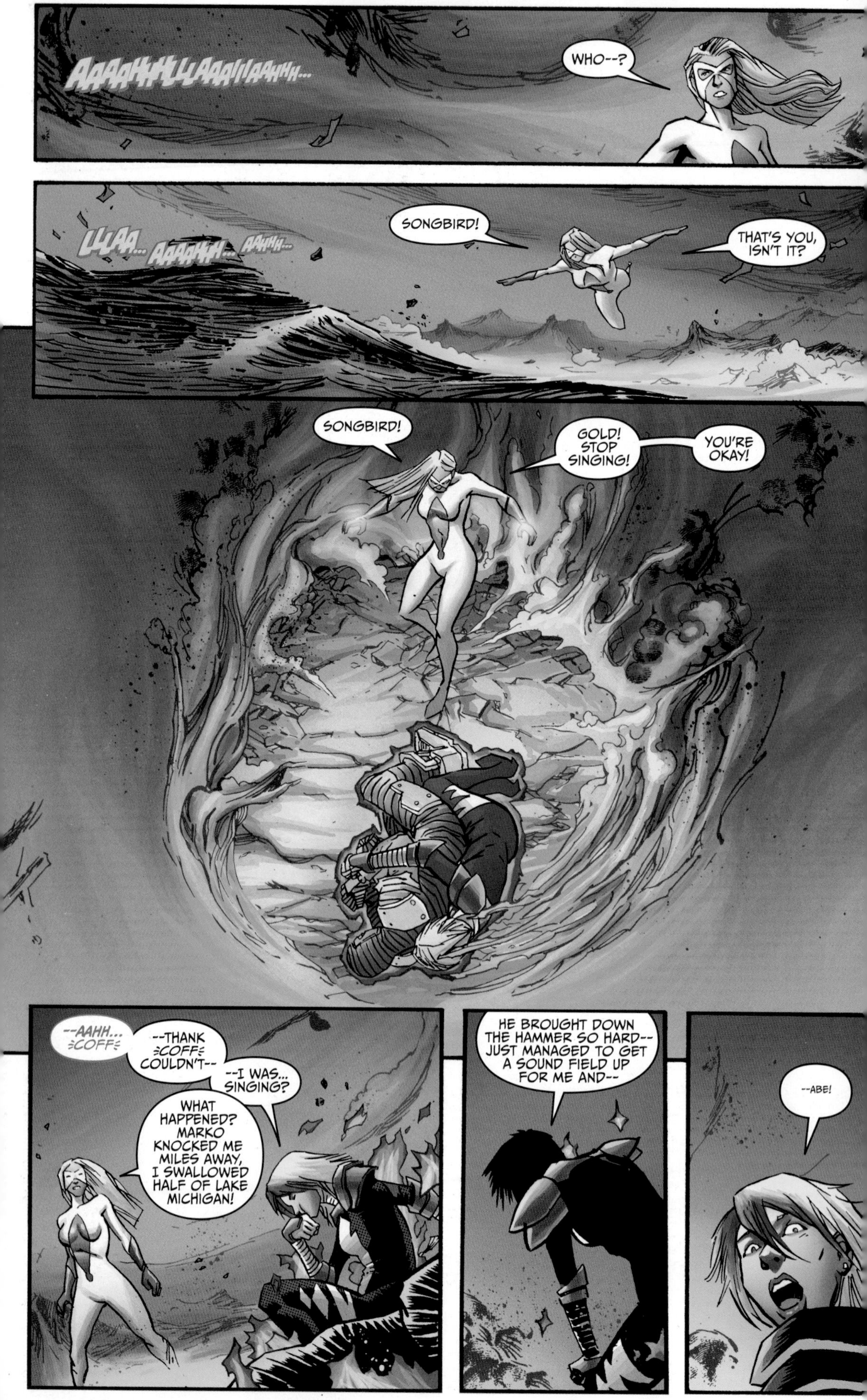
AAAHHHLLLAAAIIIAAHHH...
WHO--?
LLLAA... AAAHHHH... AAHHH...
SONGBIRD!
THAT'S YOU, ISN'T IT?
SONGBIRD!
GOLD! STOP SINGING!
YOU'RE OKAY!
--AAHH... COFF
--THANK COFF COULDN'T--
--I WAS... SINGING?
WHAT HAPPENED? MARKO KNOCKED ME MILES AWAY, I SWALLOWED HALF OF LAKE MICHIGAN!
HE BROUGHT DOWN THE HAMMER SO HARD-- JUST MANAGED TO GET A SOUND FIELD UP FOR ME AND--
--ABE!

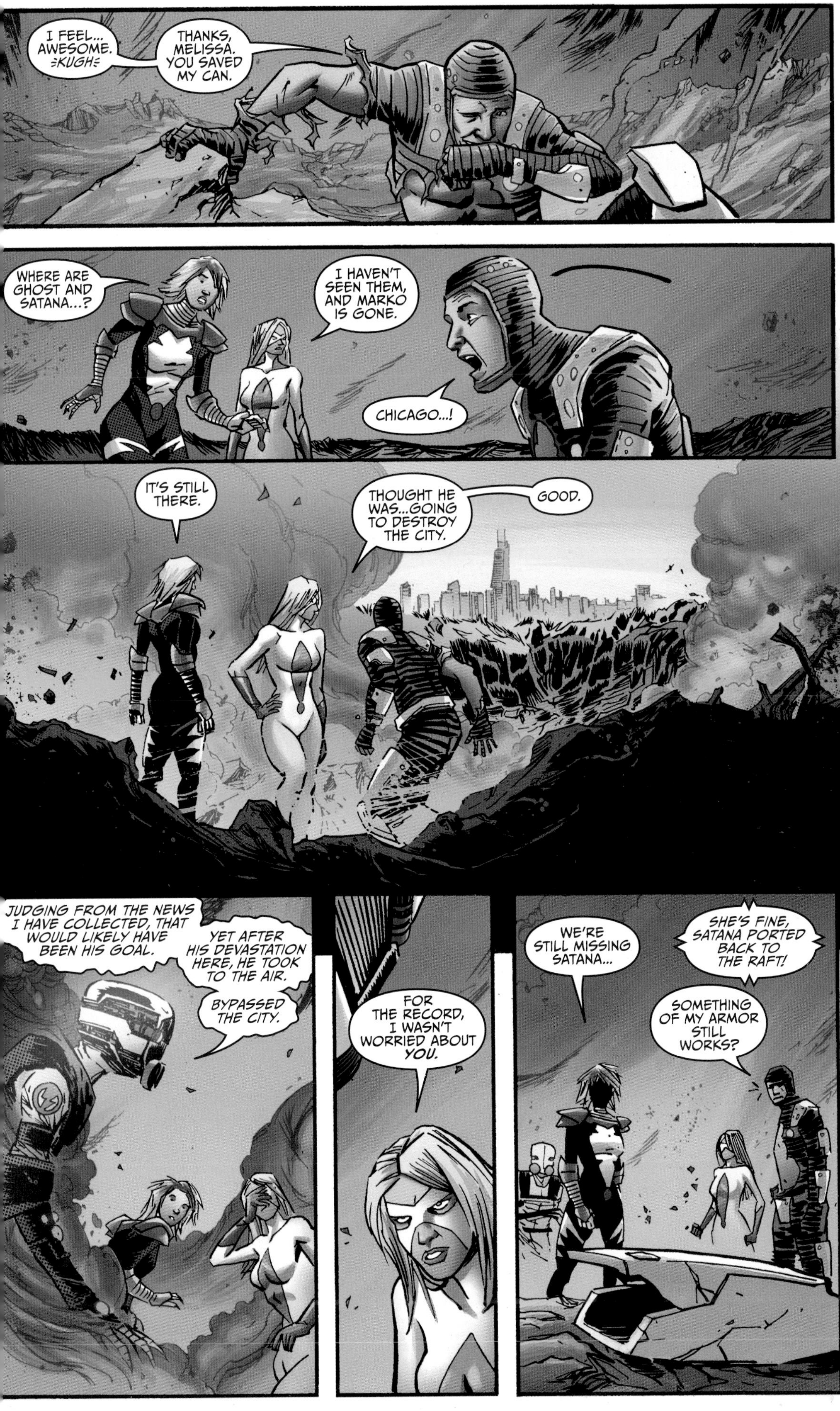
I FEEL... AWESOME. KUGH
THANKS, MELISSA. YOU SAVED MY CAN.
WHERE ARE GHOST AND SATANA...?
I HAVEN'T SEEN THEM, AND MARKO IS GONE.
CHICAGO...!
IT'S STILL THERE.
THOUGHT HE WAS...GOING TO DESTROY THE CITY.
GOOD.
JUDGING FROM THE NEWS I HAVE COLLECTED, THAT WOULD LIKELY HAVE BEEN HIS GOAL.
YET AFTER HIS DEVASTATION HERE, HE TOOK TO THE AIR.
BYPASSED THE CITY.
FOR THE RECORD, I WASN'T WORRIED ABOUT YOU.
WE'RE STILL MISSING SATANA...
SHE'S FINE, SATANA PORTED BACK TO THE RAFT!
SOMETHING OF MY ARMOR STILL WORKS?

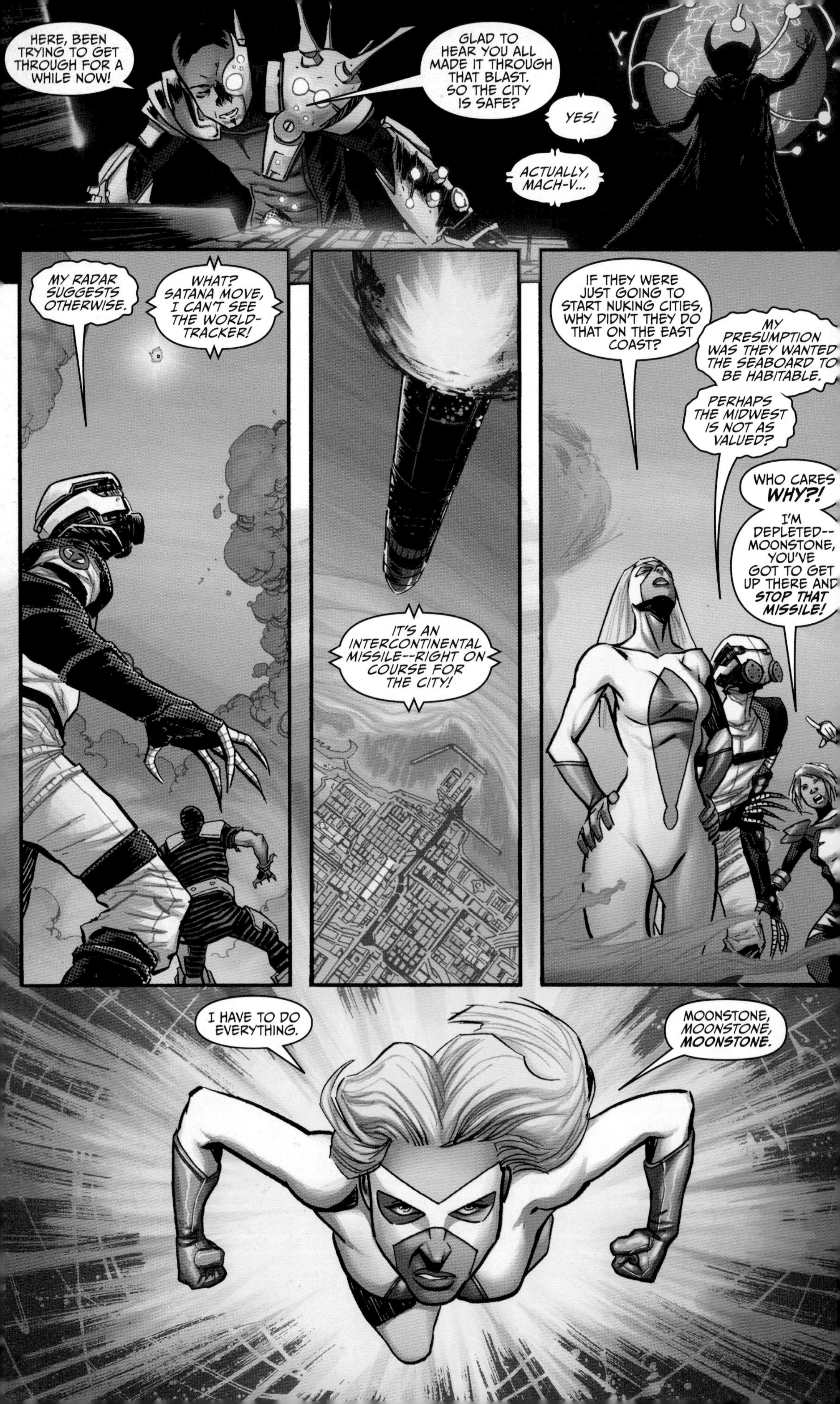
HERE, BEEN TRYING TO GET THROUGH FOR A WHILE NOW!
GLAD TO HEAR YOU ALL MADE IT THROUGH THAT BLAST. SO THE CITY IS SAFE?
YES!
ACTUALLY, MACH-V...
MY RADAR SUGGESTS OTHERWISE.
WHAT? SATANA MOVE, I CAN'T SEE THE WORLD-TRACKER!
IT'S AN INTERCONTINENTAL MISSILE--RIGHT ON COURSE FOR THE CITY!
IF THEY WERE JUST GOING TO START NUKING CITIES, WHY DIDN'T THEY DO THAT ON THE EAST COAST?
MY PRESUMPTION WAS THEY WANTED THE SEABOARD TO BE HABITABLE.
PERHAPS THE MIDWEST IS NOT AS VALUED?
WHO CARES WHY?!
I'M DEPLETED--MOONSTONE, YOU'VE GOT TO GET UP THERE AND STOP THAT MISSILE!
I HAVE TO DO EVERYTHING.
MOONSTONE, MOONSTONE, MOONSTONE.

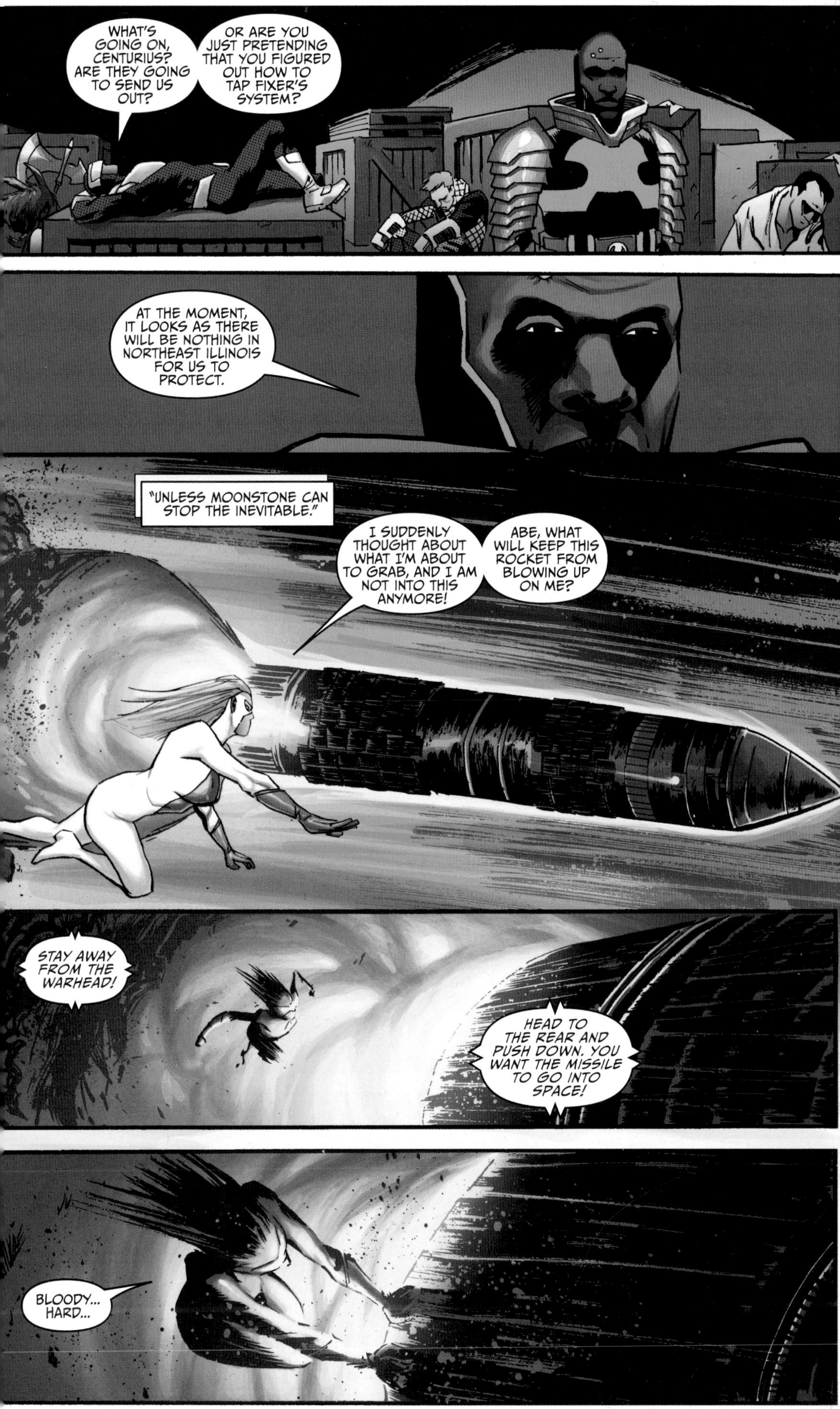
WHAT'S GOING ON, CENTURIUS? ARE THEY GOING TO SEND US OUT?
OR ARE YOU JUST PRETENDING THAT YOU FIGURED OUT HOW TO TAP FIXER'S SYSTEM?
AT THE MOMENT, IT LOOKS AS THERE WILL BE NOTHING IN NORTHEAST ILLINOIS FOR US TO PROTECT.
"UNLESS MOONSTONE CAN STOP THE INEVITABLE."
I SUDDENLY THOUGHT ABOUT WHAT I'M ABOUT TO GRAB, AND I AM NOT INTO THIS ANYMORE!
ABE, WHAT WILL KEEP THIS ROCKET FROM BLOWING UP ON ME?
STAY AWAY FROM THE WARHEAD!
HEAD TO THE REAR AND PUSH DOWN. YOU WANT THE MISSILE TO GO INTO SPACE!
BLOODY... HARD...

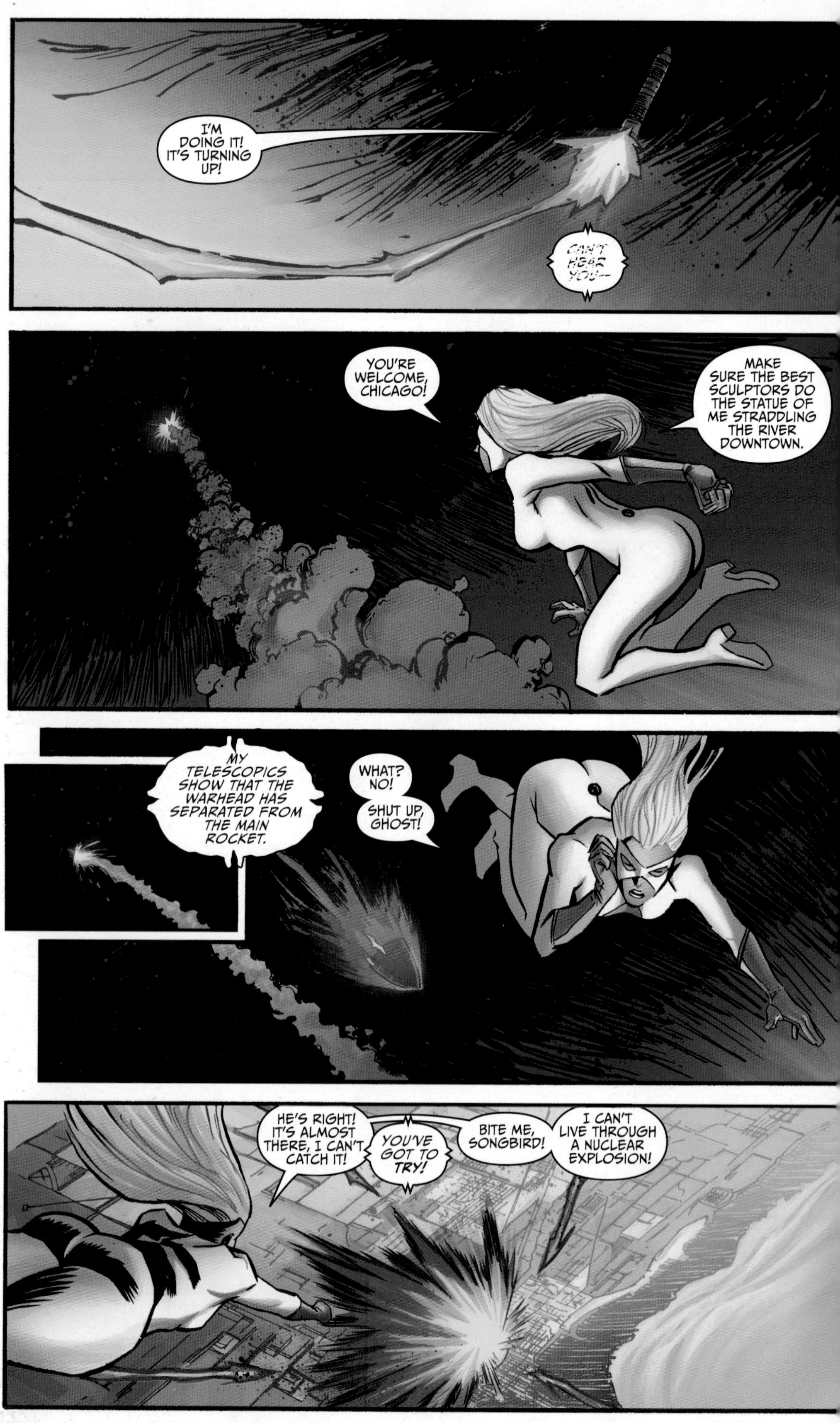
I'M DOING IT! IT'S TURNING UP!
CAN'T HEAR YOU--
YOU'RE WELCOME, CHICAGO!
MAKE SURE THE BEST SCULPTORS DO THE STATUE OF ME STRADDLING THE RIVER DOWNTOWN.
MY TELESCOPICS SHOW THAT THE WARHEAD HAS SEPARATED FROM THE MAIN ROCKET.
WHAT? NO!
SHUT UP, GHOST!
HE'S RIGHT! IT'S ALMOST THERE, I CAN'T CATCH IT!
YOU'VE GOT TO TRY!
BITE ME, SONGBIRD!
I CAN'T LIVE THROUGH A NUCLEAR EXPLOSION!

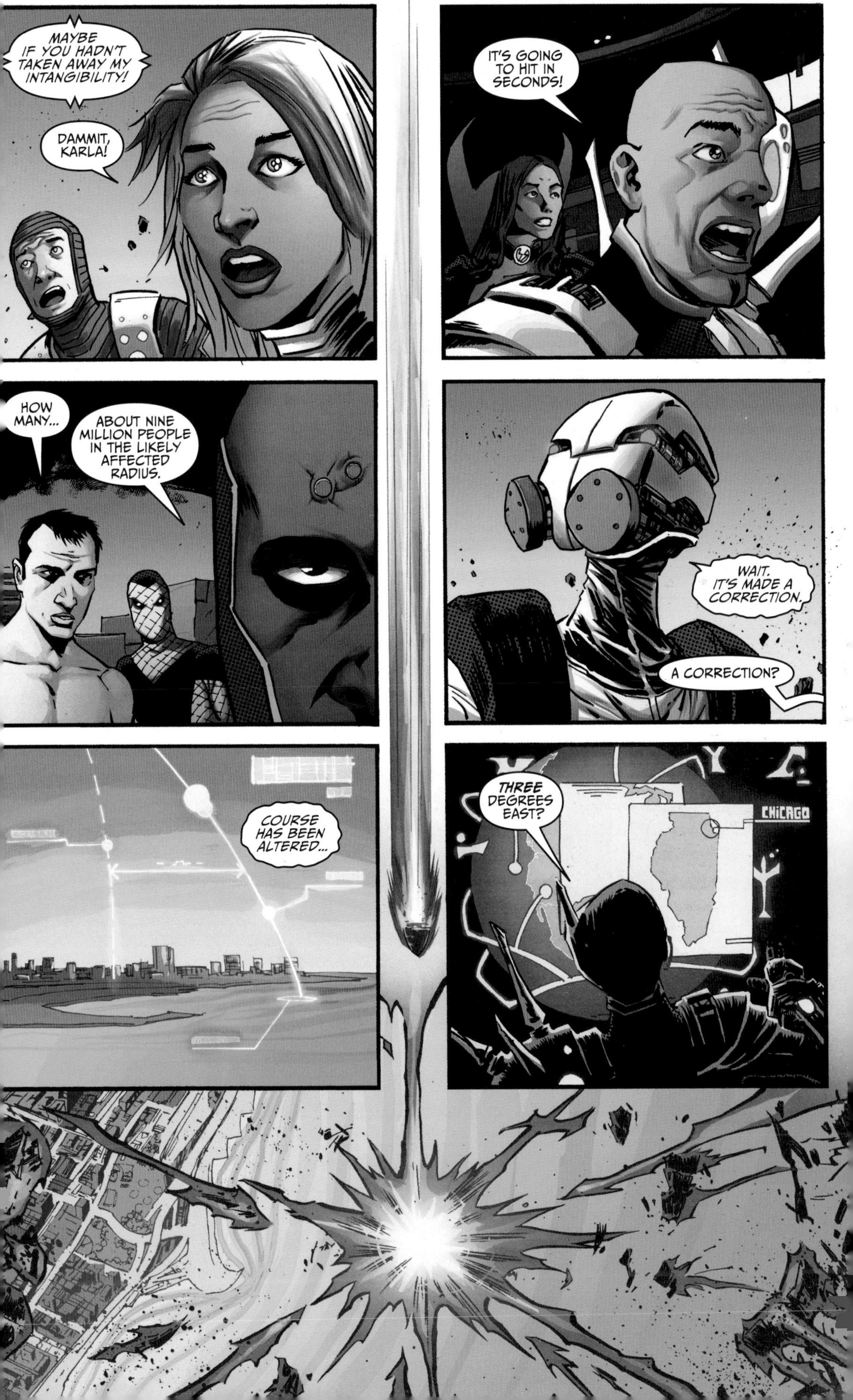

MAYBE IF YOU HADN'T TAKEN AWAY MY INTANGIBILITY!
DAMMIT, KARLA!
IT'S GOING TO HIT IN SECONDS!
HOW MANY...
ABOUT NINE MILLION PEOPLE IN THE LIKELY AFFECTED RADIUS.
WAIT. IT'S MADE A CORRECTION.
A CORRECTION?
COURSE HAS BEEN ALTERED...
THREE DEGREES EAST?
CHICAGO

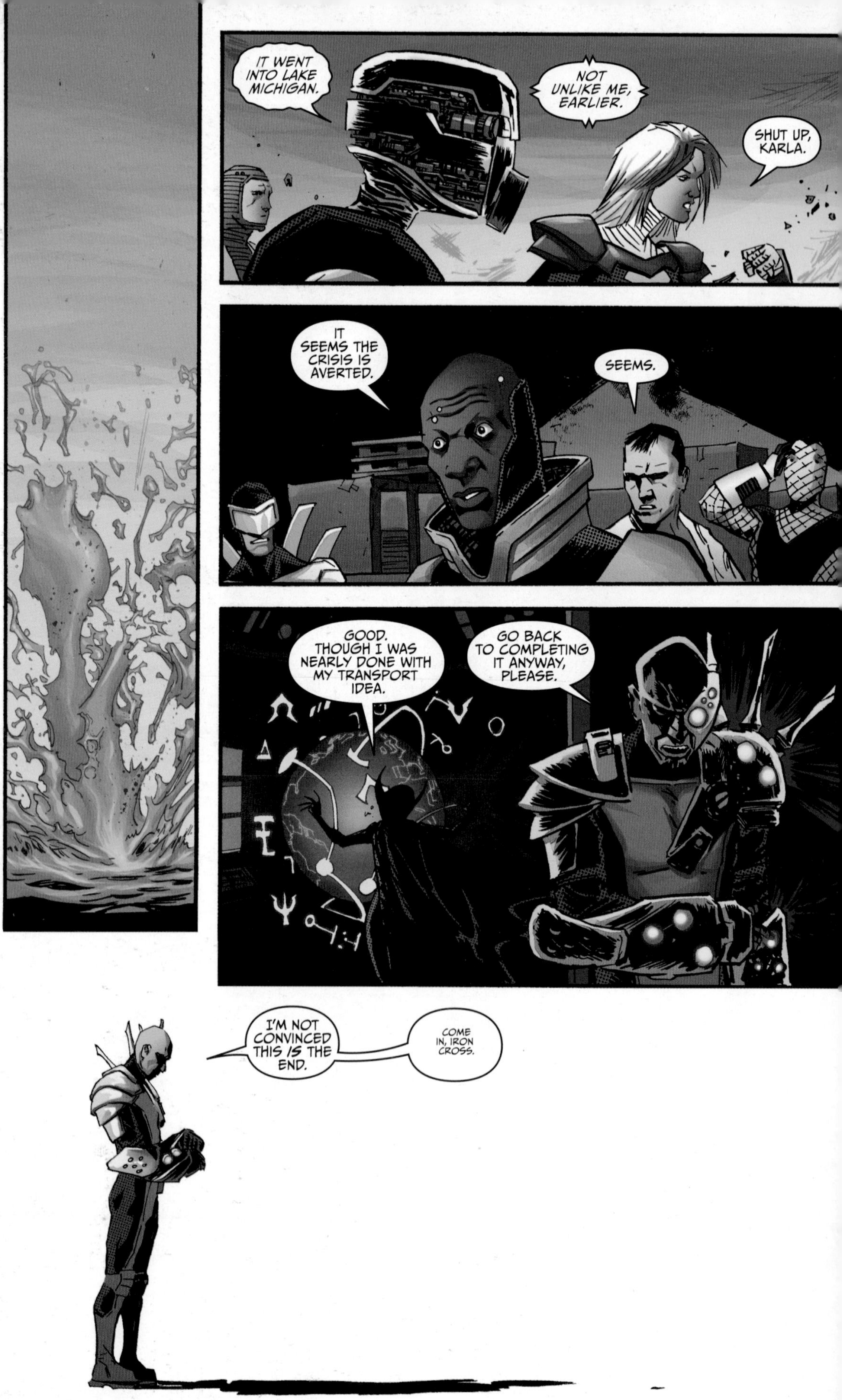
IT WENT INTO LAKE MICHIGAN.
NOT UNLIKE ME, EARLIER.
SHUT UP, KARLA.
IT SEEMS THE CRISIS IS AVERTED.
SEEMS.
GOOD. THOUGH I WAS NEARLY DONE WITH MY TRANSPORT IDEA.
GO BACK TO COMPLETING IT ANYWAY, PLEASE.
I'M NOT CONVINCED THIS *IS* THE END.
COME IN, IRON CROSS.

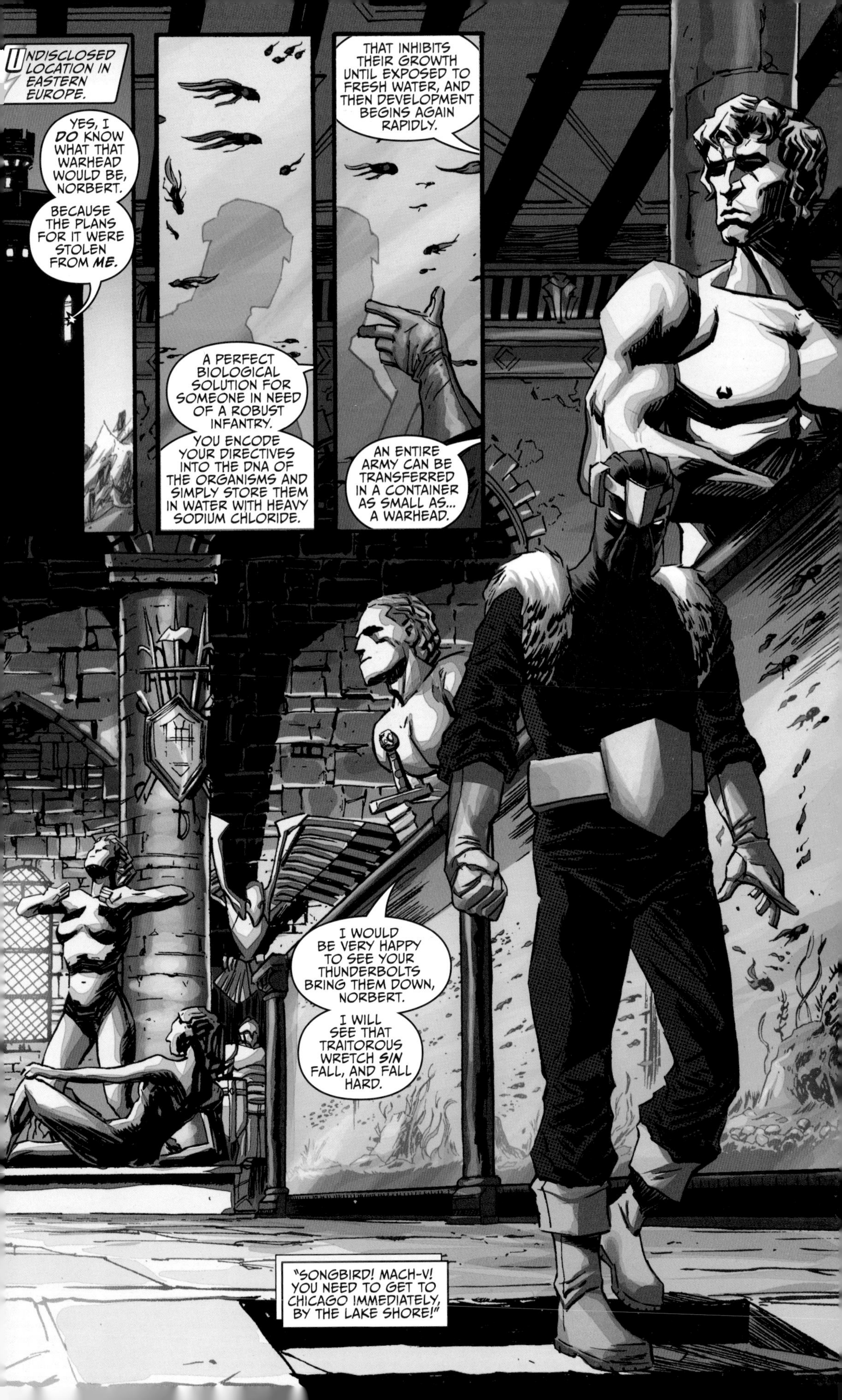
UNDISCLOSED LOCATION IN EASTERN EUROPE.
YES, I DO KNOW WHAT THAT WARHEAD WOULD BE, NORBERT.
BECAUSE THE PLANS FOR IT WERE STOLEN FROM ME.
A PERFECT BIOLOGICAL SOLUTION FOR SOMEONE IN NEED OF A ROBUST INFANTRY.
YOU ENCODE YOUR DIRECTIVES INTO THE DNA OF THE ORGANISMS AND SIMPLY STORE THEM IN WATER WITH HEAVY SODIUM CHLORIDE.
THAT INHIBITS THEIR GROWTH UNTIL EXPOSED TO FRESH WATER, AND THEN DEVELOPMENT BEGINS AGAIN RAPIDLY.
AN ENTIRE ARMY CAN BE TRANSFERRED IN A CONTAINER AS SMALL AS... A WARHEAD.
I WOULD BE VERY HAPPY TO SEE YOUR THUNDERBOLTS BRING THEM DOWN, NORBERT.
I WILL SEE THAT TRAITOROUS WRETCH SIN FALL, AND FALL HARD.
"SONGBIRD! MACH-V! YOU NEED TO GET TO CHICAGO IMMEDIATELY, BY THE LAKE SHORE!"

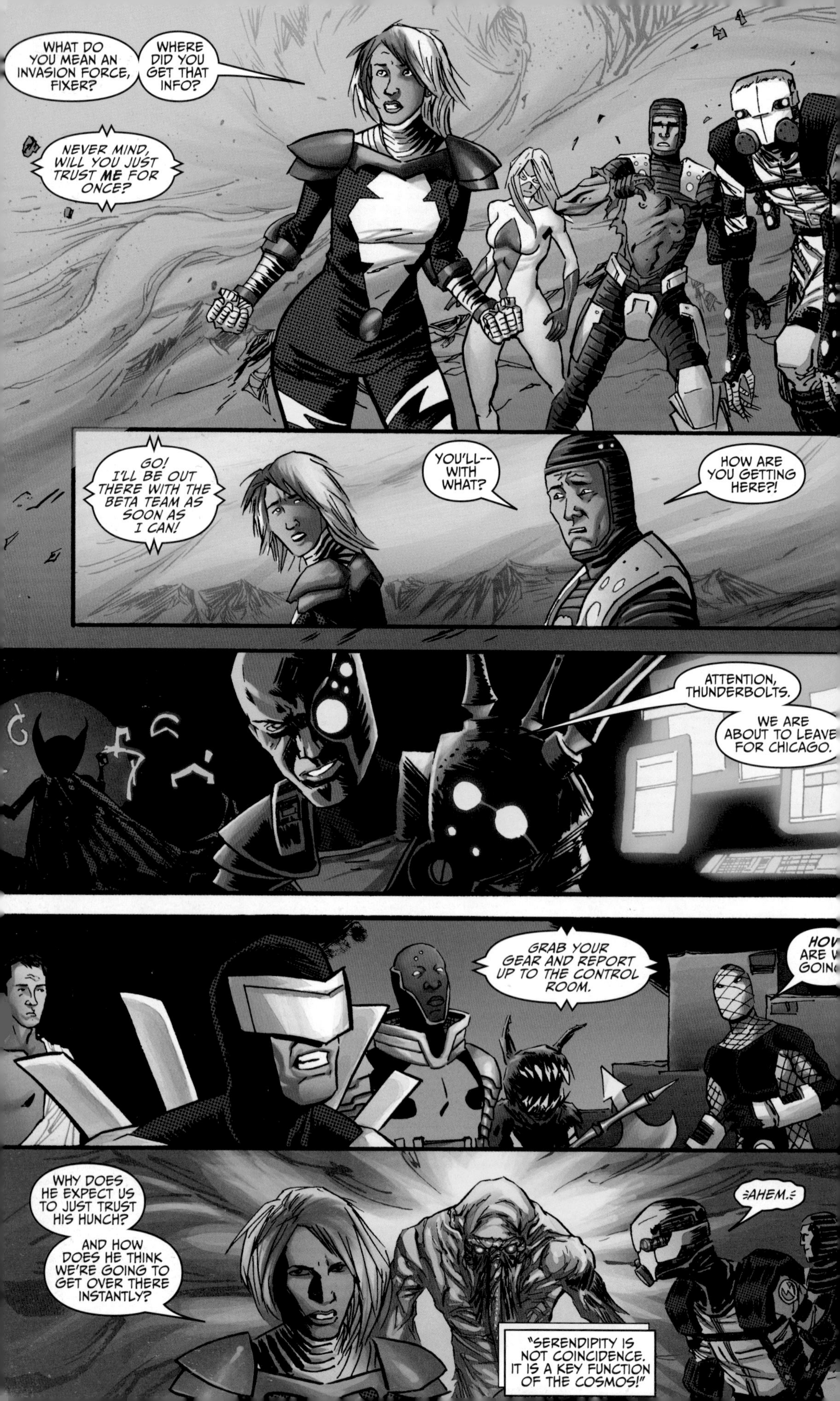
WHAT DO YOU MEAN AN INVASION FORCE, FIXER?
WHERE DID YOU GET THAT INFO?
NEVER MIND, WILL YOU JUST TRUST **ME** FOR ONCE?
GO! I'LL BE OUT THERE WITH THE BETA TEAM AS SOON AS I CAN!
YOU'LL-- WITH WHAT?
HOW ARE YOU GETTING HERE?!
ATTENTION, THUNDERBOLTS.
WE ARE ABOUT TO LEAVE FOR CHICAGO.
GRAB YOUR GEAR AND REPORT UP TO THE CONTROL ROOM.
WHY DOES HE EXPECT US TO JUST TRUST HIS HUNCH?
AND HOW DOES HE THINK WE'RE GOING TO GET OVER THERE INSTANTLY?
AHEM.
"SERENDIPITY IS NOT COINCIDENCE. IT IS A KEY FUNCTION OF THE COSMOS!"

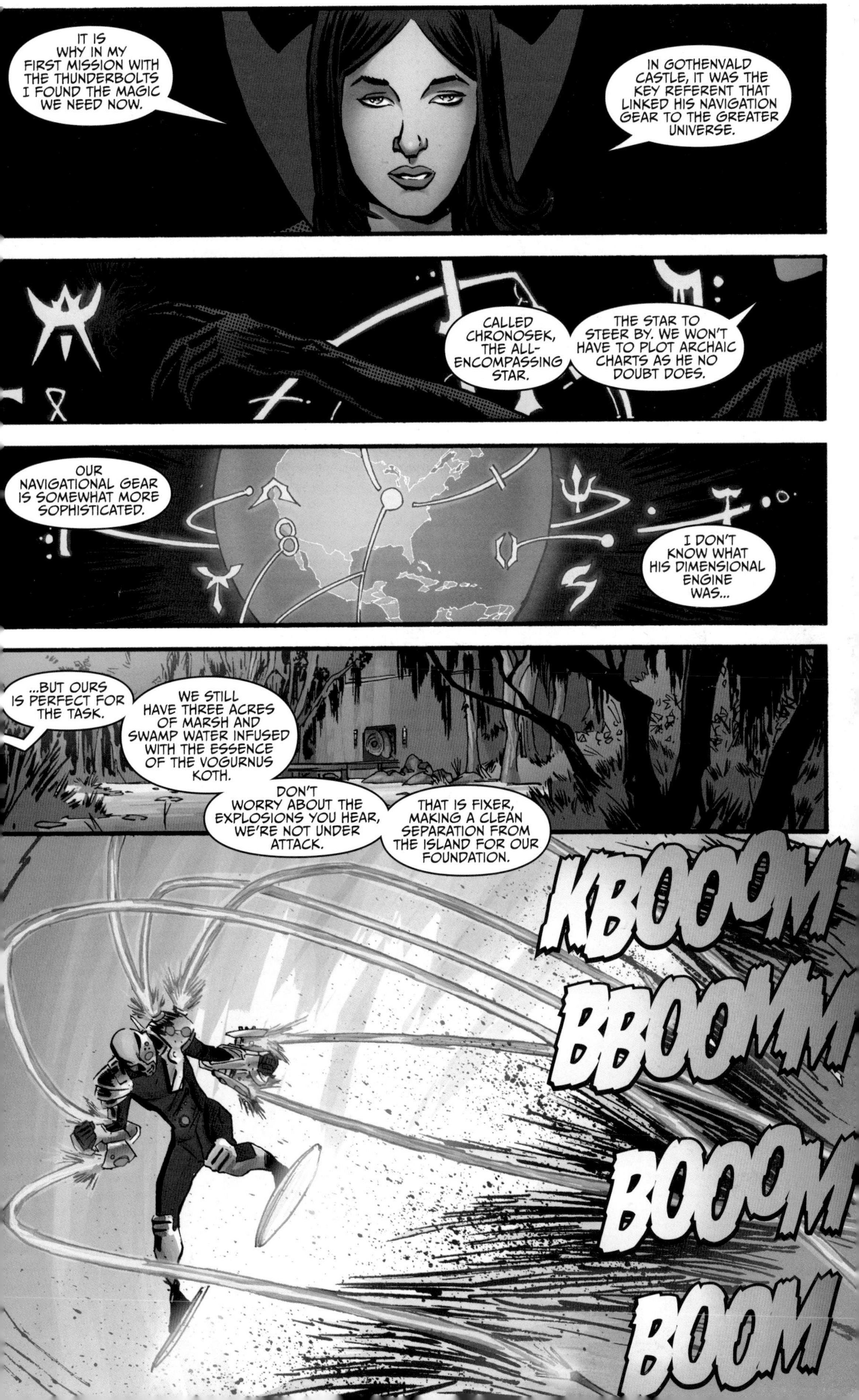

IT IS WHY IN MY FIRST MISSION WITH THE THUNDERBOLTS I FOUND THE MAGIC WE NEED NOW.
IN GOTHENVALD CASTLE, IT WAS THE KEY REFERENT THAT LINKED HIS NAVIGATION GEAR TO THE GREATER UNIVERSE.
CALLED CHRONOSEK, THE ALL-ENCOMPASSING STAR.
THE STAR TO STEER BY. WE WON'T HAVE TO PLOT ARCHAIC CHARTS AS HE NO DOUBT DOES.
OUR NAVIGATIONAL GEAR IS SOMEWHAT MORE SOPHISTICATED.
I DON'T KNOW WHAT HIS DIMENSIONAL ENGINE WAS...
...BUT OURS IS PERFECT FOR THE TASK.
WE STILL HAVE THREE ACRES OF MARSH AND SWAMP WATER INFUSED WITH THE ESSENCE OF THE VOGURNUS KOTH.
DON'T WORRY ABOUT THE EXPLOSIONS YOU HEAR, WE'RE NOT UNDER ATTACK.
THAT IS FIXER, MAKING A CLEAN SEPARATION FROM THE ISLAND FOR OUR FOUNDATION.
KBOOOM
BBOOMM
BOOOM
BOOM

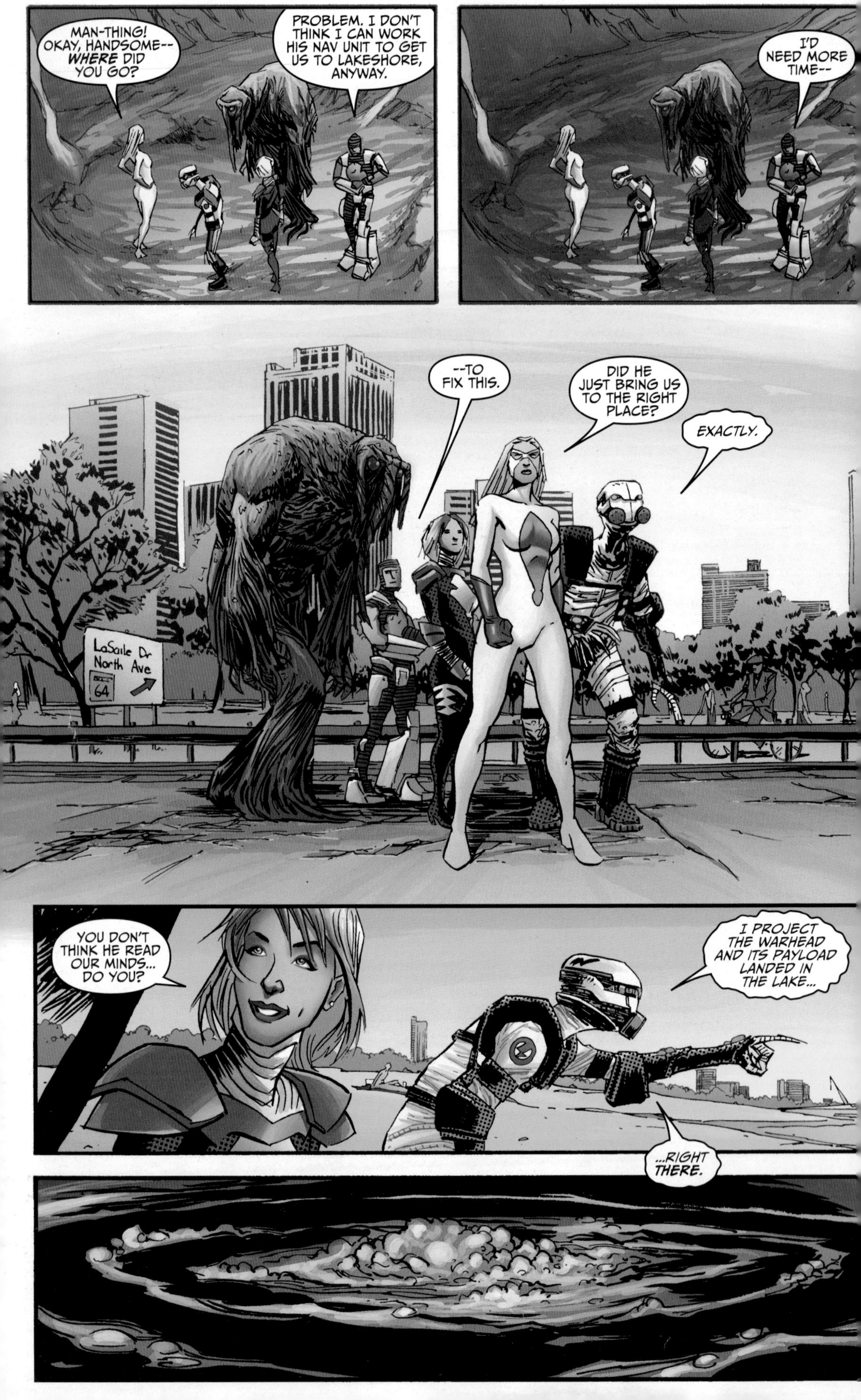
MAN-THING! OKAY, HANDSOME-- WHERE DID YOU GO?
PROBLEM. I DON'T THINK I CAN WORK HIS NAV UNIT TO GET US TO LAKESHORE, ANYWAY.
I'D NEED MORE TIME--
--TO FIX THIS.
DID HE JUST BRING US TO THE RIGHT PLACE?
EXACTLY.
LaSalle Dr
North Ave
64
YOU DON'T THINK HE READ OUR MINDS... DO YOU?
I PROJECT THE WARHEAD AND ITS PAYLOAD LANDED IN THE LAKE...
...RIGHT THERE.

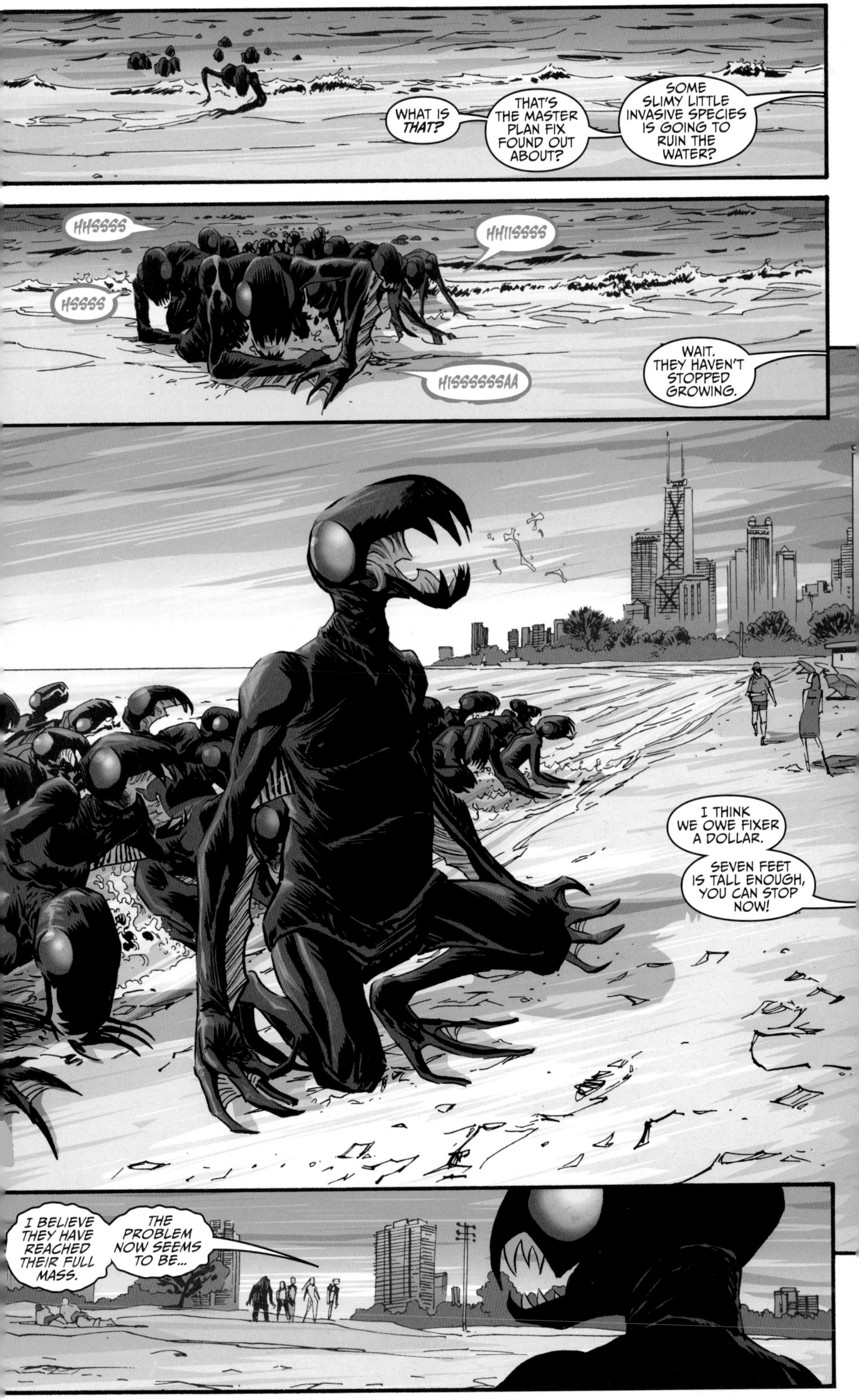
WHAT IS THAT?
THAT'S THE MASTER PLAN FIX FOUND OUT ABOUT?
SOME SLIMY LITTLE INVASIVE SPECIES IS GOING TO RUIN THE WATER?
HHSSSS
HHIISSSS
HSSSS
HISSSSSSAA
WAIT. THEY HAVEN'T STOPPED GROWING.
I THINK WE OWE FIXER A DOLLAR.
SEVEN FEET IS TALL ENOUGH, YOU CAN STOP NOW!
I BELIEVE THEY HAVE REACHED THEIR FULL MASS.
THE PROBLEM NOW SEEMS TO BE...

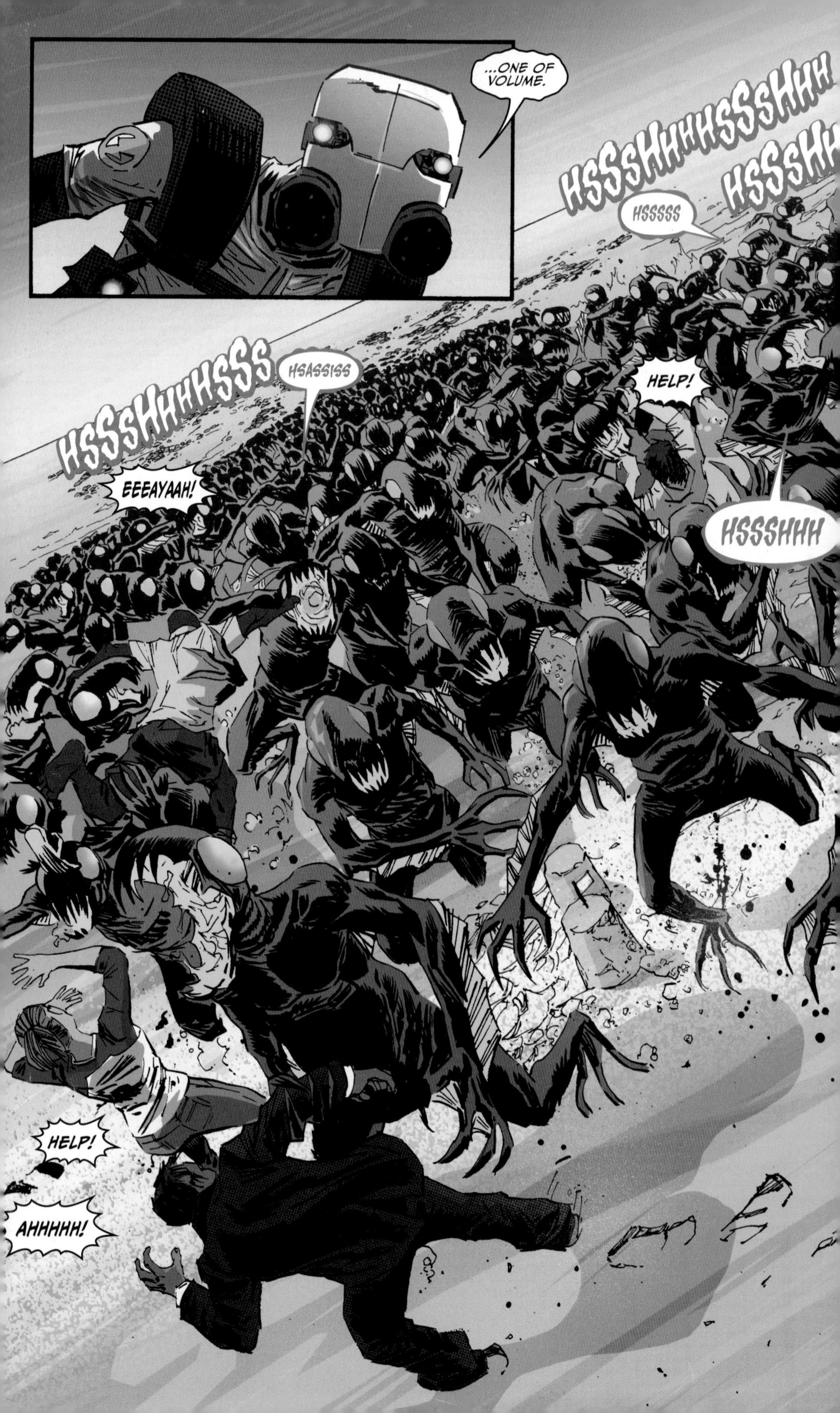
...ONE OF VOLUME.
HSSSHHHHSSSSHHH
HSSSHH
HSSSSS
HSSSHHHHSSS
HSASSISS
HELP!
EEEAYAAH!
HSSSHHH
HELP!
AHHHHH!

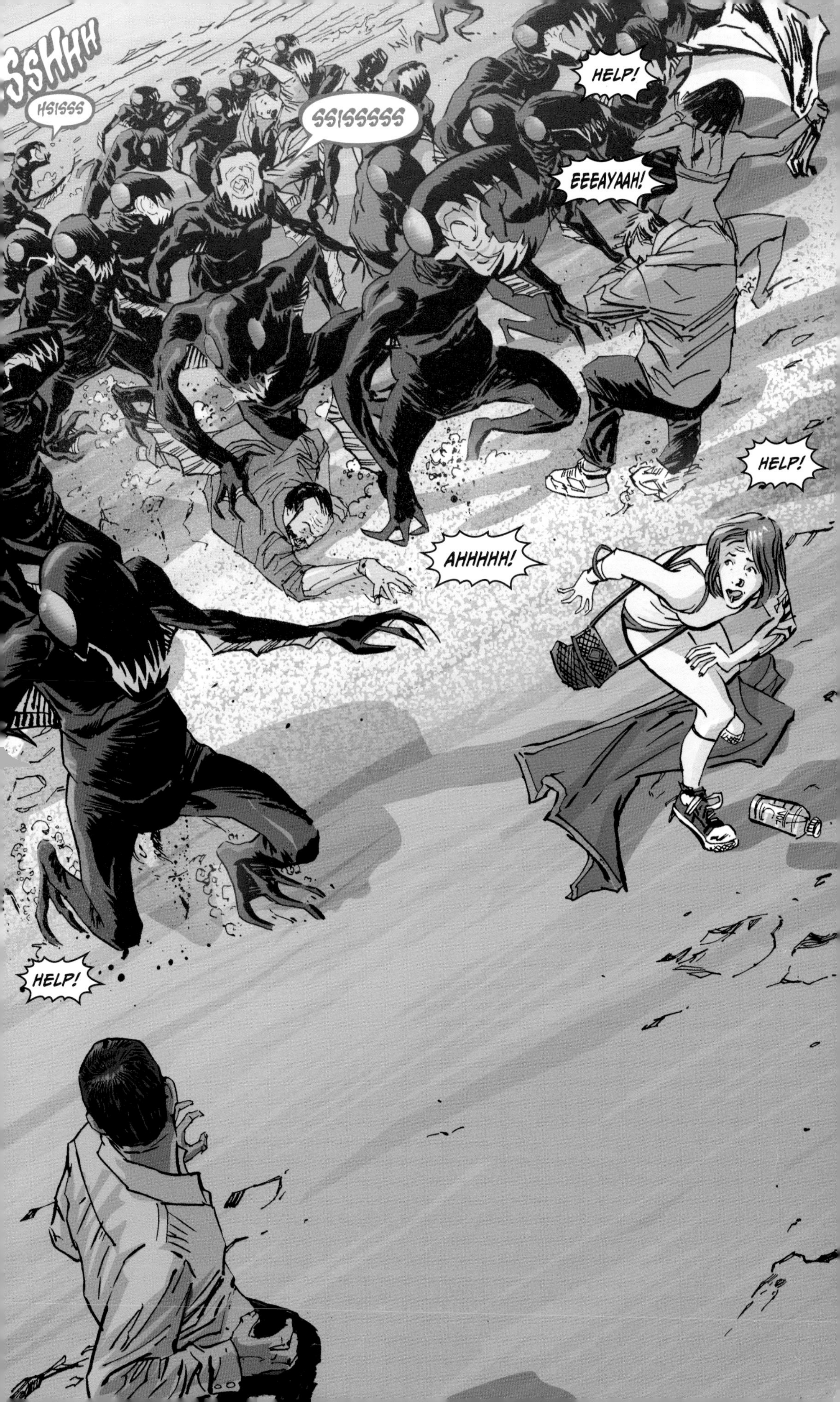
SSHHH
HSISSS
SSISSSSS
HELP!
EEEAYAAH!
HELP!
AHHHHH!
HELP!

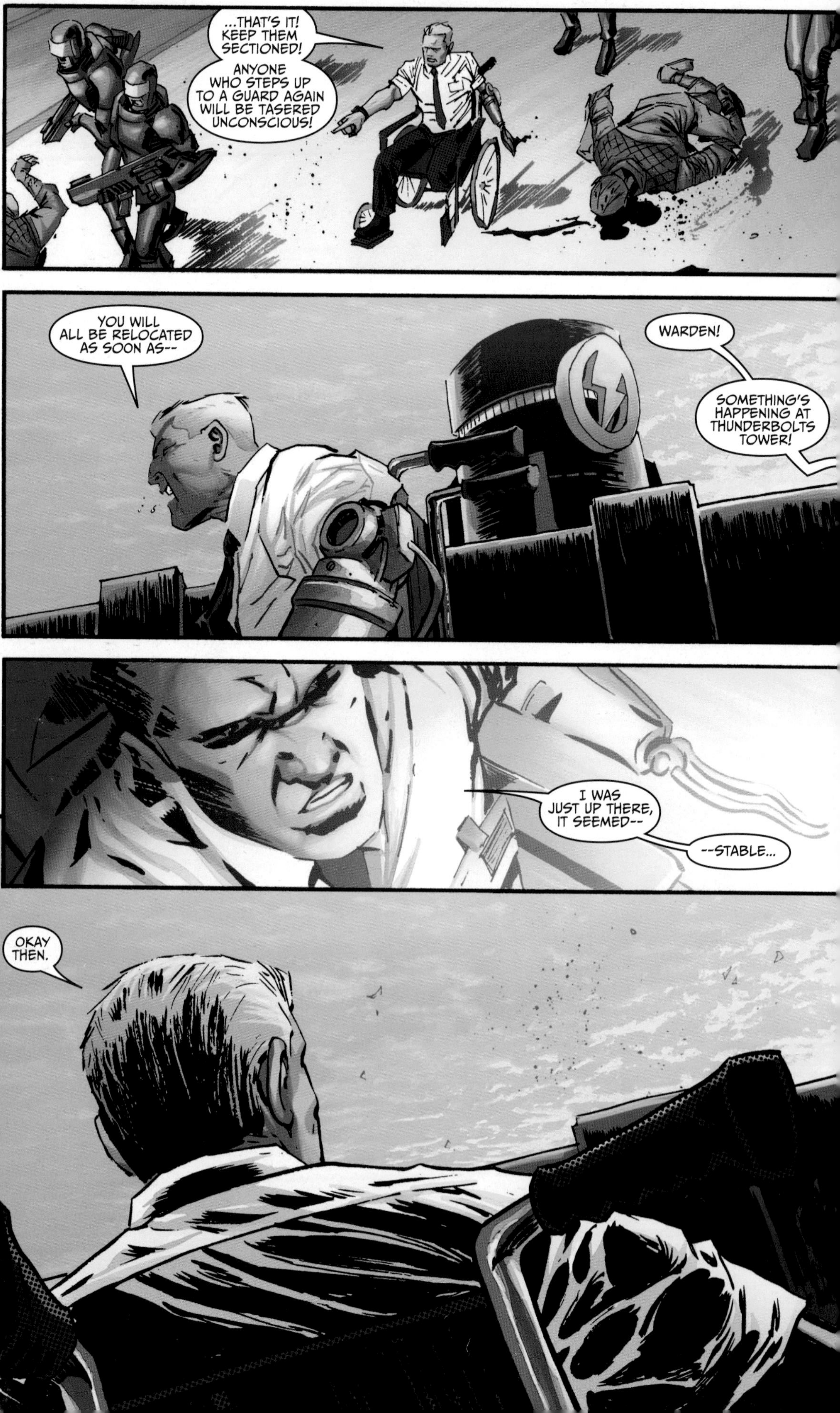
...THAT'S IT! KEEP THEM SECTIONED!
ANYONE WHO STEPS UP TO A GUARD AGAIN WILL BE TASERED UNCONSCIOUS!
YOU WILL ALL BE RELOCATED AS SOON AS--
WARDEN!
SOMETHING'S HAPPENING AT THUNDERBOLTS TOWER!
I WAS JUST UP THERE, IT SEEMED--
--STABLE...
OKAY THEN.

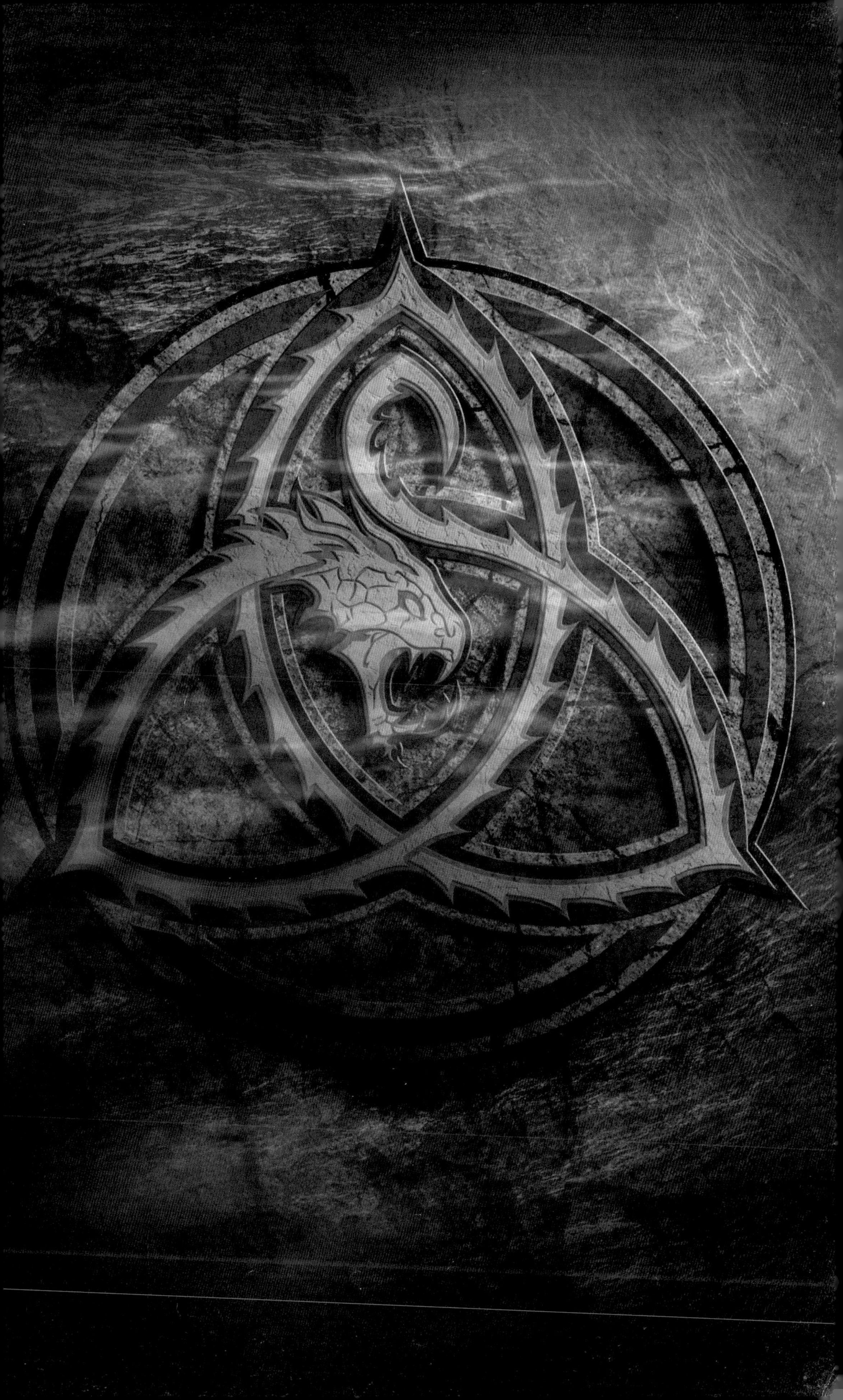

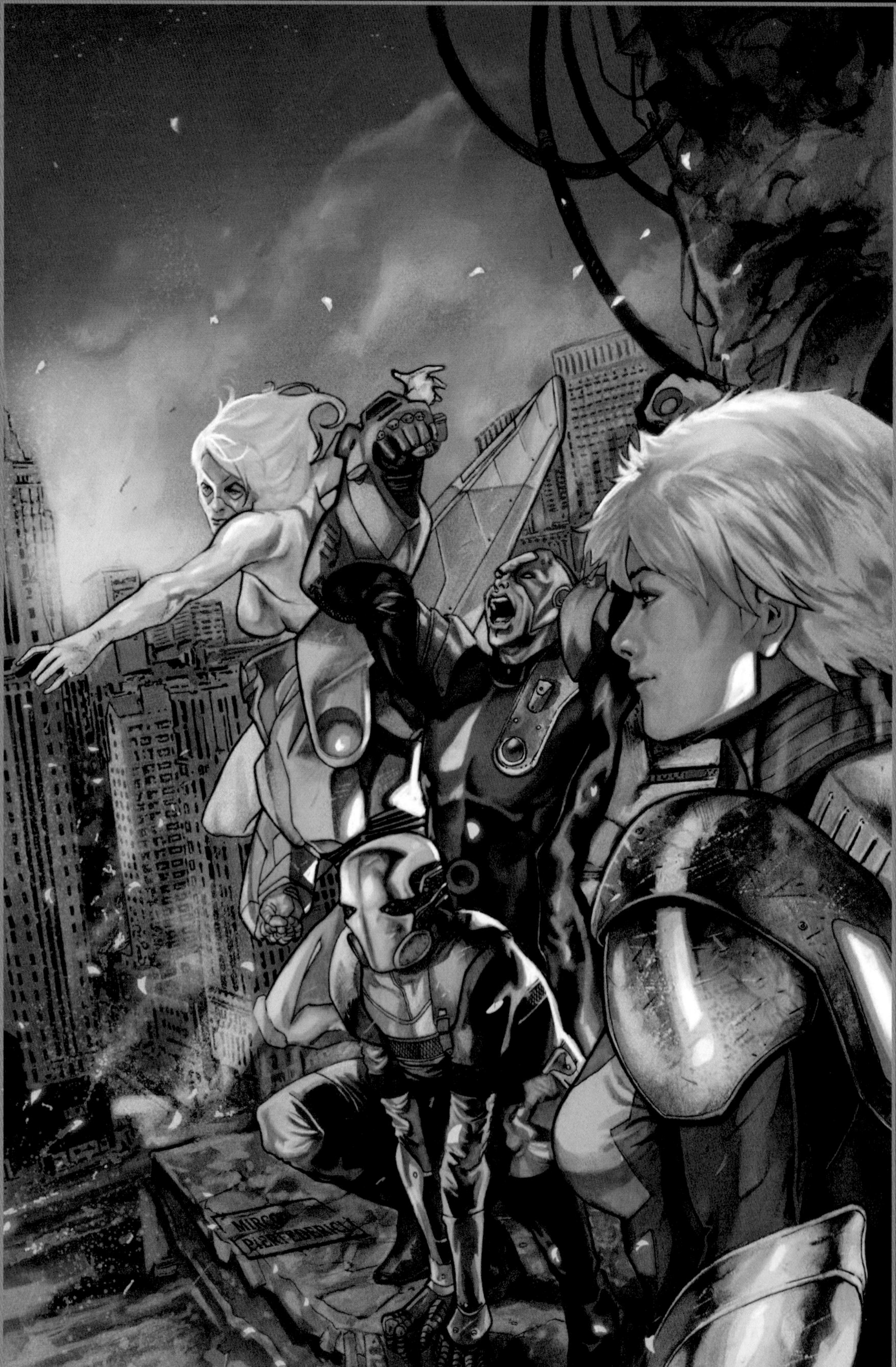

THUNDERBOLTS #162

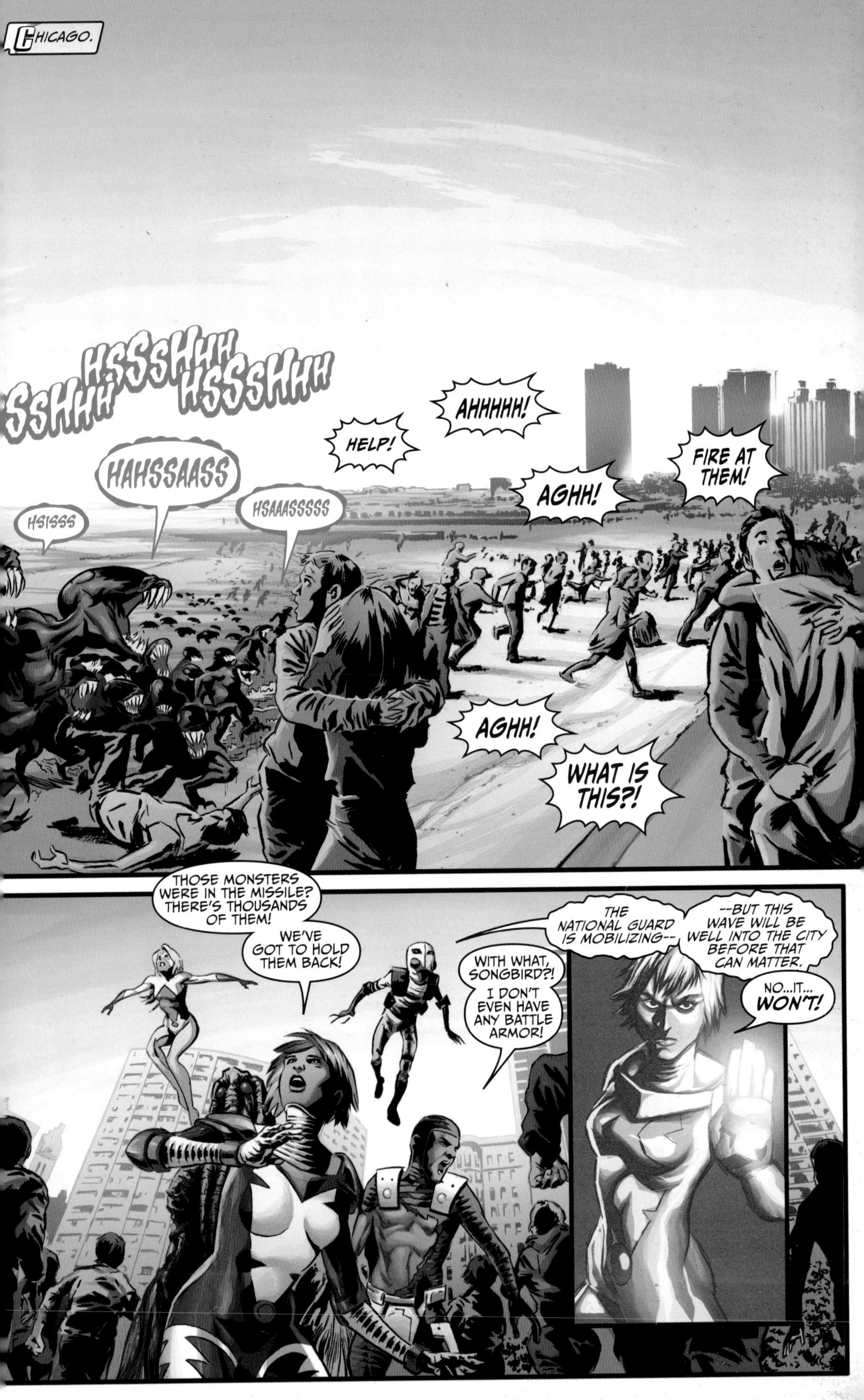
CHICAGO.
SSHHH
HSSSHHH
HSSSHHH
HSISSS
HAHSSAASS
HSAAASSSSS
HELP!
AHHHHH!
AGHH!
FIRE AT THEM!
AGHH!
WHAT IS THIS?!
THOSE MONSTERS WERE IN THE MISSILE? THERE'S THOUSANDS OF THEM!
WE'VE GOT TO HOLD THEM BACK!
WITH WHAT, SONGBIRD?!
I DON'T EVEN HAVE ANY BATTLE ARMOR!
THE NATIONAL GUARD IS MOBILIZING--
--BUT THIS WAVE WILL BE WELL INTO THE CITY BEFORE THAT CAN MATTER.
NO...IT... WON'T!

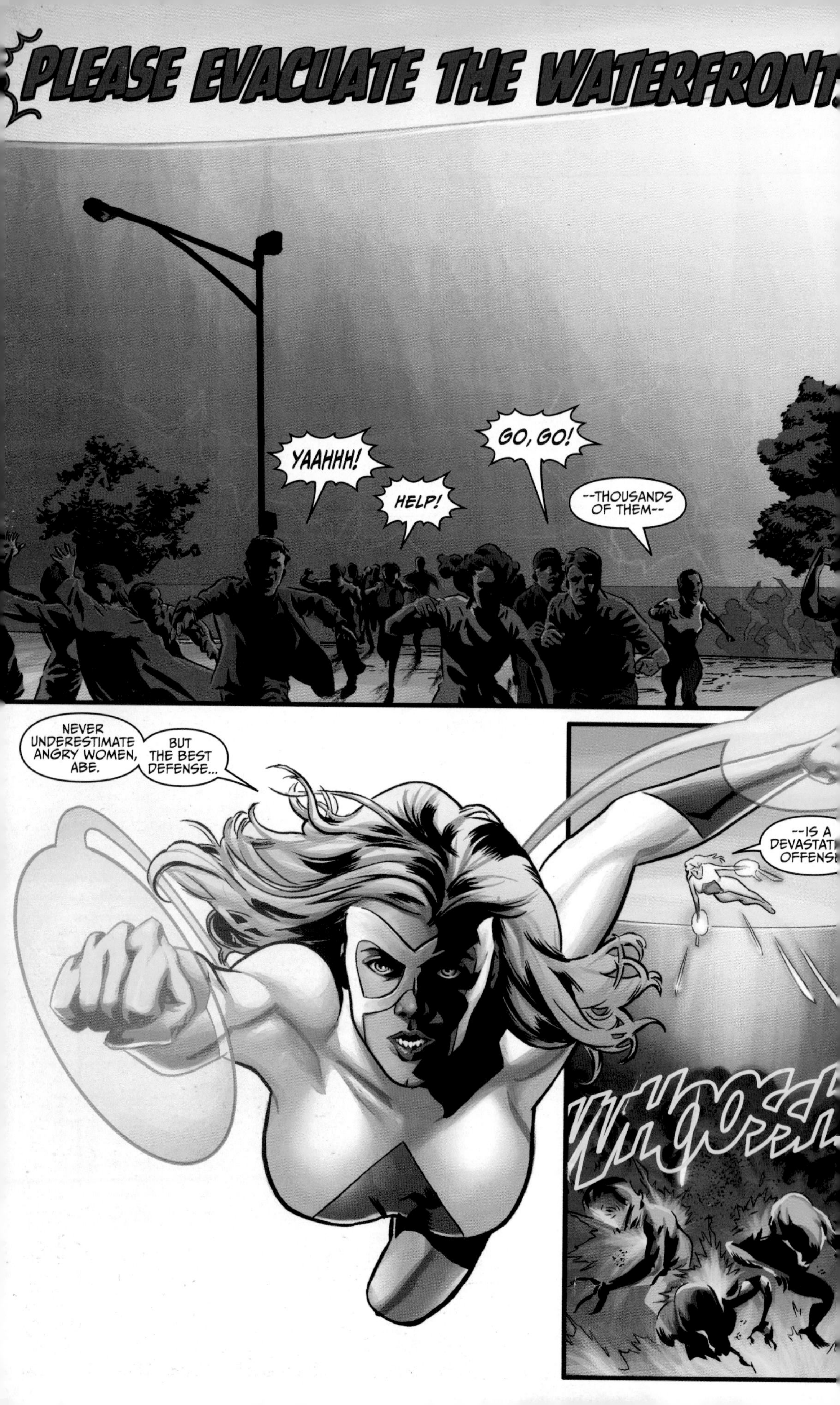

PLEASE EVACUATE THE WATERFRONT
YAAHHH!
HELP!
GO, GO!
--THOUSANDS OF THEM--
NEVER UNDERESTIMATE ANGRY WOMEN, ABE.
BUT THE BEST DEFENSE...

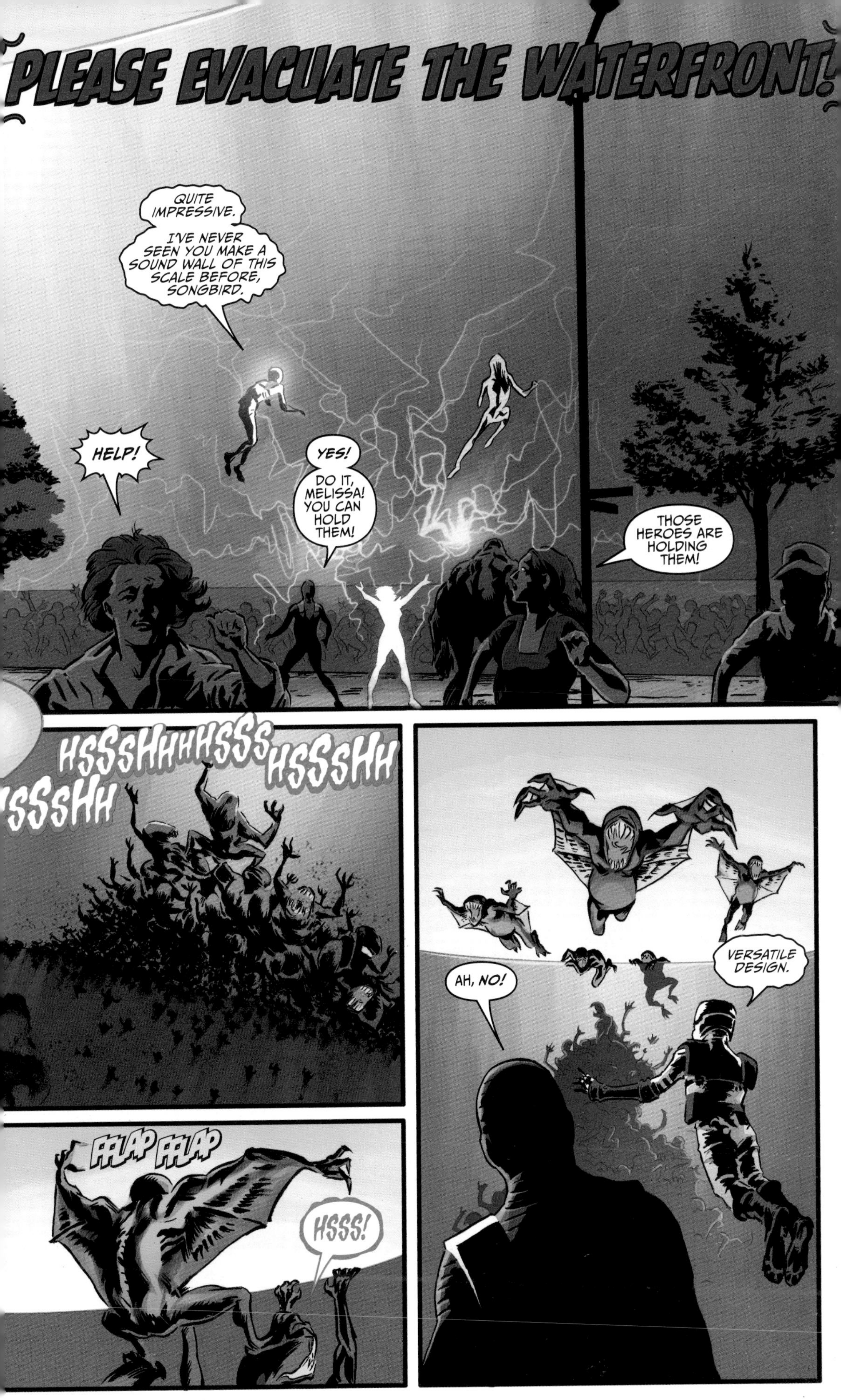
PLEASE EVACUATE THE WATERFRONT!
QUITE IMPRESSIVE.
I'VE NEVER SEEN YOU MAKE A SOUND WALL OF THIS SCALE BEFORE, SONGBIRD.
HELP!
YES!
DO IT, MELISSA! YOU CAN HOLD THEM!
THOSE HEROES ARE HOLDING THEM!
HSSSHHHHSSS HSSSHH
SSSSHH
FFLAP FFLAP
HSSS!
VERSATILE DESIGN.
AH, NO!

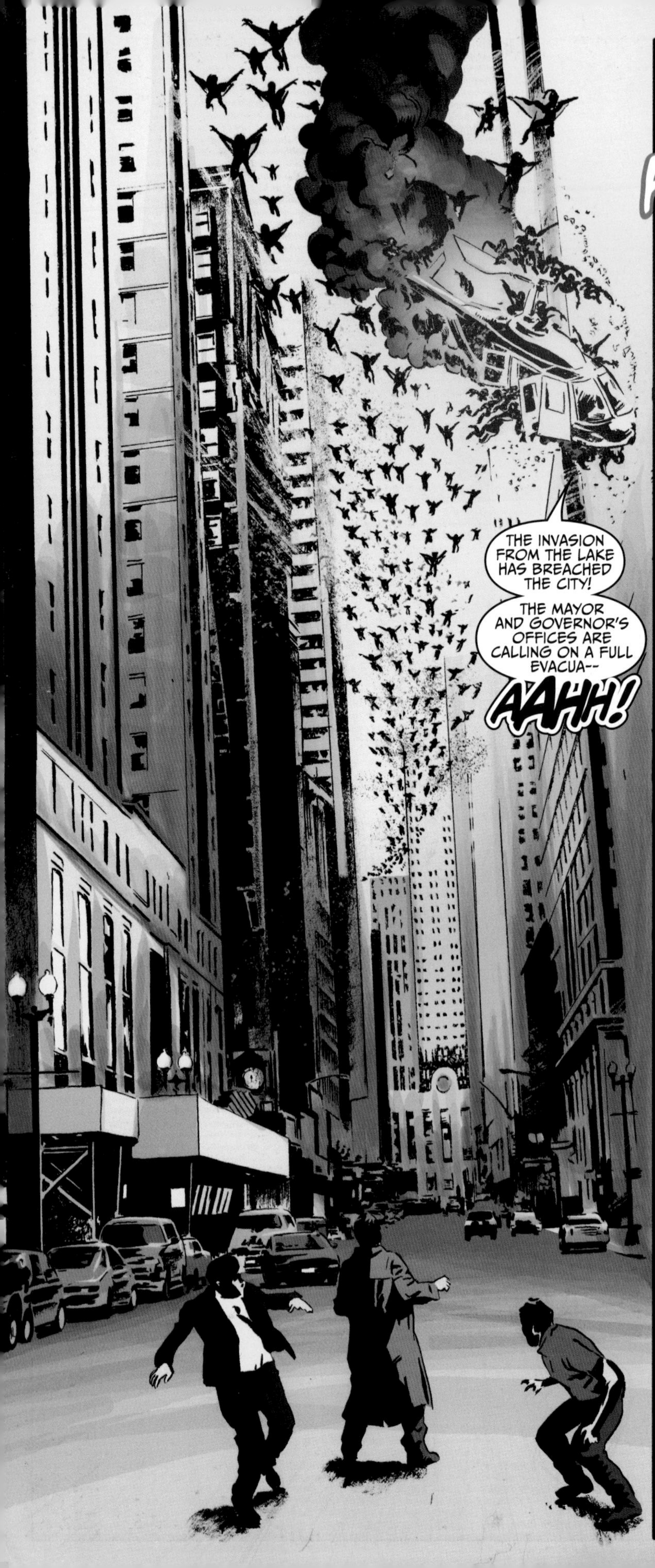
THE INVASION FROM THE LAKE HAS BREACHED THE CITY!
THE MAYOR AND GOVERNOR'S OFFICES ARE CALLING ON A FULL EVACUA--
AAHH!

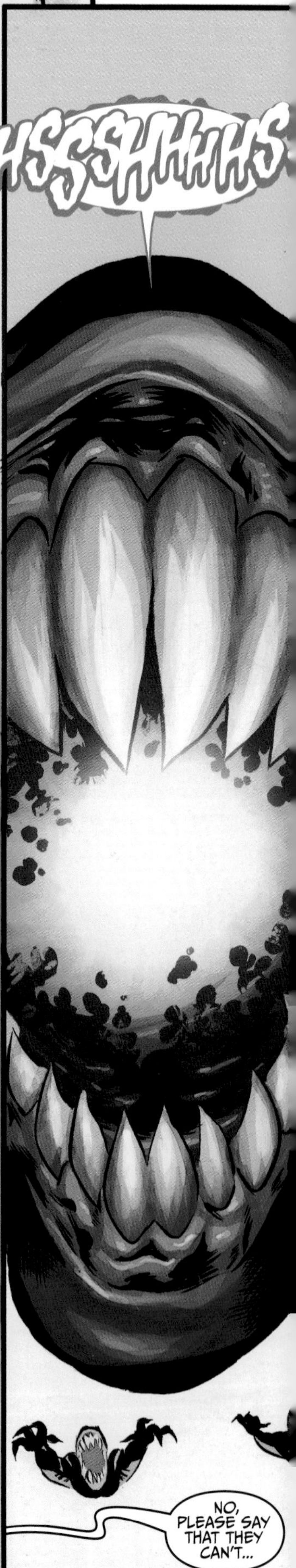
HSSSHHHHS
NO, PLEASE SAY THAT THEY CAN'T...

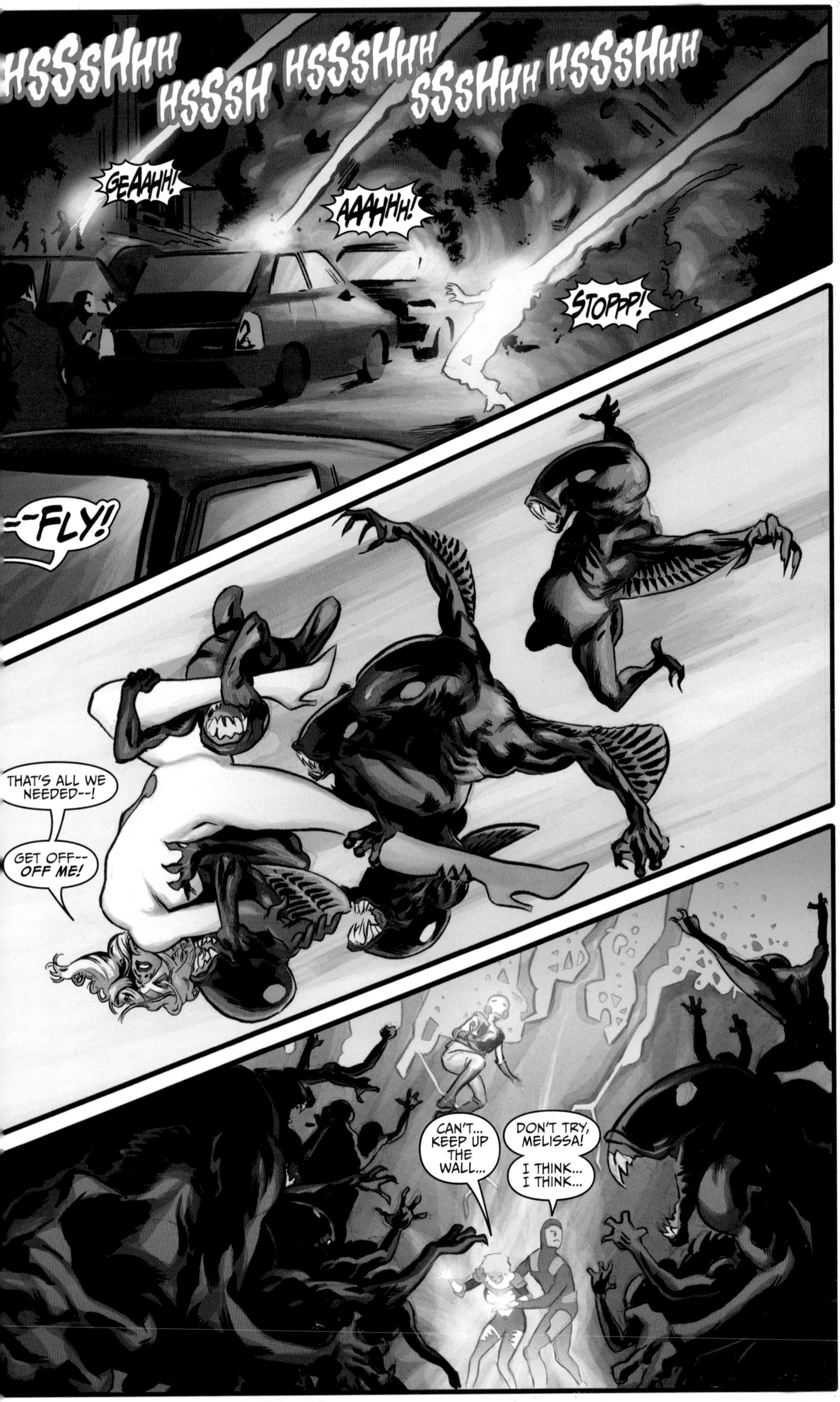
HSSSHHH
HSSSH HSSSHHH
SSSHHH HSSSHHH
GEAAHH!
AAAHHH!
STOPPP!
--FLY!
THAT'S ALL WE NEEDED--!
GET OFF-- OFF ME!
CAN'T... KEEP UP THE WALL...
DON'T TRY, MELISSA!
I THINK... I THINK...

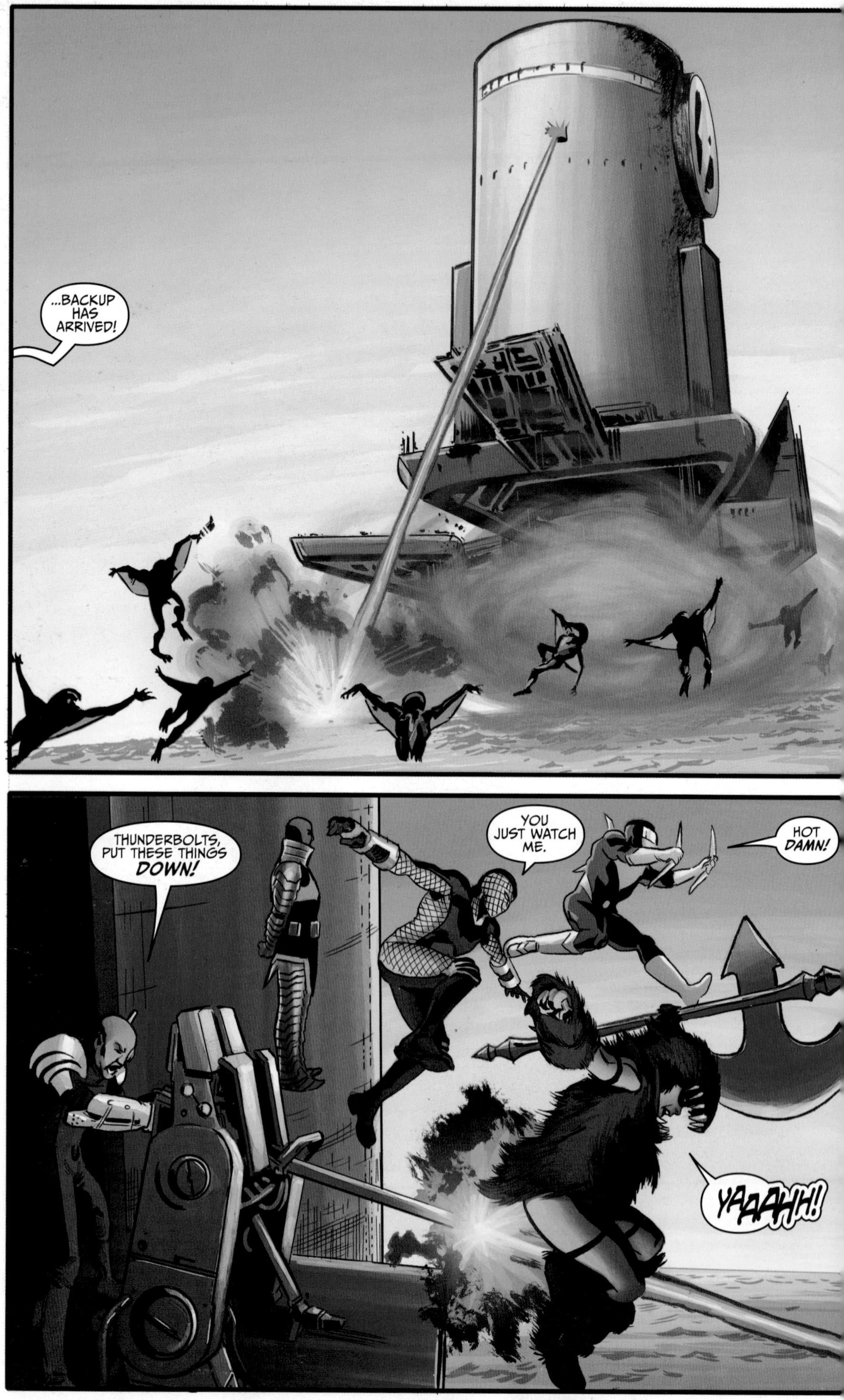
...BACKUP HAS ARRIVED!
THUNDERBOLTS, PUT THESE THINGS DOWN!
YOU JUST WATCH ME.
HOT DAMN!
YAAAHH!

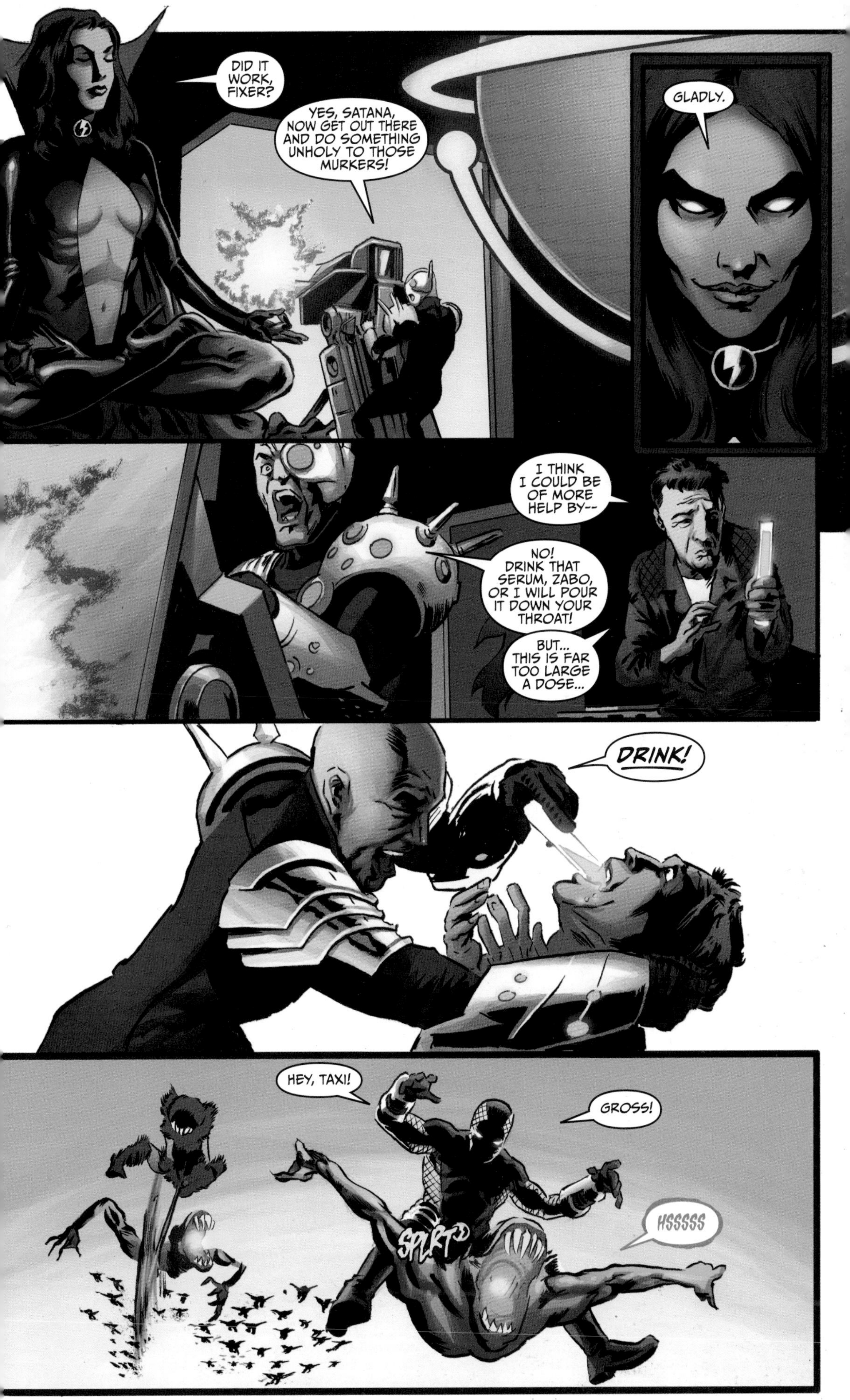
DID IT WORK, FIXER?
YES, SATANA, NOW GET OUT THERE AND DO SOMETHING UNHOLY TO THOSE MURKERS!
GLADLY.
I THINK I COULD BE OF MORE HELP BY--
NO! DRINK THAT SERUM, ZABO, OR I WILL POUR IT DOWN YOUR THROAT!
BUT... THIS IS FAR TOO LARGE A DOSE...
DRINK!
HEY, TAXI!
GROSS!
SPLRT
HSSSSS

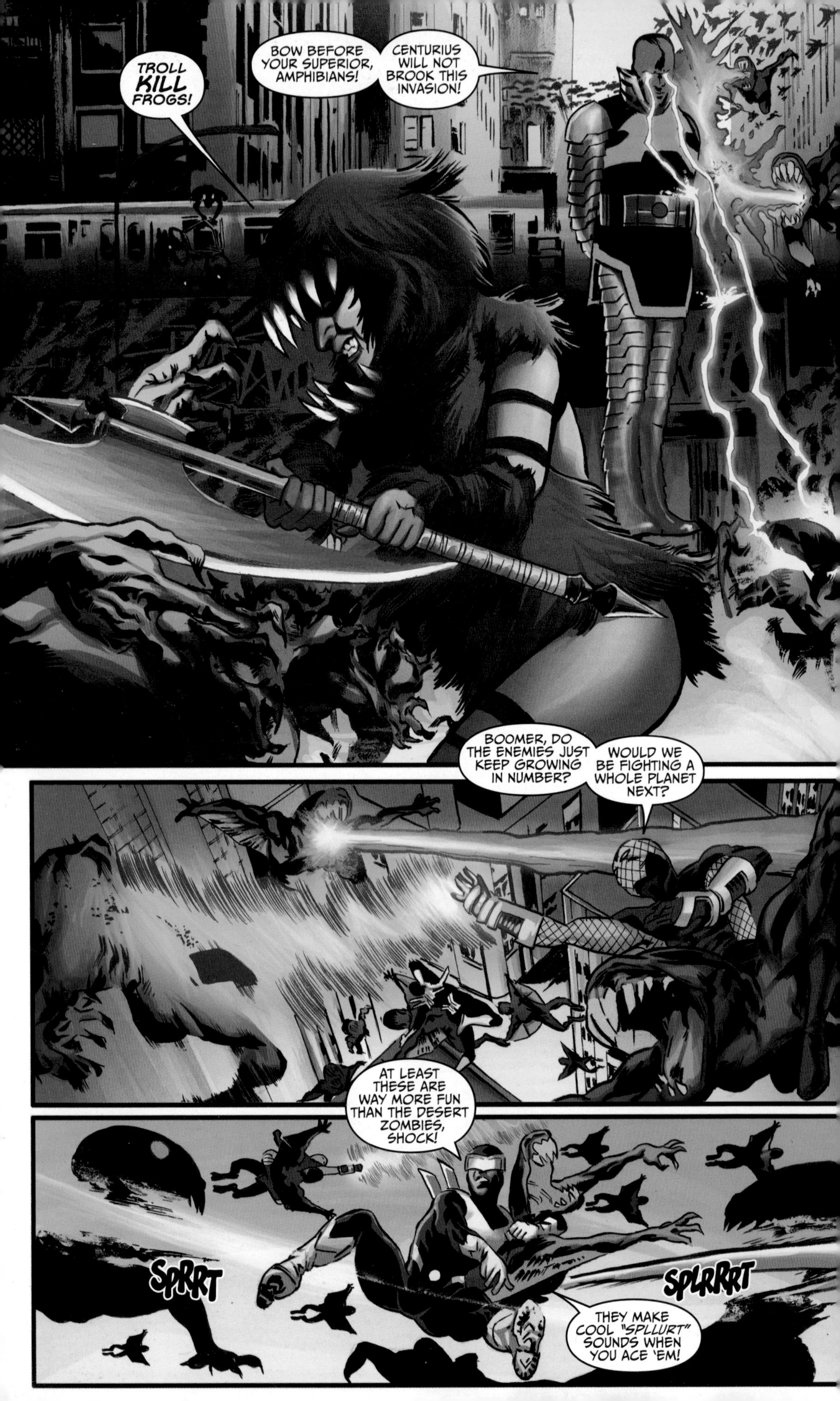
TROLL KILL FROGS!
BOW BEFORE YOUR SUPERIOR, AMPHIBIANS!
CENTURIUS WILL NOT BROOK THIS INVASION!
BOOMER, DO THE ENEMIES JUST KEEP GROWING IN NUMBER?
WOULD WE BE FIGHTING A WHOLE PLANET NEXT?
AT LEAST THESE ARE WAY MORE FUN THAN THE DESERT ZOMBIES, SHOCK!
SPRRT
SPLRRRT
THEY MAKE COOL "SPLLURT" SOUNDS WHEN YOU ACE 'EM!

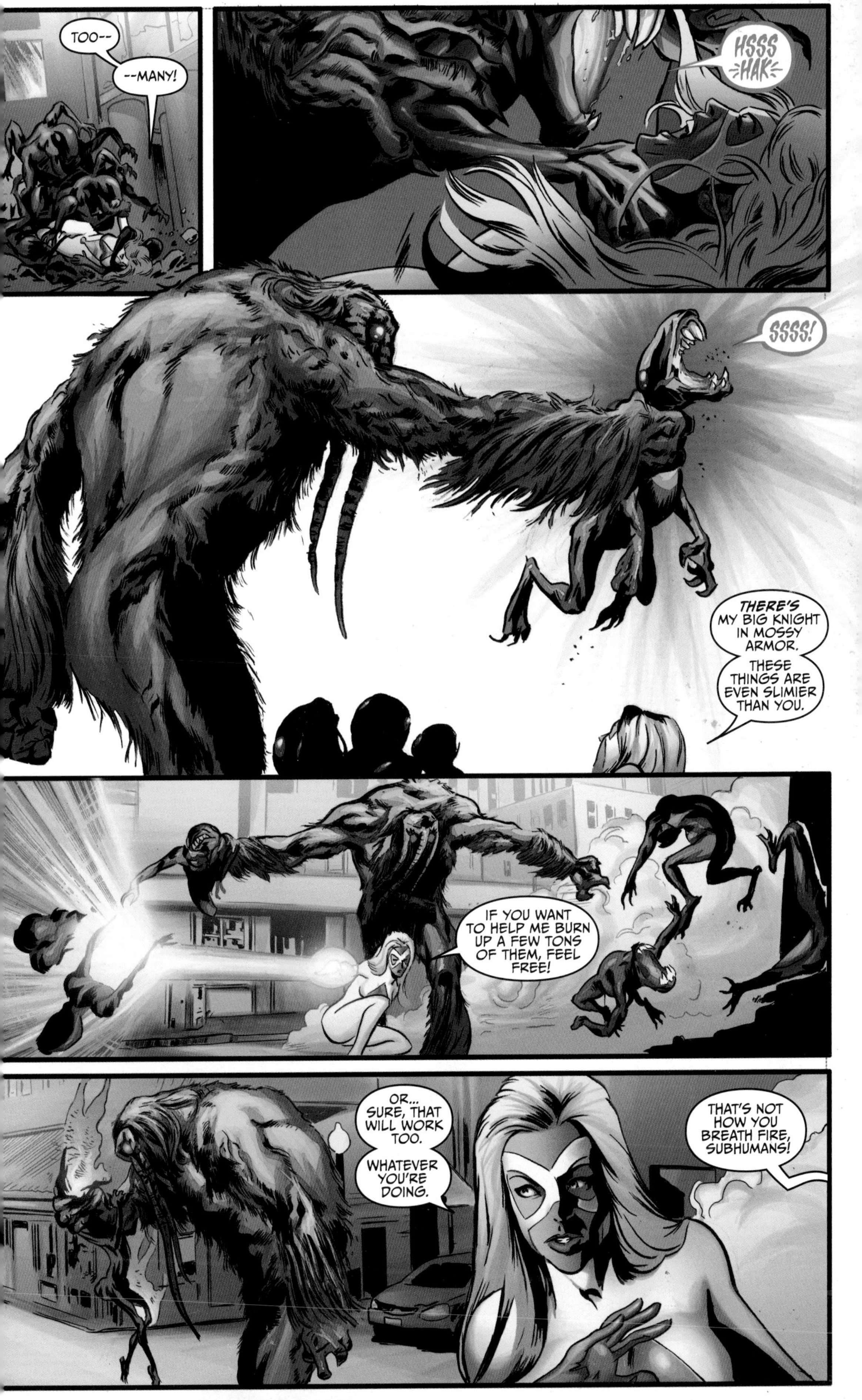
TOO--
--MANY!
HSSS HAK
SSSS!
THERE'S MY BIG KNIGHT IN MOSSY ARMOR.
THESE THINGS ARE EVEN SLIMIER THAN YOU.
IF YOU WANT TO HELP ME BURN UP A FEW TONS OF THEM, FEEL FREE!
OR... SURE, THAT WILL WORK TOO.
WHATEVER YOU'RE DOING.
THAT'S NOT HOW YOU BREATH FIRE, SUBHUMANS!

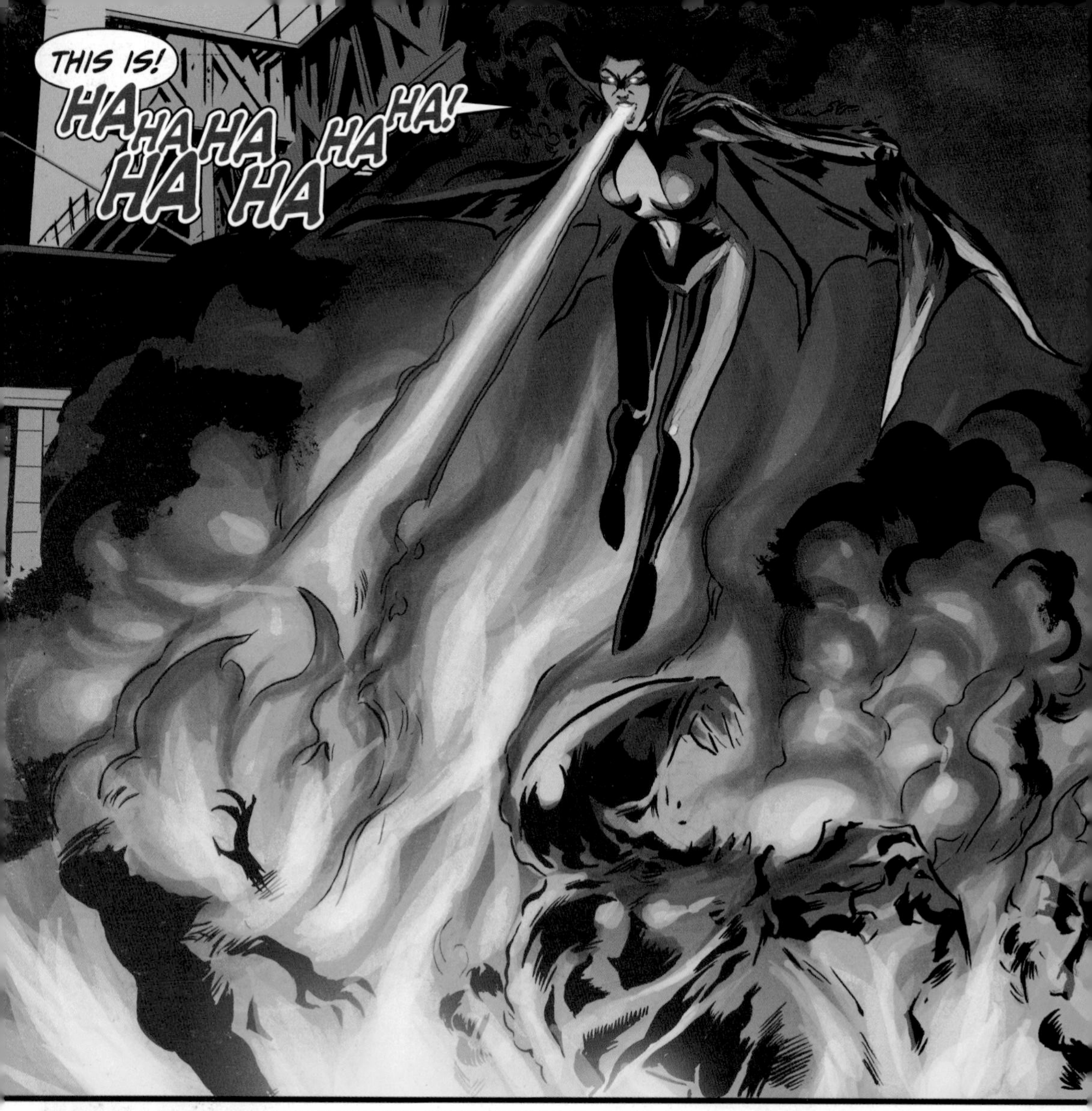
THIS IS!
HA HA HA HA HA HA HA HA!
HA HA

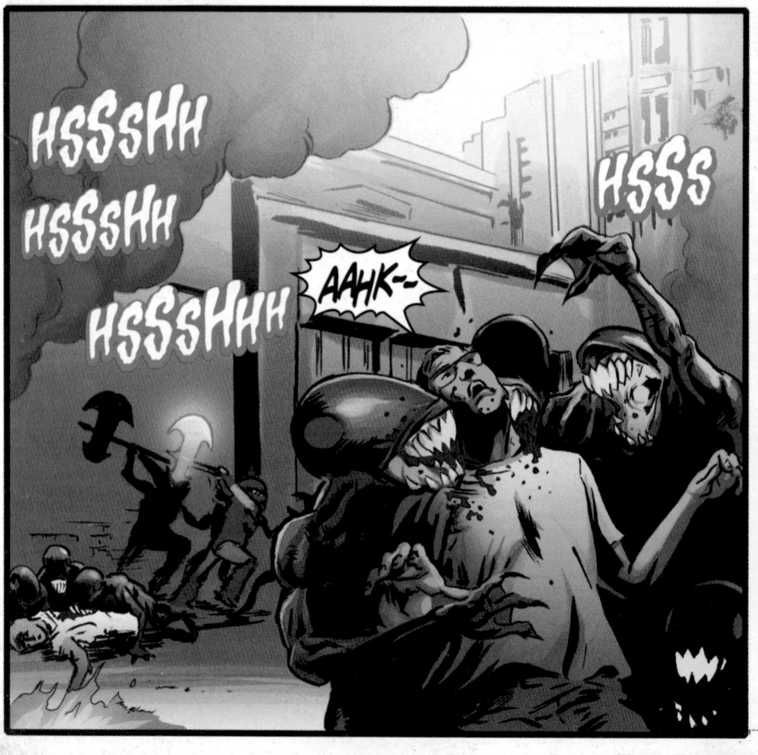
HSSSHH
HSSSHH
HSSSHHH
HSSS
AAHK--

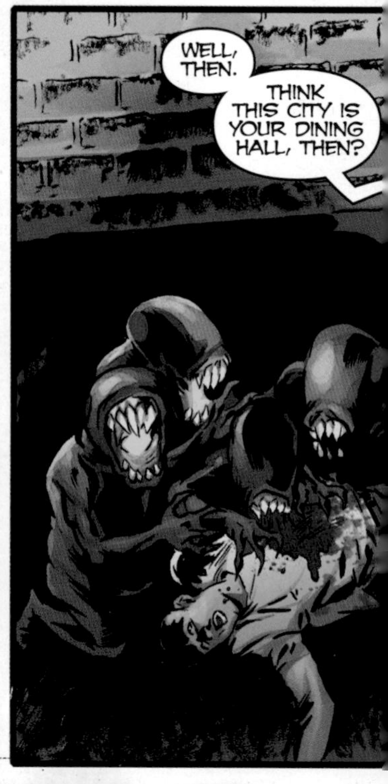
WELL, THEN.
THINK THIS CITY IS YOUR DINING HALL, THEN?

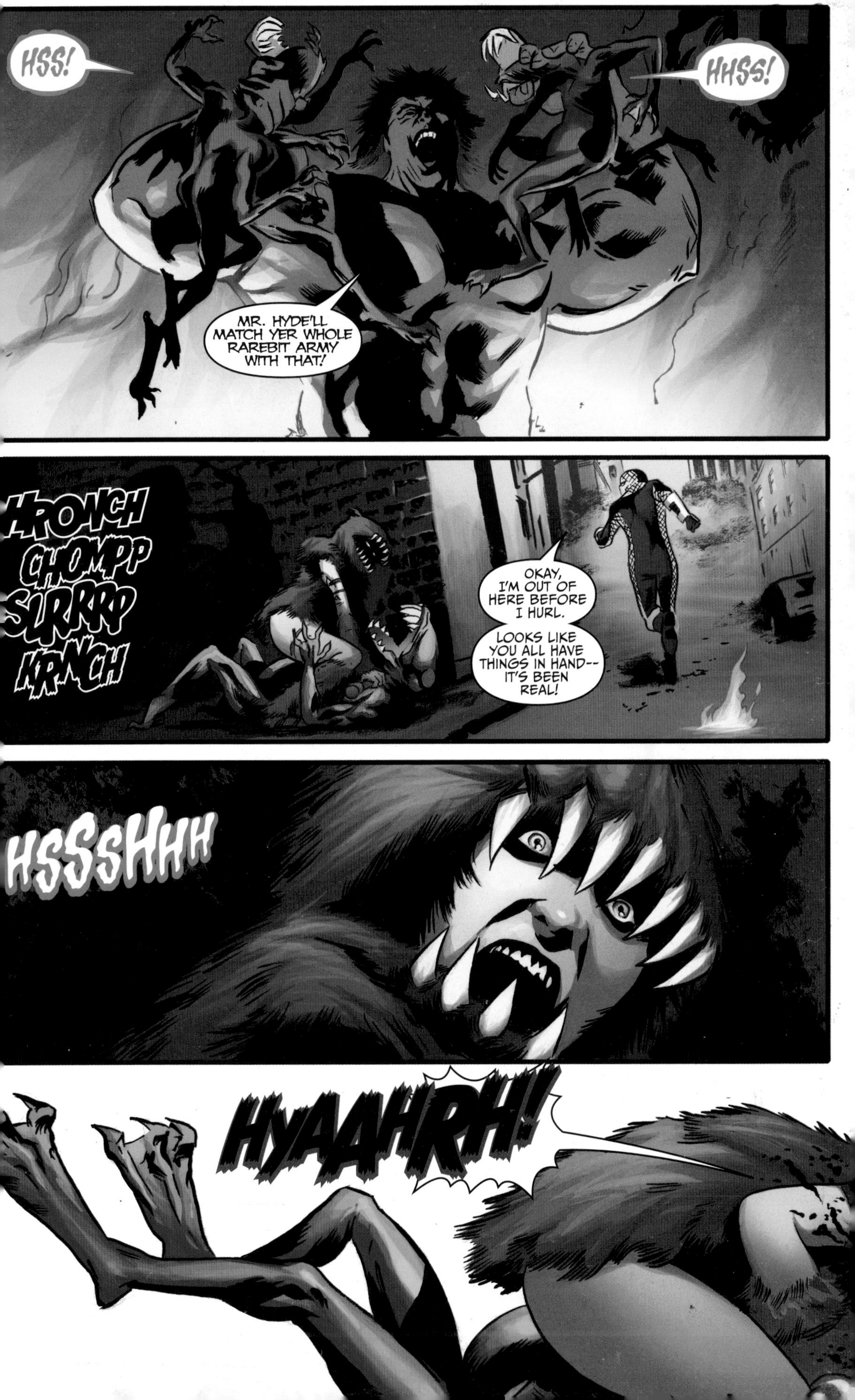
HSS!
HHSS!
MR. HYDE'LL MATCH YER WHOLE RAREBIT ARMY WITH THAT!
HRONCH CHOMPP SLRRRP KRNCH
OKAY, I'M OUT OF HERE BEFORE I HURL.
LOOKS LIKE YOU ALL HAVE THINGS IN HAND-- IT'S BEEN REAL!
HSSSHHH
HYAAHRH!

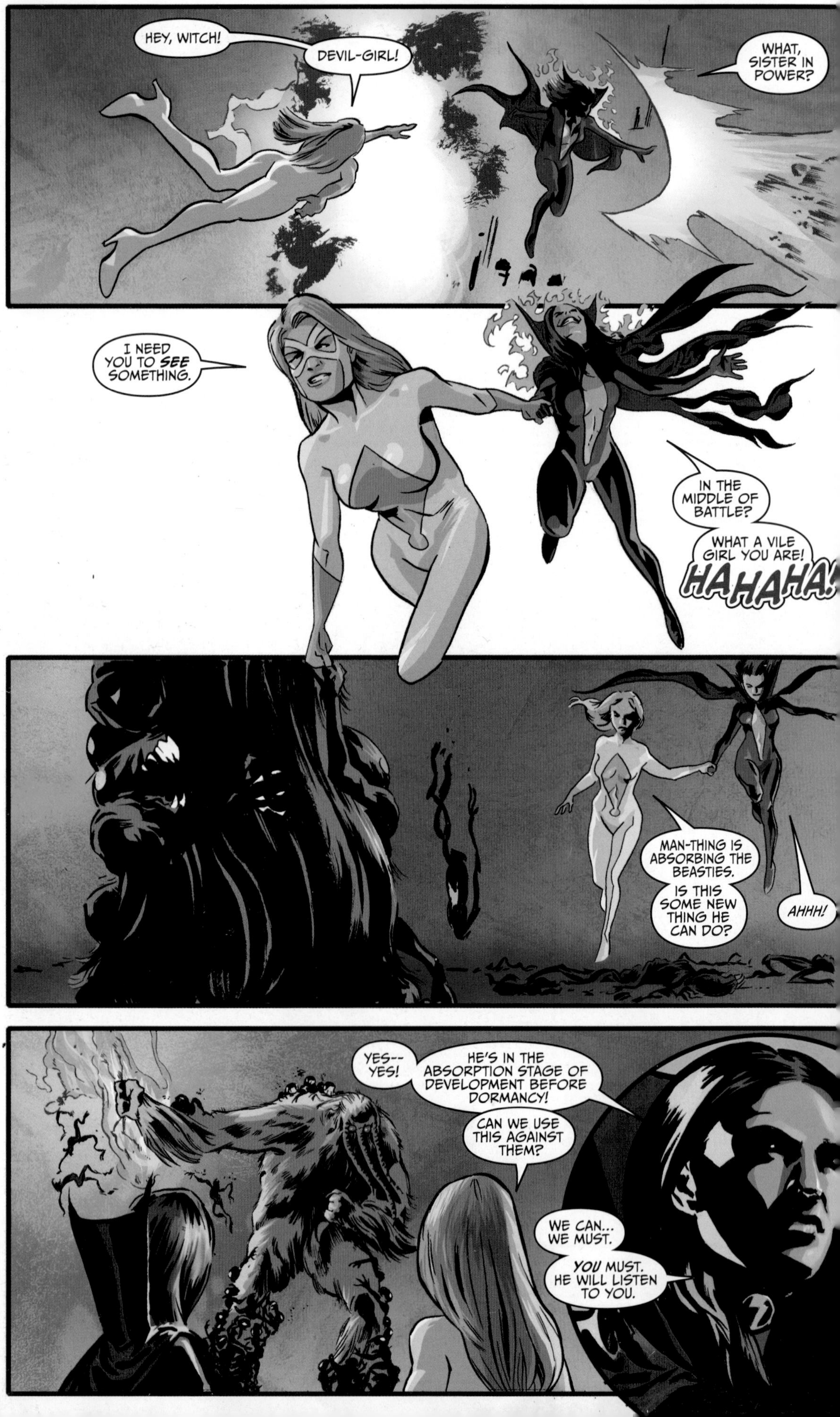
HEY, WITCH!
DEVIL-GIRL!
WHAT, SISTER IN POWER?
I NEED YOU TO SEE SOMETHING.
IN THE MIDDLE OF BATTLE?
WHAT A VILE GIRL YOU ARE!
HAHAHA!
MAN-THING IS ABSORBING THE BEASTIES.
IS THIS SOME NEW THING HE CAN DO?
AHHH!
YES-- YES!
HE'S IN THE ABSORPTION STAGE OF DEVELOPMENT BEFORE DORMANCY!
CAN WE USE THIS AGAINST THEM?
WE CAN... WE MUST.
YOU MUST. HE WILL LISTEN TO YOU.

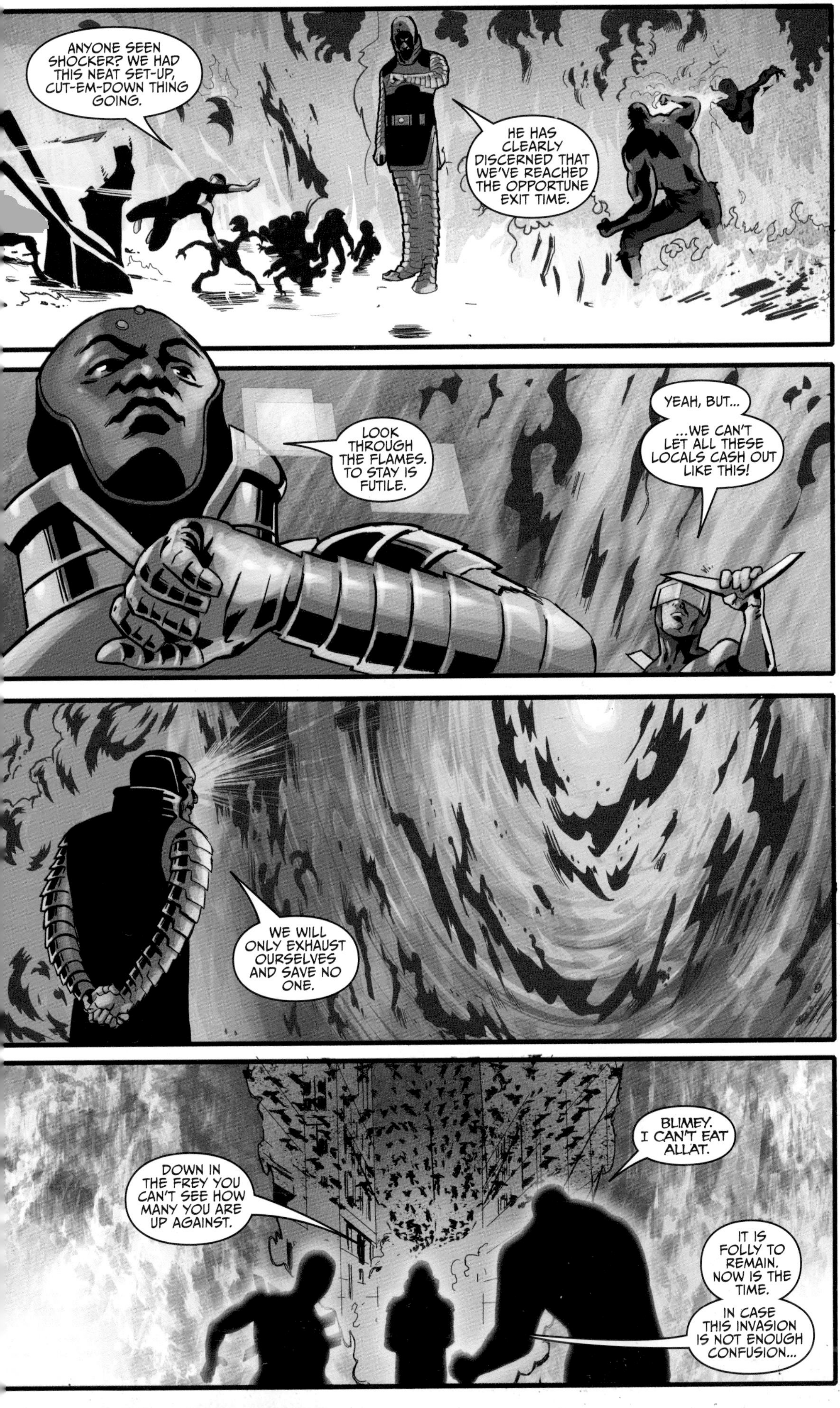
ANYONE SEEN SHOCKER? WE HAD THIS NEAT SET-UP, CUT-EM-DOWN THING GOING.
HE HAS CLEARLY DISCERNED THAT WE'VE REACHED THE OPPORTUNE EXIT TIME.
LOOK THROUGH THE FLAMES. TO STAY IS FUTILE.
YEAH, BUT...
...WE CAN'T LET ALL THESE LOCALS CASH OUT LIKE THIS!
WE WILL ONLY EXHAUST OURSELVES AND SAVE NO ONE.
DOWN IN THE FREY YOU CAN'T SEE HOW MANY YOU ARE UP AGAINST.
BLIMEY. I CAN'T EAT ALLAT.
IT IS FOLLY TO REMAIN. NOW IS THE TIME.
IN CASE THIS INVASION IS NOT ENOUGH CONFUSION...

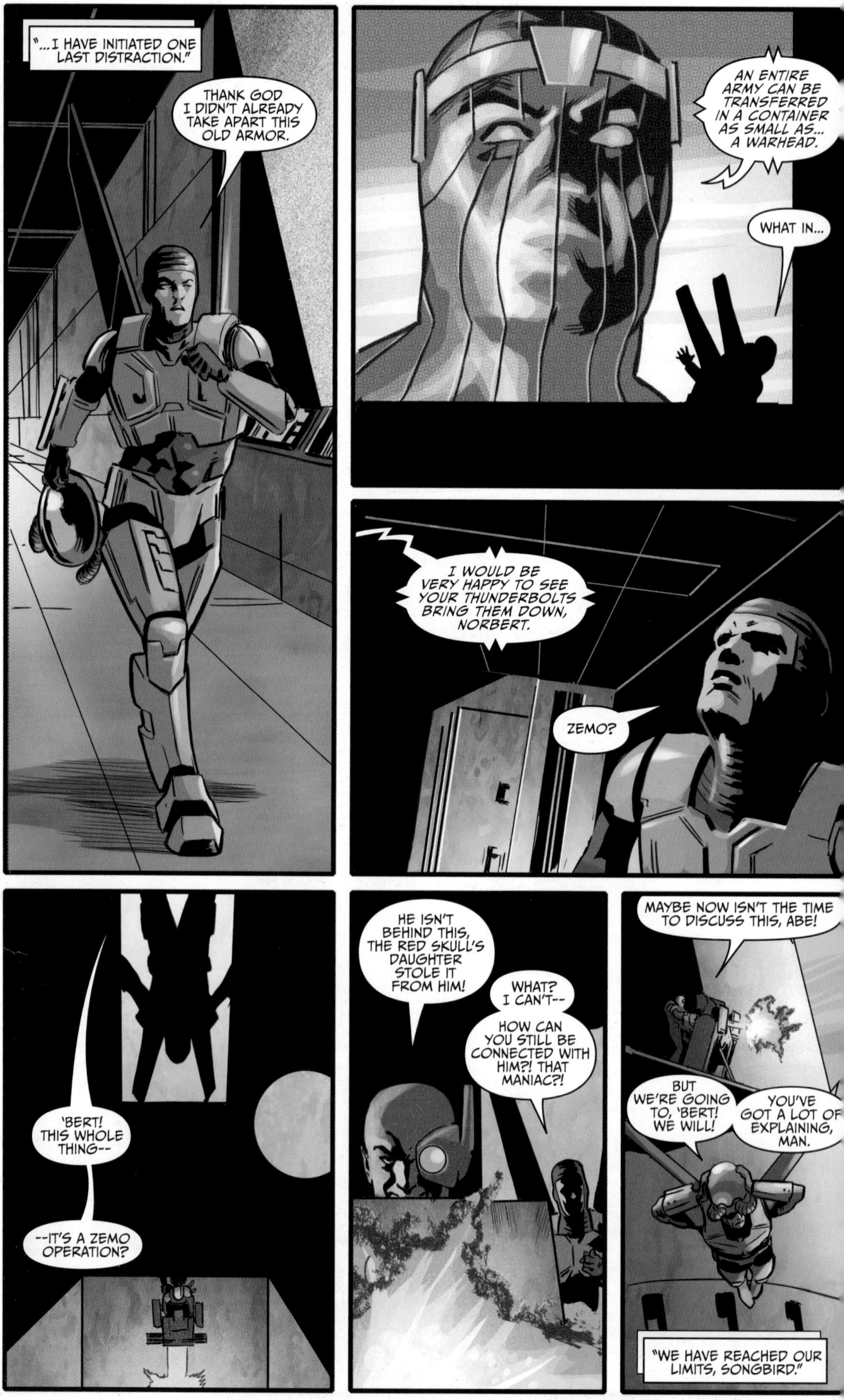
"...I HAVE INITIATED ONE LAST DISTRACTION."
THANK GOD I DIDN'T ALREADY TAKE APART THIS OLD ARMOR.
AN ENTIRE ARMY CAN BE TRANSFERRED IN A CONTAINER AS SMALL AS... A WARHEAD.
WHAT IN...
I WOULD BE VERY HAPPY TO SEE YOUR THUNDERBOLTS BRING THEM DOWN, NORBERT.
ZEMO?
'BERT! THIS WHOLE THING--
--IT'S A ZEMO OPERATION?
HE ISN'T BEHIND THIS, THE RED SKULL'S DAUGHTER STOLE IT FROM HIM!
WHAT? I CAN'T--
HOW CAN YOU STILL BE CONNECTED WITH HIM?! THAT MANIAC?!
MAYBE NOW ISN'T THE TIME TO DISCUSS THIS, ABE!
BUT WE'RE GOING TO, 'BERT! WE WILL!
YOU'VE GOT A LOT OF EXPLAINING, MAN.
"WE HAVE REACHED OUR LIMITS, SONGBIRD."

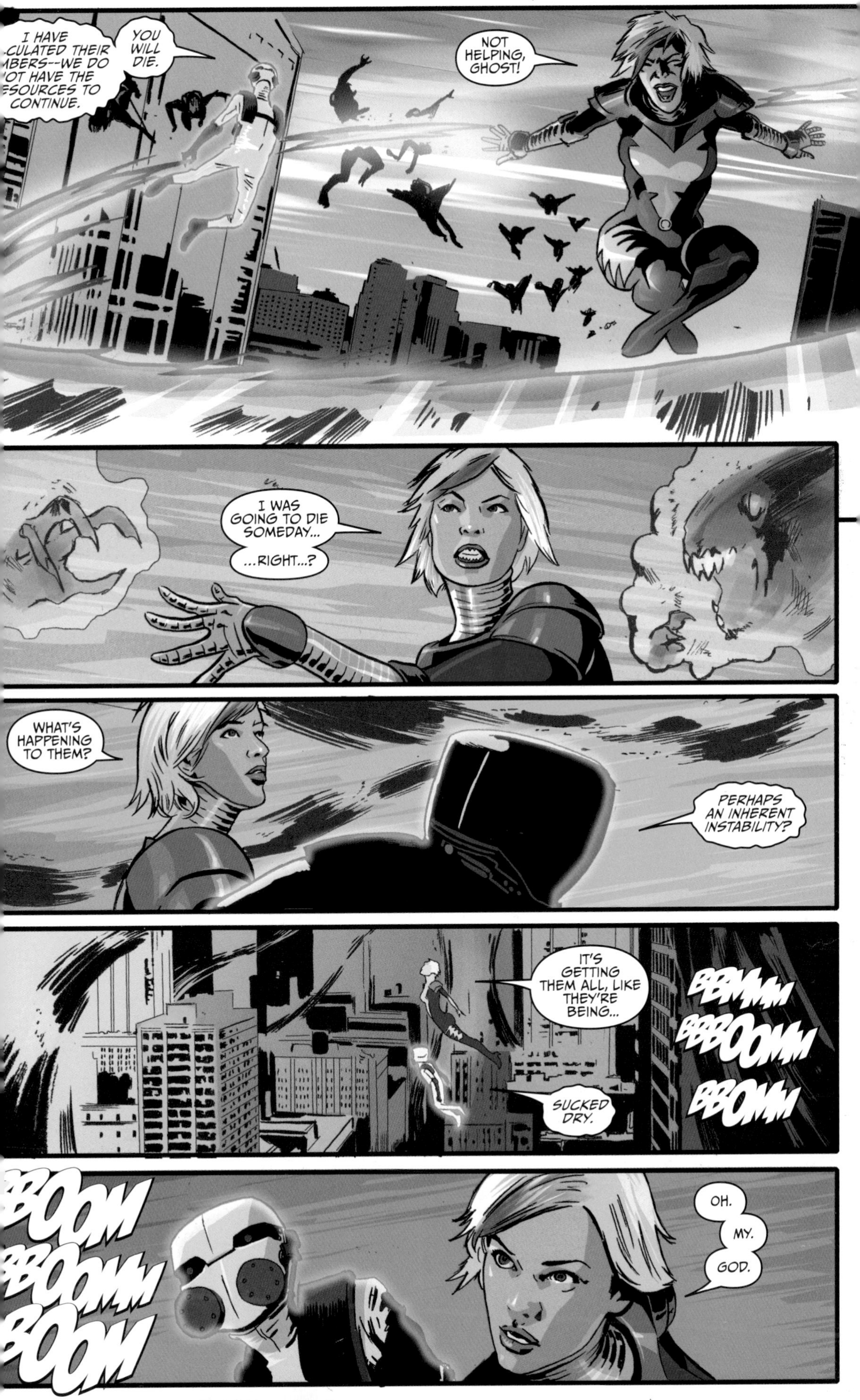

I HAVE
CULATED THEIR
MBERS--WE DO
OT HAVE THE
ESOURCES TO
CONTINUE.
YOU WILL DIE.
NOT HELPING, GHOST!
I WAS GOING TO DIE SOMEDAY...
...RIGHT...?
WHAT'S HAPPENING TO THEM?
PERHAPS AN INHERENT INSTABILITY?
IT'S GETTING THEM ALL, LIKE THEY'RE BEING...
SUCKED DRY.
BBMMM
BBBOOMM
BBOMM
BOOM
BOOMM
BOOM
OH.
MY.
GOD.

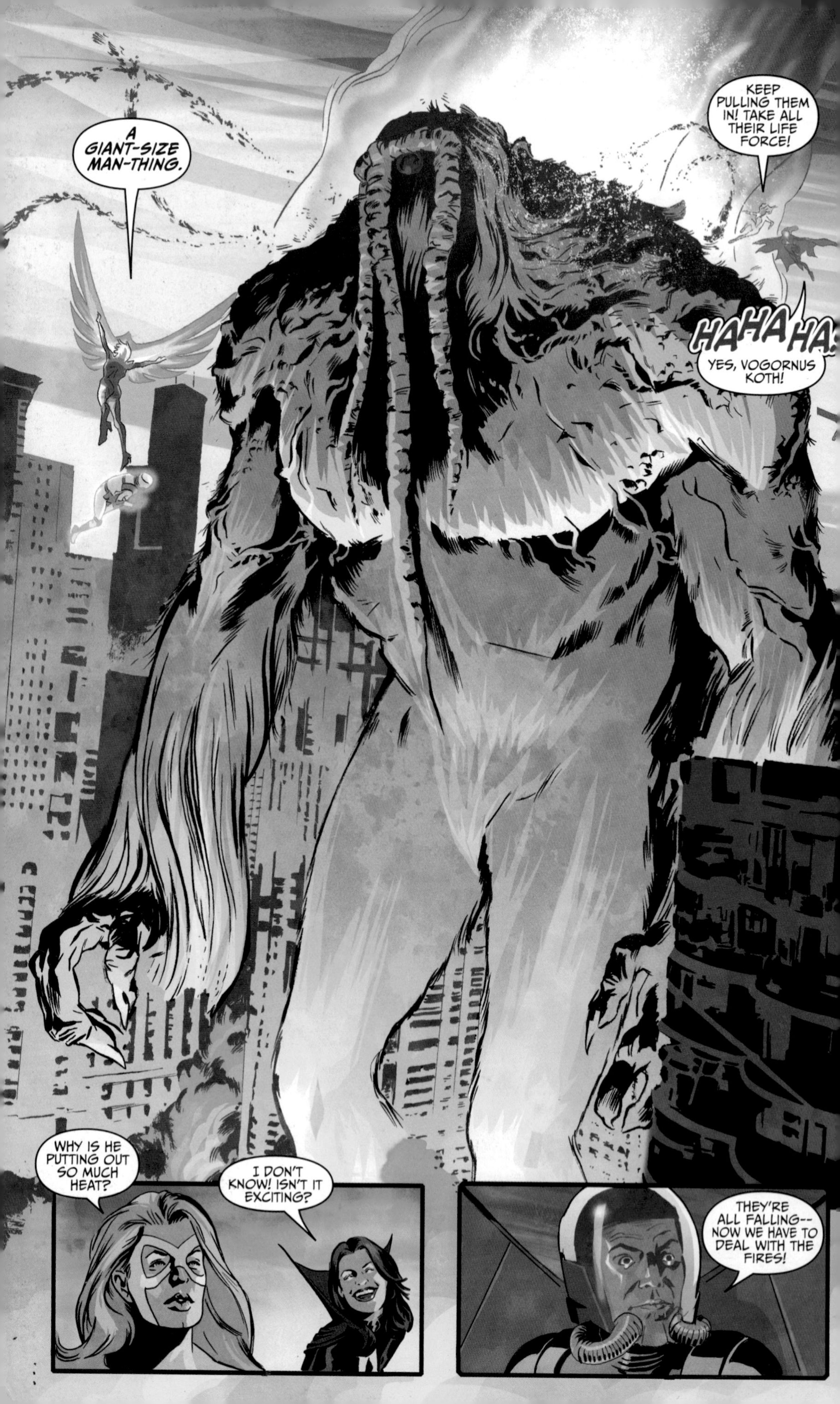
A GIANT-SIZE MAN-THING.
KEEP PULLING THEM IN! TAKE ALL THEIR LIFE FORCE!
HAHAHA! YES, VOGORNUS KOTH!
WHY IS HE PUTTING OUT SO MUCH HEAT?
I DON'T KNOW! ISN'T IT EXCITING?
THEY'RE ALL FALLING-- NOW WE HAVE TO DEAL WITH THE FIRES!

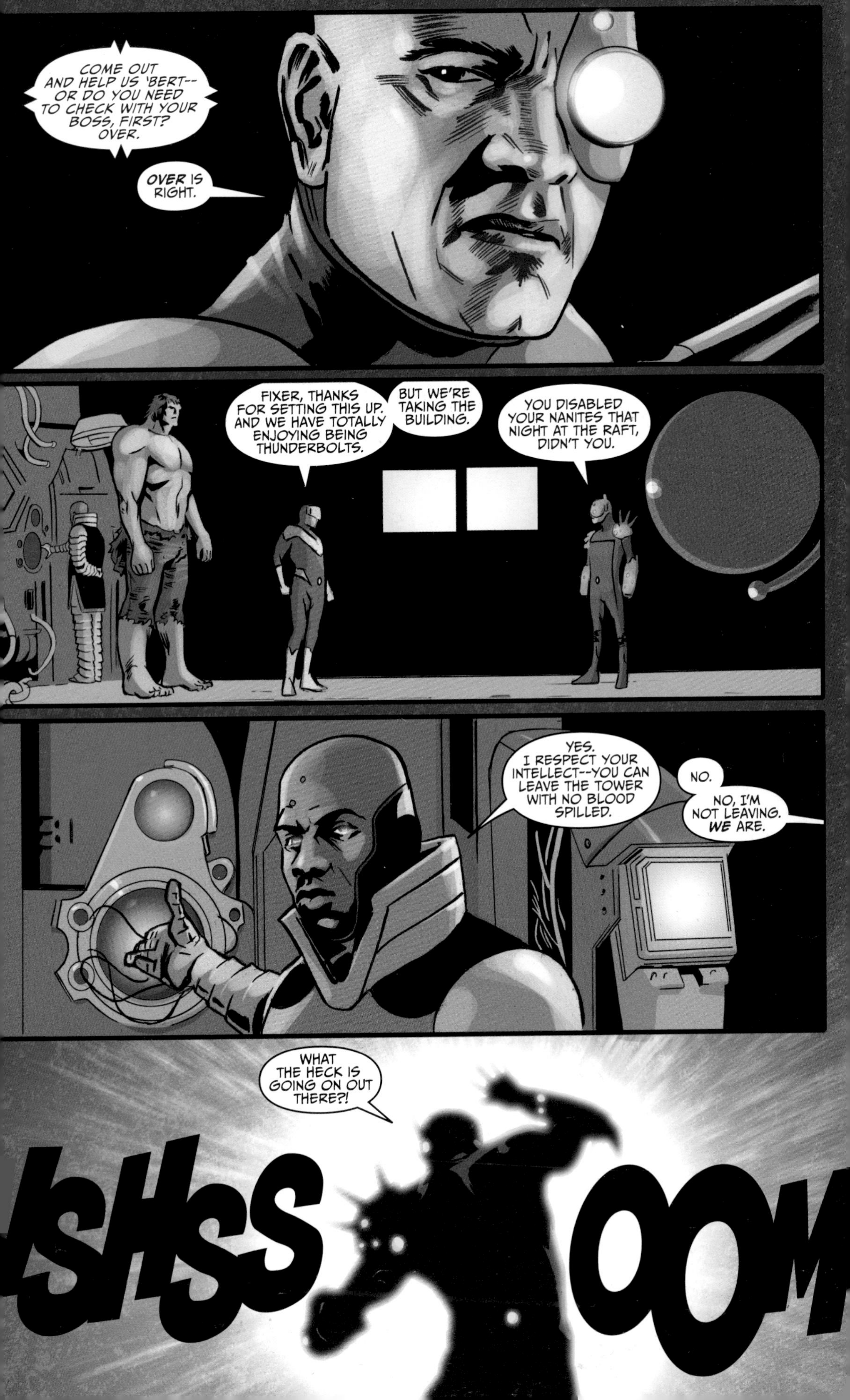

COME OUT AND HELP US 'BERT-- OR DO YOU NEED TO CHECK WITH YOUR BOSS, FIRST? OVER.
OVER IS RIGHT.
FIXER, THANKS FOR SETTING THIS UP. AND WE HAVE TOTALLY ENJOYING BEING THUNDERBOLTS.
BUT WE'RE TAKING THE BUILDING.
YOU DISABLED YOUR NANITES THAT NIGHT AT THE RAFT, DIDN'T YOU.
YES. I RESPECT YOUR INTELLECT--YOU CAN LEAVE THE TOWER WITH NO BLOOD SPILLED.
NO.
NO, I'M NOT LEAVING. WE ARE.
WHAT THE HECK IS GOING ON OUT THERE?!
SHSS
OOM

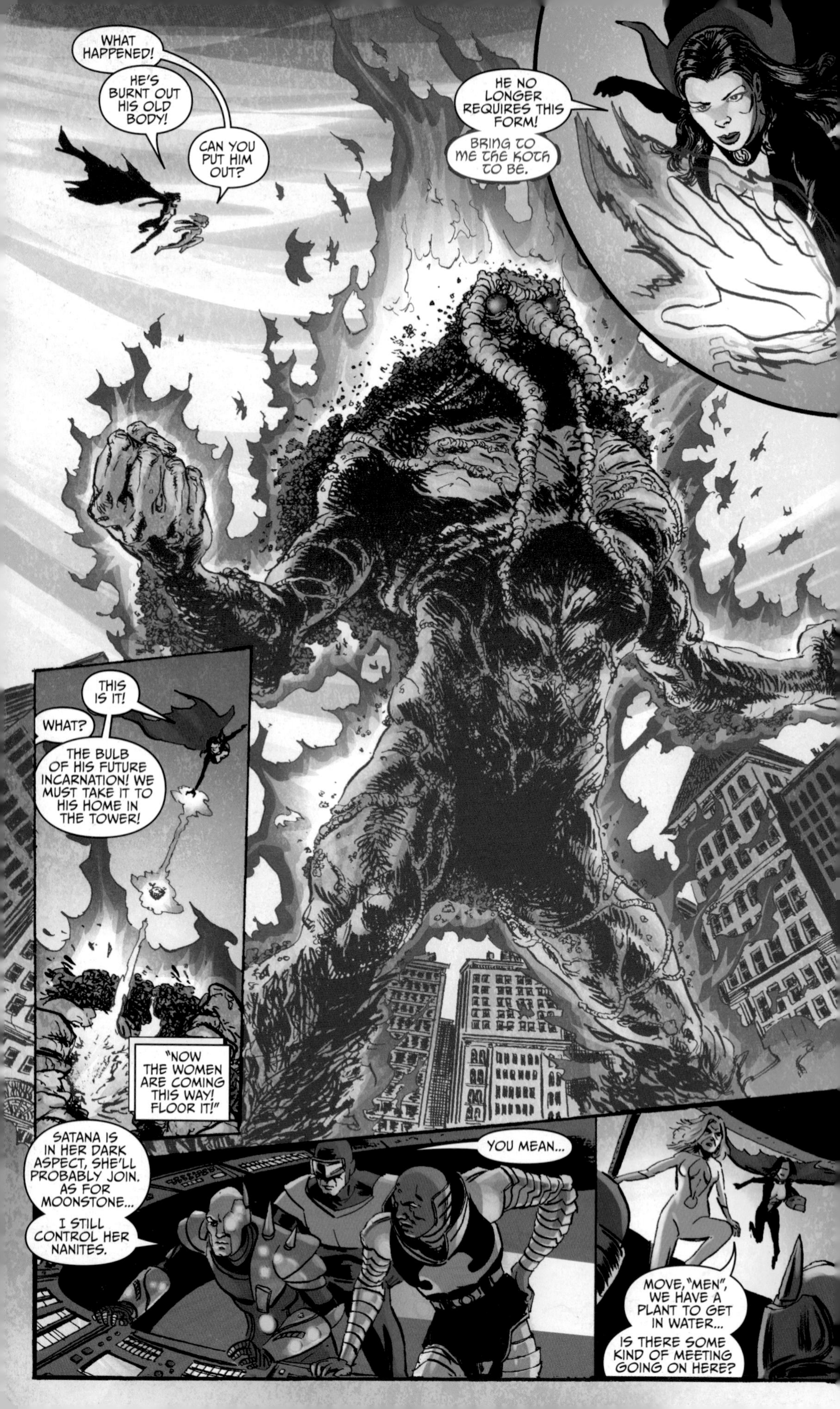
WHAT HAPPENED!
HE'S BURNT OUT HIS OLD BODY!
CAN YOU PUT HIM OUT?
HE NO LONGER REQUIRES THIS FORM!
BRING TO ME THE KOTH TO BE.
THIS IS IT!
WHAT?
THE BULB OF HIS FUTURE INCARNATION! WE MUST TAKE IT TO HIS HOME IN THE TOWER!
"NOW THE WOMEN ARE COMING THIS WAY! FLOOR IT!"
SATANA IS IN HER DARK ASPECT, SHE'LL PROBABLY JOIN. AS FOR MOONSTONE...
I STILL CONTROL HER NANITES.
YOU MEAN...
MOVE, "MEN", WE HAVE A PLANT TO GET IN WATER...
IS THERE SOME KIND OF MEETING GOING ON HERE?

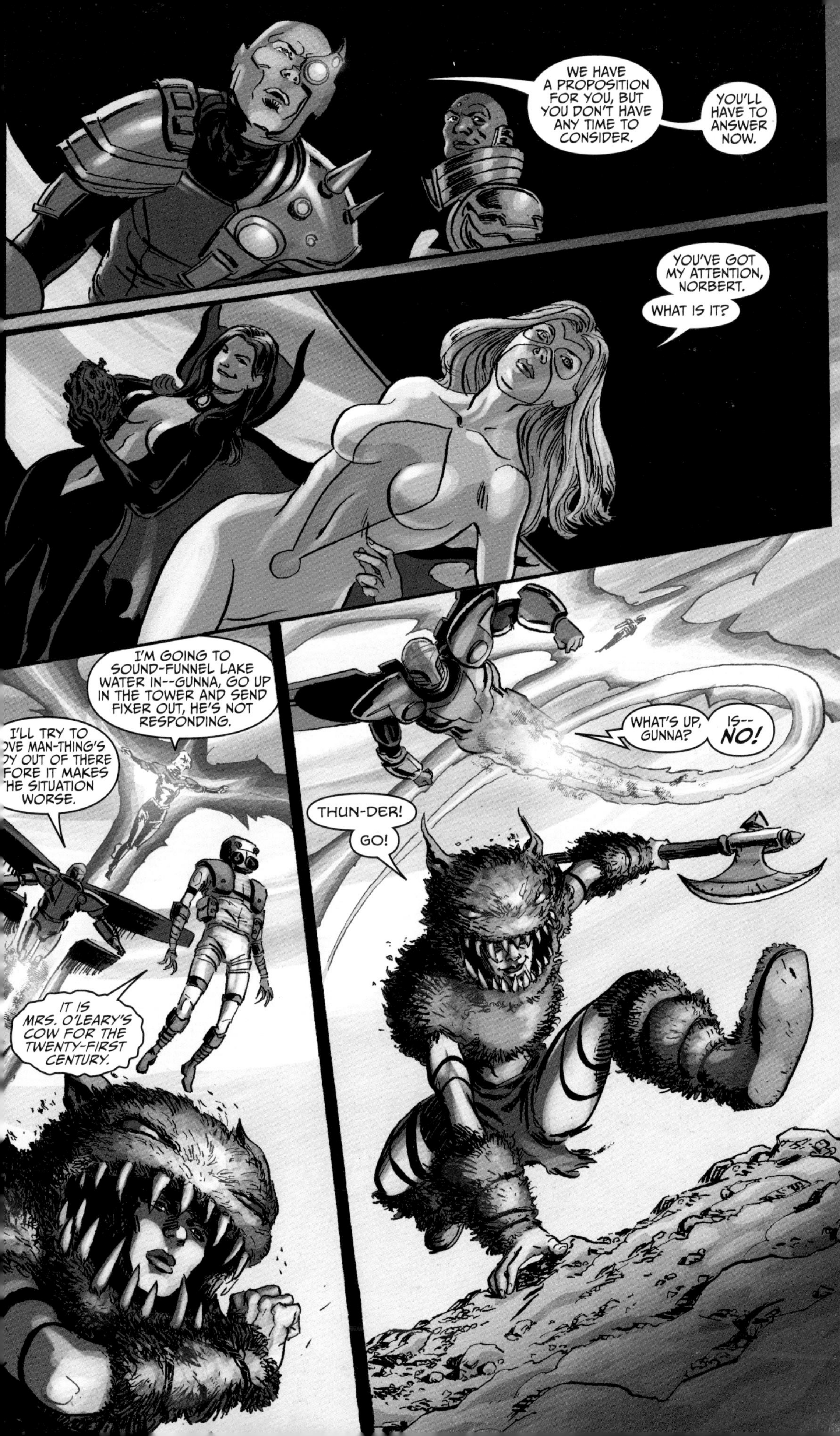
WE HAVE A PROPOSITION FOR YOU, BUT YOU DON'T HAVE ANY TIME TO CONSIDER.
YOU'LL HAVE TO ANSWER NOW.
YOU'VE GOT MY ATTENTION, NORBERT.
WHAT IS IT?
I'M GOING TO SOUND-FUNNEL LAKE WATER IN--GUNNA, GO UP IN THE TOWER AND SEND FIXER OUT, HE'S NOT RESPONDING.
I'LL TRY TO
FORE IT MAKES
THE SITUATION WORSE.
IT IS MRS. O'LEARY'S COW FOR THE TWENTY-FIRST CENTURY.
WHAT'S UP, GUNNA?
IS-- NO!
THUN-DER!
GO!

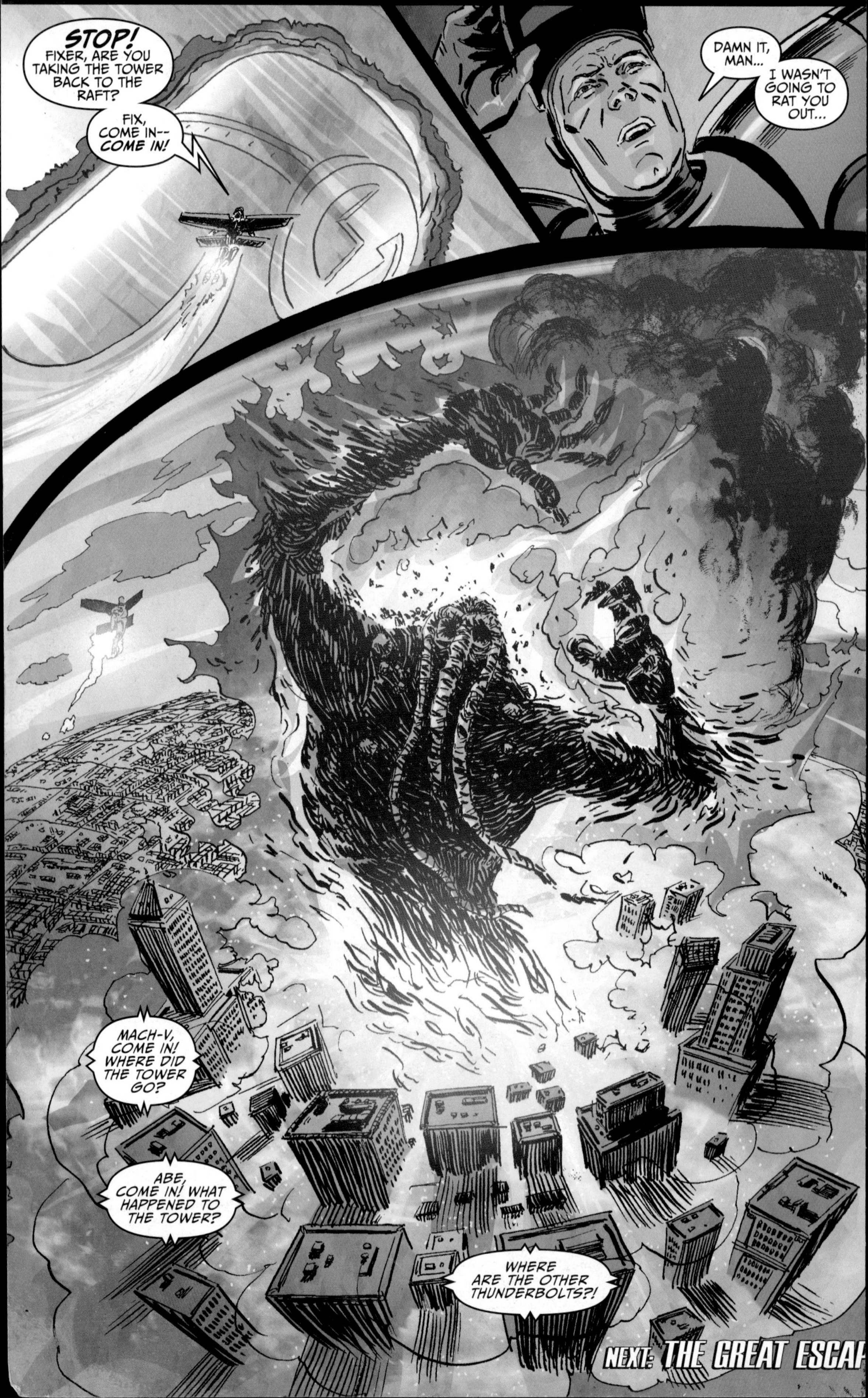
STOP! FIXER, ARE YOU TAKING THE TOWER BACK TO THE RAFT?
FIX, COME IN-- COME IN!
DAMN IT, MAN... I WASN'T GOING TO RAT YOU OUT...
MACH-V, COME IN! WHERE DID THE TOWER GO?
ABE, COME IN! WHAT HAPPENED TO THE TOWER?
WHERE ARE THE OTHER THUNDERBOLTS?!
NEXT: THE GREAT ESCAP

BULLPEN EXTRA!

THUNDERBOLTS CLASSIC!

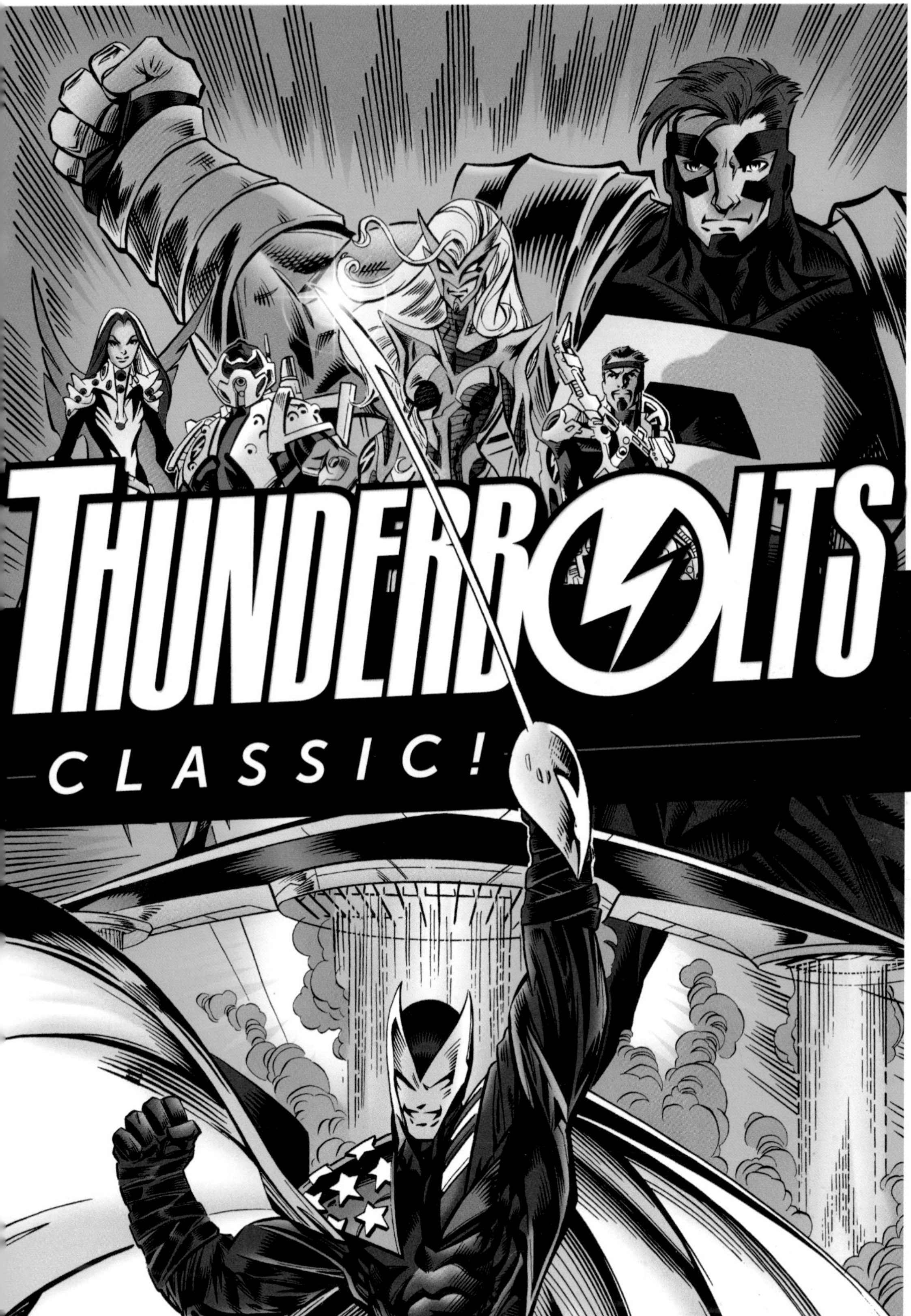

ORIGINAL THUNDERBOLTS ENSEMBLE FROM *THUNDERBOLTS #1*, ART BY MARK BAGLEY.

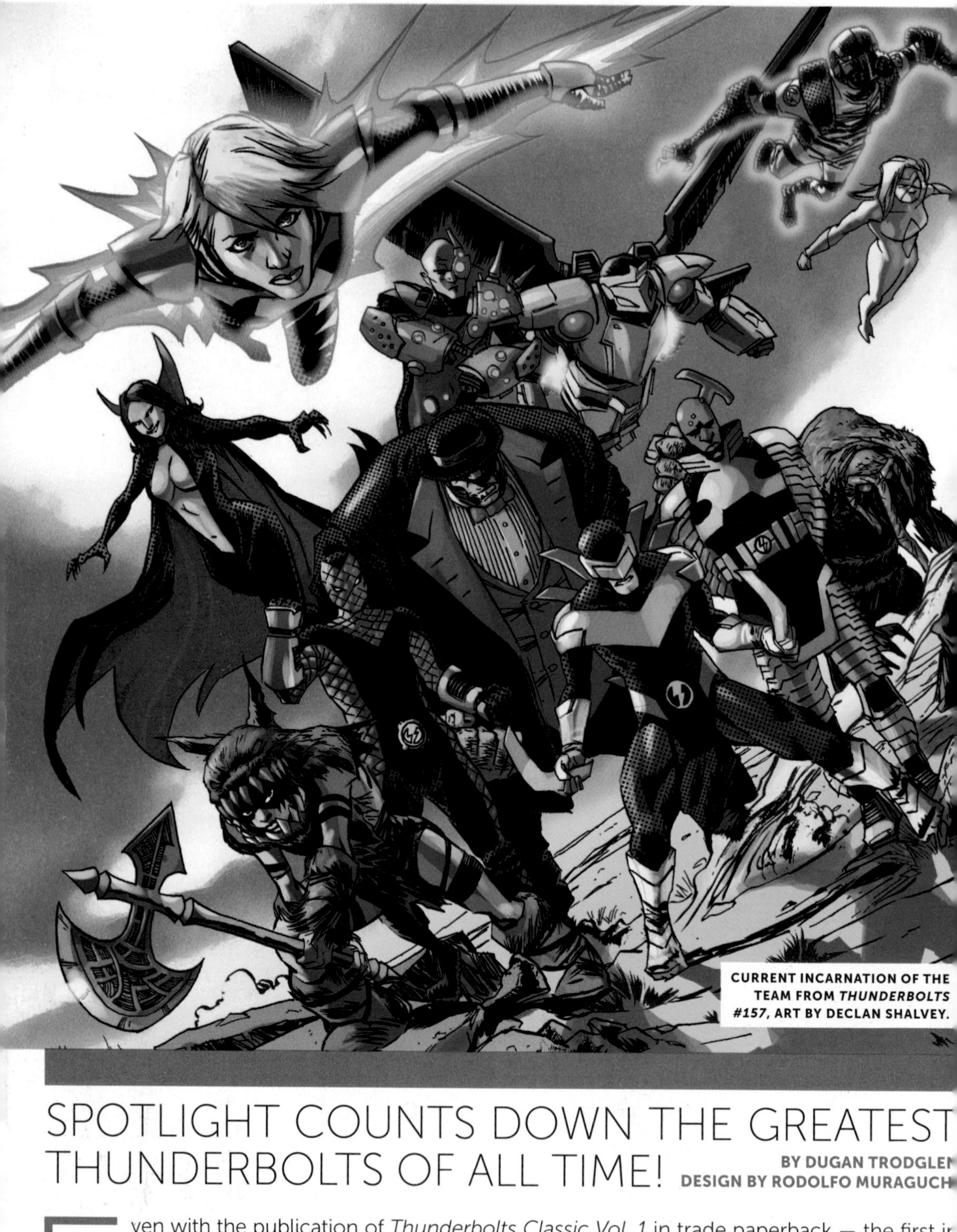

CURRENT INCARNATION OF THE TEAM FROM *THUNDERBOLTS* #157, ART BY DECLAN SHALVEY.

SPOTLIGHT COUNTS DOWN THE GREATEST THUNDERBOLTS OF ALL TIME!

BY DUGAN TRODGLE
DESIGN BY RODOLFO MURAGUCH

Even with the publication of *Thunderbolts Classic Vol. 1* in trade paperback — the first ir a series — it's hard to believe *Thunderbolts* has sailed past 150 issues. The last fifteer years have been a rough time for new concepts to find solid footing in the world o super-hero comics, but the T-Bolts are an exception to that trend. One of the book's secrets is that it has redefined itself several times, especially during the last few years But if there's one thing that has remained a constant, it's strong characters. The team has seer many members come and go since Kurt Busiek and Mark Bagley launched the series in 1997; the current incarnation — led by Luke Cage and featuring such off-the-wall membership choices as Juggernaut, Ghost and Man-Thing — is a particularly strong one. We thought it would be fun tc rank the five greatest Thunderbolts of all time.

5 GHOST

The mysterious Ghost is a relative newcomer to the team. Norman Osborn recruited Ghost when he was put in charge of the Thunderbolts program in the wake of *Secret Invasion* and is the only Osborn recruit to remain with Luke Cage's team. *Thunderbolts* has a tradition of characters with their own agendas — Fixer, Moonstone, etc - an important part of the book's dynamic. Ghost fits nat bill nicely. He takes anti-capitalist, anti-corporatist aranoia to new heights and makes everyone around him ncomfortable — adding up to a fascinating, thoroughly ntertaining character. One gets the impression he could et away with leaving anytime — but sticks around, nyway. Sometimes he acts heroically, sometimes not. ut he's always really, really creepy.

EY ISSUE: *Thunderbolts #151*
n an origin issue dedicated solely to Ghost, we finally get ome background on this old Iron Man villain — and it's s unnerving as you'd expect.

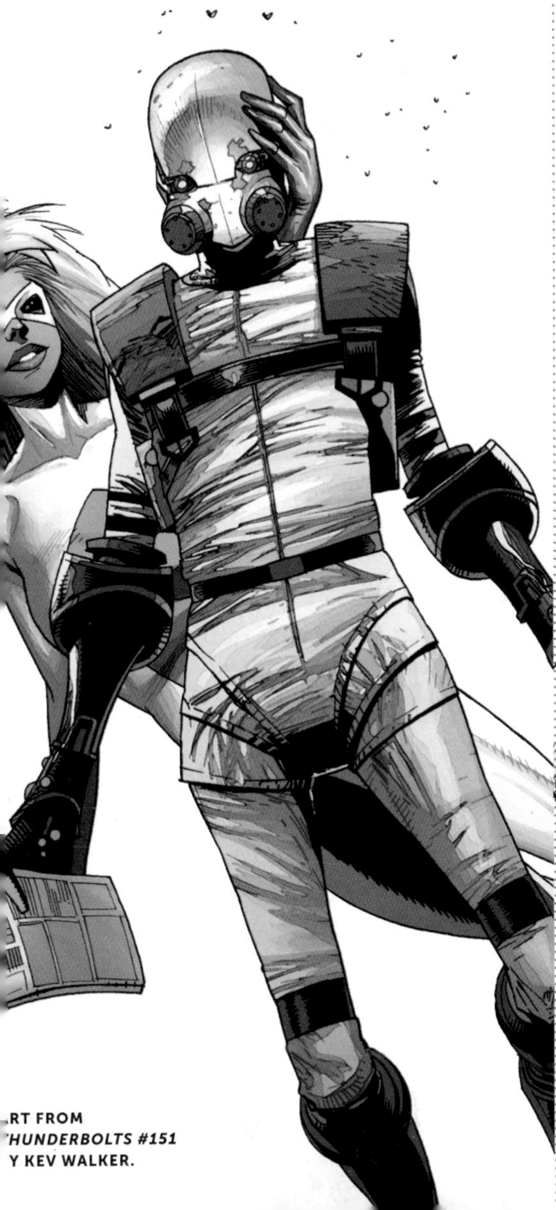

RT FROM
HUNDERBOLTS #151
Y KEV WALKER.

4 MACH V

Abner Jenkins has had one of the more unusual character arcs in *Thunderbolts* history and has embodied the book's theme of striving for redemption. Originally the Beetle, foe of Spider-Man and the Human Torch from Marvel's early days, he became a member of the Masters of Evil and later the original T-Bolts — donning a much cooler suit of battle armor than the Beetle had. He began as MACH I, has since moved up several notches to MACH V and even went through a period as a surgically altered black man! One of the members to catch the "hero bug" early on, he rebelled against T-Bolts founder Baron Zemo and even went so far as to serve jail time to legitimize himself. Today, he is a member of the Thunderbolts support staff, helping keep the new team in line.

KEY ISSUES:

Spider-Man Team-Up #7
While still the Masters of Evil disguised as heroes, the Thunderbolts found themselves teaming up with Spider-Man. This caused Abe to see Spidey from a new perspective, something that started him on the path to heroism.

Thunderbolts #23
When Hawkeye took over as leader of the Thunderbolts in an attempt to steer the team to the side of the angels, it became clear the right thing for Abe to do was serve his sentence for the serious crimes he had committed. In one of the book's more powerful moments, he did just that — selflessly turning himself in. It was a gut punch to himself; his then-girlfriend, Songbird; and the reader.

ART FROM
THUNDERBOLTS #23
BY MARK BAGLEY.

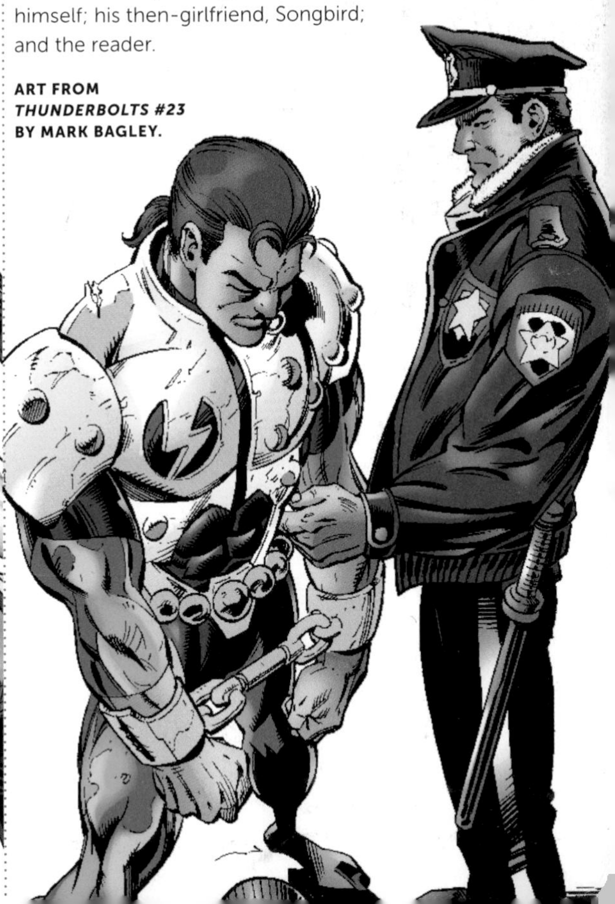

3 BARON ZEMO

We said greatest. That doesn't mean they all have to be good guys, right? Every leader the Thunderbolts have ever had — Hawkeye, Luke Cage, even Norman Osborn — must be judged next to the team's charismatic founder: Baron Helmut Zemo. Originally assuming the mantle of obscure WWII hero Citizen V, Zemo masterminded the team to fill the void of the assumed-dead Avengers and Fantastic Four. He planned to gain the trust of the powers-that-be to access valuable information he would eventually use to rule the world! No, it didn't work out as planned — with his own team turning against him — but that was only after defeating the recently returned Avengers. After a time away from the team, Zemo returned with an altered outlook that had him taking a more heroic approach to leading the squad — albeit with his own more complex agenda. But we all remember him best for his lead role with the original team. These days, he seems to be back to his villainous ways in the pages of *Captain America* — recently going up against the man he thought he'd killed, James "Bucky" Barnes.

KEY ISSUE: *Thunderbolts #1*
What else? Not just a key moment for Zemo, but one of the great moments in recent comic-book history. It was the comics equivalent of "I see dead people," and it raised the bar for all the other super villains out there: Top this for style and chutzpah. After an entire double-sized issue with the Marvel Universe and the reader thinking this was just another random group of new super heroes, we learn that, no, this is Zemo's greatest plot yet!

ART FROM *THUNDERBOLTS #1* BY BAGLEY

2 MOONSTONE

Finding Moonstone has always been easy: locate the Thunderbolts leader, and there Karla Sofen is — whispering in his ear, nudging him in whatever direction she wants him or the team to go, never fully supporting (or rejecting) his leadership. Moonstone — she long ago dropped her "heroic" alias Meteorite — is the essence of a character with her own agenda. Having been part of most Thunderbolts incarnations, she's an expert at knowing which way the wind is blowing, when to go with it and when it's time to make it blow her way. Although Moonstone has generally remained the same character with the same motivations — unlike some of her original teammates — what makes her fascinating is the way she plays off of and manipulates the variety of personalities that have comprised the team over time, from Jolt to Hawkeye to Osborn's loonies like Bullseye. Luke Cage is having none of it so far, knowing full well to keep his distance. What does that mean for Karla? I'm sure we'll find out!

KEY ISSUE: *Thunderbolts #14*
The Thunderbolts are fresh from turning their backs on Zemo, ready to walk the straight and narrow, when they're transported to the dimension called Kosmos. After being imprisoned there, Moonstone kills the king to make good their escape — an omen that Karla Sofen was still no angel.

ART FROM *THUNDERBOLTS #144* BY WALKER.

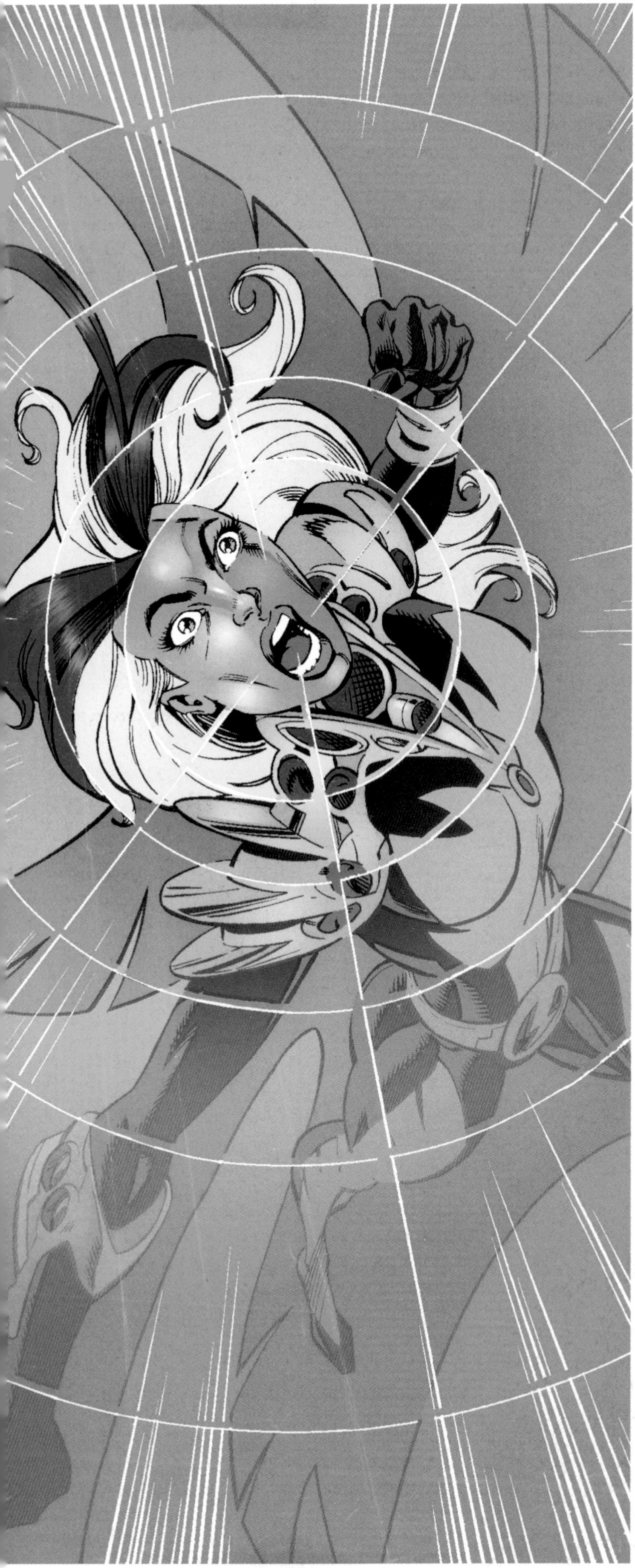

SONGBIRD

1 Aside from being cute as a button, Melissa Gold is our easy pick for greatest Thunderbolt of all time. Her character has grown from the insanely shrewish Screaming Mimi into a young woman beginning to change her tune into the embodiment of strength under fire. And we mean under fire! She's even been besieged by fellow Thunderbolts on multiple occasions. We're talking the likes of Baron Zemo and Norman Osborn!

Along with Moonstone, Songbird has logged the most issues as a Thunderbolt. She was one of the original Masters of Evil in disguise. When the team returned in the pages of *New Thunderbolts*, she was there. And she even found herself on a team full of villains handpicked and led by Osborn when he had control of the team. She's now part of Luke Cage's staff — training and leading the new crop of Thunderbolts, and not afraid to jump in and join the action or go up against a rogue T-Bolts member.

And her character design — with her one-of-a-kind dyed-purple hair, with remnants of her vintage Screaming Mimi white roots still showing in substantially long shocks, and a striking super-hero costume that's one of the best holdovers from the late '90s — remains compellingly dynamic to this day.

Congratulations, Songbird — you are the greatest Thunderbolt of all time!

KEY ISSUES:

Thunderbolts #8
Fighting alone against the Elements of Doom after the rest of the team had been defeated, it was during this battle that a then-unsure Melissa came into her own as a hero.

Thunderbolts #127
Things were falling apart for Osborn, and he decided Songbird couldn't be trusted — so he sent Bullseye and Venom to kill her. The odds were not in her favor — but then, they never had been. Songbird 1, Norman Osborn 0.

ART FROM *THUNDERBOLTS #21* BY BAGLEY.

This list was obviously heavy on the original Thunderbolts, but that's no surprise. Besides the fact some of them are still contributing to the team, being the first of something earns you lots of points. But hey, if you have other thoughts on the greatest — or worst — Thunderbolts of all time, let us know!

HONORABLE MENTIONS

ART FROM *THUNDERBOLTS #20* BY BAGLEY.

ART FROM *THUNDERBOLTS #145* BY WALKER.

COVER ART FROM *THUNDERBOLTS #4* BY BAGLEY.

HAWKEYE: His earnest tenure as T-Bolts leader returned Clint Barton to greatness in the Marvel Universe after years of mediocrity.

JUGGERNAUT: Currently the team's "big dumb guy" (see Atlas), Jugs has been making all the right moves, but is constantly worried it's not going to matter in the long run. Of course, that was before he found a certain hammer in *Fear Itself*.

JOLT: The original team's naïve ingénue, the young Jolt didn't even know they were villains, and it was her shiny optimism that helped pull characters like Songbird and MACH I into the world of genuine heroes.

DISHONORABLE MENTIONS

CROSSBONES: A true washout. Crossbones recently proved some villains aren't redeemable — or even close, really. He killed a cop!

SWORDSMAN: Not a terrible character, but his end was so ignominious — completely manipulated and ultimately killed by Norman Osborn — his T-Bolts legacy is one of shame.

HEADSMAN: Headsman shares a similar name and similarly pitiful ending with Swordsman. Briefly on Norman Osborn's Dark Reign-era squad, Headsman was blown away by teammate Scourge when the latter mistakenly shot through a hologram of Norman Osborn.

CROSSBONES TOPS THE LIST OF THUNDERBOLTS WASHOUTS. ART FROM *THUNDERBOLTS #145* BY WALKER.